Culture and
Customs of
the Dominican Republic

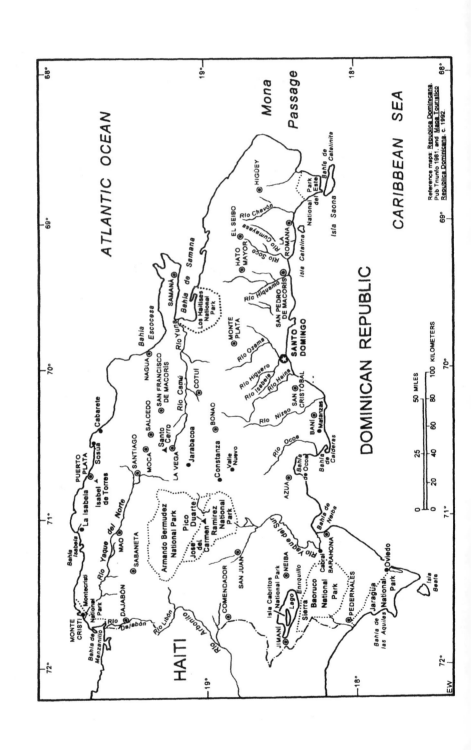

Culture and Customs of the Dominican Republic

Isabel Zakrzewski Brown

Culture and Customs of Latin America
and the Caribbean
Peter Standish, Series Editor

GREENWOOD PRESS
Westport, Connecticut • London

Library of Congress Cataloging-in-Publication Data

Brown, Isabel Zakrzewski.
    Culture and customs of the Dominican Republic / Isabel Zakrzewski
Brown.
        p.   cm.—(Culture and customs of Latin America and the
Caribbean, ISSN 1521–8856)
        Includes bibliographical references and index.
        ISBN 0–313–30314–2 (alk. paper)
        1. Dominican Republic—Civilization—20th century.   2. Popular
culture—Dominican Republic.   I. Title.   II. Series.
F1938.45.B76   1999
972.93—dc21   99–27184

British Library Cataloguing in Publication Data is available.

Library of Congress Catalog Card Number: 99–27184
ISBN: 978-0-313-36055-8
ISSN: 1521–8856

First published in 1999

Greenwood Press, 88 Post Road West, Westport, CT 06881
An imprint of Greenwood Publishing Group, Inc.
www.greenwood.com

Printed in the United States of America

The paper used in this book complies with the
Permanent Paper Standard issued by the National
Information Standards Organization (Z39.48–1984).

10   9   8   7   6

Copyright Acknowledgments

The author and publisher gratefully acknowledge permission for use of the following material:
Frontispiece map reproduced courtesy of Eugene M. Wilson.

To Billy, Gregory, Michael,
and Katherine

Contents

Illustrations

Series Foreword

"CULTURE" is a problematic word. In everyday language we tend to use it in at least two senses. On the one hand we speak of cultured people and places full of culture, uses that imply a knowledge or presence of certain forms of behavior or of artistic expression that are socially prestigious. In this sense large cities and prosperous people tend to be seen as the most cultured. On the other hand, there is an interpretation of "culture" that is broader and more anthropological; culture in this broader sense refers to whatever traditions, beliefs, customs, and creative activities characterize a given community—in short, it refers to what makes that community different from others. In this second sense, everyone has culture; indeed, it is impossible to be without culture.

The problems associated with the idea of culture have been exacerbated in recent years by two trends: less respectful use of language and a greater blurring of cultural differences. Nowadays, "culture" often means little more than behavior, attitude, or atmosphere. We hear about the culture of the boardroom, of the football team, of the marketplace; there are books with titles like *The Culture of War* by Richard Gabriel (Greenwood, 1990) or *The Culture of Narcissism* by Christopher Lasch (1979). In fact, as Christopher Clausen points out in a recent article published in the *American Scholar* (Summer 1996), we have gotten ourselves into trouble by using the term so sloppily.

People who study culture generally assume that culture (in the anthropological sense) is learned, not genetically determined. Another general assumption made in these days of multiculturalism has been that cultural differences should be respected rather than put under pressure to change. But these assumptions, too, have sometimes proved to be problematic. For instance, multiculturalism is a fine ideal, but in practice it is not always easy to reconcile with the beliefs of the very people who advocate it: for example, is female circumcision an issue of human rights or just a different cultural practice?

The blurring of cultural differences is a process that began with the steamship, increased with radio, and is now racing ahead with the Internet. We are becoming globally homogenized. Since the English-speaking world (and the United States in particular) is the dominant force behind this process of homogenization, it behooves us to make efforts to understand the sensibilities of members of other cultures.

This series of books, a contribution toward that greater understanding, deals with the neighbors of the United States, with people who have just as much right to call themselves Americans. What are the historical, institutional, religious, and artistic features that make up the modern culture of such peoples as the Haitians, the Chileans, the Jamaicans, and the Guatemalans? How are their habits and assumptions different from our own? What can we learn from them? As we familiarize ourselves with the ways of other countries, we come to see our own from a new perspective.

Each volume in the series focuses on a single country. With slight variations to accommodate national differences, each begins by outlining the historical, political, ethnic, geographical, and linguistic context, as well as the religious and social customs, and then proceeds to a discussion of a variety of artistic activities, including the press, the media, the cinema, music, literature, and the visual and performing arts. The authors are all intimately acquainted with the countries concerned: some were born or brought up in them, and each has a professional commitment to enhancing the understanding of the culture in question.

We are inclined to suppose that our ways of thinking and behaving are normal. And so they are . . . for us. We all need to realize that ours is only one culture among many, and that it is hard to establish by any rational criteria that ours as a whole is any better (or worse) than any other. As individual members of our immediate community, we know that we must learn to respect our differences from one another. Respect for differences between cultures is no less vital. This is particularly true of the United States, a nation of immigrants, but one that sometimes seems to be bent on destroying variety at home, and, worse still, on having others follow suit. By learning about other people's cultures, we come to understand and respect them; we earn their respect for us; and, not least, we see ourselves in a new light.

Peter Standish
East Carolina University

Acknowledgments

I am eternally indebted to Virginia Cabral and José Alcántara Almánzar for their friendship, encouragement, and faith in this project. Their love for their homeland and their excitement about promoting it made it possible to write this study whose objective is to familiarize people with this enchanting country.

I am also deeply grateful for the unwavering support I have received from Dr. Bernard J. Quinn, chair of the Department of Foreign Languages and Literatures at the University of South Alabama, my colleagues in that department, and from the Dean of the College of Arts and Sciences at the University of South Alabama, Dr. Larry Allen. Likewise, I wish to recognize the University of South Alabama's Research Council for awarding me with funds to travel to the Dominican Republic to gather primary materials for this study.

Finally, I wish to thank my parents Wanda and Gustavo for their enthusiastic approval of all that I do.

Introduction

The Dominican Republic, best known for its beautiful beaches, lavish resorts, and for being the first place that Christopher Columbus and his men settled in the New World, is an island nation in the Caribbean. There is much more to this country, beginning with its people whose optimistic, energetic, and cheerful character is immediately engaging and endearing. Dominicans are a proud people who have withstood innumerable setbacks due to an unstable political history and to physical devastation occasioned by hurricanes and earthquakes. It has been an independent republic since 1844.

To introduce Dominican culture and customs it is important to have a sense of the country's physical geography, its history, and its people. Dominican geography is rich in mountains, valleys, virtually unexplored and unexploited coves and bays, and natural habitats of rare species of flora and fauna. Dominican history is different from that of any other country in Latin America because this is the only country to receive independence not from Spain, but rather from a neighboring Latin American country. The explanation of how Haiti came to rule the whole island is fascinating as is the history of the Taíno Indians who occupied the island at the time of Columbus' arrival. The history of the Dominican Republic is also tragically unique because of the brutality of the long dictatorship of Rafael Leonidas Trujillo. Other countries in Latin America have suffered tyrannical dictatorships, but Trujillo's rule is considered among the most savage. At the end of the twentieth century, the Dominican Republic has a democratically elected president who was born and raised in New York City. As a people, Dominicans are generally described as gregarious, kind, and generous. These admirable qualities extend across racial lines, class stratifications, rural and urban dwellers, males and females, and those Dominicans who have migrated to New York City. Generalities, however, do not adequately address the distinctions that also characterize Dominicans and are likewise identified and divided by their race, social status, geographic habitat, and gender. The Dominicans who migrated to New York City have not turned their backs on their country. On the contrary, their success in the United States accounts for a significant revenue for the Dominican Republic, and the work of artists in New York City cannot be separated from that of the island. It is seen, instead, as an extension of that which the island has to offer.

The chapter on religion in the Dominican Republic examines Dominicans' religious practices, which on the surface, at least, are almost totally inspired by Catholicism. Probing beneath this surface one finds that Haitian voodoo has been extremely influential in vast rural areas as well as in the outskirts of major urban centers. The voodoo that is practiced in the Dominican Republic is different from that practiced in Haiti, as it reflects an evolution that stems from Taíno, Catholic, and Haitian voodoo beliefs. With regard to Catholicism, Dominicans have sustained a few religious practices that date back to the Middle Ages in Spain. For the most part, though, Dominican Catholicism is struggling for supremacy in an environment that is increasingly attracting evangelists from many different Protestant denominations.

The Dominican way of life, celebrating national and religious holidays, and speaking is treated in the chapter on social customs. What distinguishes Dominican customs and idiom from those of other Hispanic nations is explained primarily as a product of Dominican history from the times of the Taíno Indians, colonial years, independence, through today. Despite the proximity of other Hispanic island nations such as Cuba and Puerto Rico, Dominicans have developed distinctive customs and language that make them unique and not directly comparable to their neighbors.

The comparison with Cuba and Puerto Rico is sustained in the discussion of culture in the Dominican Republic. From literature, the media, to performing and visual arts, Dominican artists have carved an impressive and lasting niche for themselves. For example, the national dance, the *merengue*, has become popular throughout the world, as has the music that accompanies it. Cultural studies based both in the United States and in Europe have tended to focus mostly on cultural works from Cuba and Puerto Rico. One of the reasons the Dominican Republic, particularly with regard to customs and culture, has thus far been overlooked may be attributed to Trujillo's dictatorship and its aftermath, which has extended in some ways into the

1990s. The dictatorship suppressed creative activity and, in any event, did not provide it with means of global diffusion. The aftermath of the dictatorship included a civil war followed by fluctuations in economic stability. This environment was not conducive to artistic expression. During this dark period, Dominicans had little or no information about artistic life beyond their borders. A case in point is that of Dominican writer in exile Juan Bosch. His short stories and novels, written from the 1940s on, were known throughout Latin America, but Dominicans did not have the privilege of reading his works until after Trujillo's assassination.

Studying the Dominican Republic has become increasingly more popular in recent years. Marginalized by its own history and peculiar circumstances, the country, its people, its customs, and its culture are only now coming into the focus of those involved in cultural studies, as evidenced by the sudden proliferation of books on the market about the Dominican Republic in English. This book serves as an expansion of the study of the Dominican Republic. The wide and deep scope of its perspective on the country, its people, customs, and culture contributes to the endeavor of placing the Dominican Republic front and center, thus carrying out a service that has been long overdue.

Chronology

Pre-11 A.D.	Taíno people establish themselves on Quisqueya
December 5, 1492	Christopher Columbus makes landfall on the island he names La Española
December 21, 1492	Columbus meets Guacanagarix
December 25, 1492	First settlement of the New World—La Navidad
August 4, 1496	Santo Domingo, the capital, is founded
1520	Twenty-four sugar mills and four sugar processing plants are in operation
1530	Blacks are the predominant race on Hispaniola
1538	First university in the western world is established
1550	Virtually all Taínos are decimated by this time
Seventeenth century	French settle the western half of the island and call it Sainte Domingue
1605	Depopulation of the northern coast of Hispaniola
1793	Slavery is abolished on the French side of the island

January 1, 1804	Republic of Haiti is born
December 1, 1821	Spanish side of the island becomes independent from Spain and is renamed Haití Español
February 27, 1844	Haití Español becomes independent from Haiti and becomes the Dominican Republic. Birth of the First Republic
March 18, 1861	Dominican Republic is annexed to Spain
1861–1865	War of Restoration
May 1865	Birth of the Second Republic
1882	Ulíses Heureux (Lilís) is elected president—the beginning of the Dominican Republic's first dictatorship
1899	Ulíses Heureux is assassinated
May 16, 1916	First U.S. Marines occupation
May 1924	U.S. Marines depart
1930	Rafael Leonidas Trujillo is installed as president—beginning of the Dominican Republic's second dictatorship
1936	Name of capital is changed to Ciudad Trujillo
1957	World's Fair is held in Ciudad Trujillo
November 25, 1959	Mirabal sisters are killed
May 30, 1961	Trujillo is assassinated, ending one of the longest dictatorships on record in world history
1962	State Council composed of three members takes over
1963	Seven-month presidency of Juan Bosch
1963–1965	Triumverate rules the country
April 1965	Civil war and second occupation by U.S. Marines
1965	Installation of Hector García Godoy as president

1966	Joaquín Balaguer, vice-president in the Trujillo regime, is elected and rules through 1978—the "twelve years"
1978	Silvestre Antonio Guzmán is elected president
1982	Jorge Blanco is elected president
1986	Joaquín Balaguer returns to power
1996	Current president, Leonel Fernández Reyna, is elected

1

The Dominican Republic: The Land, Its History, and Its People

The Dominican Republic shares the island of Hispaniola with Haiti. The two-thirds of the island that the Dominican Republic occupies is replete with beautiful bays and beaches. It is also a country of expansive fertile valleys, mountain ranges, natural parks, and a sanctuary to unique flora and fauna. It is the second largest of the Spanish-speaking countries of the Greater Antilles, which refers to the four largest Caribbean islands (Cuba, Puerto Rico, and Jamaica are the other three). The history of the Dominican Republic is different from that of any other Latin American nation because the Dominican Republic received its independence from Haiti, not Spain. Its history begins with the presence of the Taíno Indians whose legacy Dominicans are proud to uphold. After independence from Spain the new republic was subjected to a long power struggle between those who wanted to remain independent and those who supported the annexation of the young country to either Spain or the United States. The consequence of these conflicts led alternately to dictatorships and to occupation by U.S. forces. Energized by the vicissitudes of their history, Dominicans, both on the island and in New York, where a large number have migrated, remain a vitally optimistic people, united in their zeal to confirm a national identity.

GEOGRAPHIC AND GEOLOGIC DETAILS

¡Quisqueya la bella! ("Quisqueya the Beautiful!") Quisqueya—the Taíno name given to the island that Christopher Columbus called La Española—added to the phrase "the beautiful," is a sentimentally popular expression with which Dominicans praise their country. Quisqueya, in Taíno, the language of the indigenous population of the same name, means mother of the lands. It is popularly repeated, as well, that La Española (known as Hispaniola in English) was the land that Columbus loved most. Today the Dominican Republic continues to be a country of great natural beauty. One is torn between the awesome fertility of the inland country and the breathtaking beauty of the coastal areas. Although some parts of the country have given way to capitalist exploitation since colonial times, much of it remains virginal.

The eastern third of the country is by far the most developed. A mountain range extends from the northwest corner of the country to the southwest. The effect of the mountain range is that of a comma, thus isolating the western and southwestern part of the country from development. To this day this area remains the least explored and the most mysterious because its rugged terrain makes travel difficult. Being the least developed portion of the island signals, on the negative side, extreme conditions of poverty and neglect, but also, perhaps paradoxically, an area of virtually unexplored, great beauty.

The Dominican Republic is 30,101.85 square miles (48,442 square kilometers) in size. The border between it and Haiti is 241.1 miles (388 kilometers) long. The coastline is 978.7 miles (1,575 kilometers) long and runs along the Atlantic Ocean, the Caribbean Sea, and the Mona Passage which separates the Dominican Republic from Puerto Rico. It has 20 geomorphologic regions ranging from peaks well over 10,000 feet above sea level to Lake Enriquillo in the southwestern part of the country, a salt-water lake that lies below sea level and is said to have the same salt content as the Dead Sea.

The four mountain ranges in the Dominican Republic are the Cordillera del Norte ("Northern Range"), which extends from the town of Montecristi in the northwestern-most corner of the country, along the northern coast, to the town of San Francisco de Macorís. The largest range and the one with the highest mountains is the Cordillera Central ("Central Range") also referred to as the spinal cord of the country. Beginning in Haiti, it runs from northwest to southeast and subdivides, one branch stretching southward toward Baní, and the other extending eastward, named the Cordillera Oriental or Sierra del Seibo ("Eastern Range" or "Seibo Mountains"). Nearby, in the Cordillera Central are modest reserves of gold, iron, silver, and bauxite mines. The Eastern Range runs parallel to the Atlantic Coast in the northeast near the region of Higüey, where several tourist resorts are located.

A popular hiking destination, Pico Duarte, in the Cordillera Central, is the highest peak in all of the Antilles, reaching 10,417 feet (3,174 meters) above sea level. The trail begins in Constanza and goes through designated water spots and beaches near waterfalls. Another important elevation is Santo Cerro ("Holy Hill") on top of which is the first sanctuary in the New World dedicated to the Virgin Mary. It also marks the spot where Columbus planted the first cross of the Americas. Columbus founded the Fuerte de la Concepción ("Conception Fort") at the foot of the same hill in 1494. Legend has it that Columbus, upon his deathbed, requested that a church be constructed on the Santo Cerro hill. The church that was in fact built was then dedicated to *Nuestra Señora de Las Mercedes* ("Our Lady of Mercy"). This church was destroyed by an earthquake in 1842 and then again by a hurricane in 1869. During its reconstruction in 1880, an important painting was stolen depicting what is popularly remembered as the definitive battle for the conquest of the island during which the Virgin Mary appeared. Nowadays the church on top of Holy Hill is a site for religious pilgrimages.

The Sierra de Neiba ("Neiba Range") extends 62 miles (100 kilometers) from the Haitian border to the Yaque del Sur river. It is about 50 miles (80 kilometers) long and has peaks as high as 1,367 feet (2,200 meters). The fourth mountain range is the Sierra de Baoruco ("Baoruco Range"), which extends from Haiti into the southwestern part of the Dominican Republic. The valleys and depressions of this range contain beautiful lakes and lagoons, including Lake Enriquillo.

The Dominican Republic has 108 rivers, most of whose sources are in the Cordillera Central. Only three of them, the Ozama, the Higuamo, and the Yuna, are suitable for the navigation of large ships. The Yuna river is the largest, flowing into Manzanillo Bay in the northwest. The longest and most important rivers for navigation and irrigation are the Yaque del Norte (184 miles [296 kilometers] long) and the Yaque del Sur (114 miles [183 kilometers] long). Both begin in the Central Range; the northern Yaque empties into Manzanillo Bay and the southern Yaque empties into Neiba Bay, in the southwest.

Lake Enriquillo's drainage basin includes 10 minor river systems and covers an area of more than 1,864 square miles (3,000 square kilometers). Rivers that run from east to west along the southern coast include the Yuma, the Chavón, the Cumayasa, the Soco, the Ozama, the Isabela, the Haina, the Nizao, and the Ocoa. There are numerous dams and artificial lakes. Some of these, such as the one close to Cotuí, provide for excellent trout and bass fishing.

The Cibao valley in the Cordillera del Norte was designated La Vega Real ("Royal Valley") by Columbus. It is also known as the "Garden of the Antilles." La Vega Real is the main supplier of agricultural products for the country. Considered the geographic center of the country, the Cibao includes

The Cibao Valley. Courtesy of *Listín Diario*.

the provinces of Santiago, Monseñor Nouel, Duarte, Espaillat, La Vega, Sánchez Ramírez, and Salcedo. Columbus founded numerous forts and towns in the Cibao including Concepción de La Vega Real, Santiago de los Treinta Caballeros, and Bonao.

The Constanza Valley, in the middle of the Cordillera Central, is considered by some to be the Dominican Shangrila. Most vegetables for local consumption are grown here, as are flowers and other products that would seem exotic for a tropical country, such as strawberries, raspberries, peaches, pears, and apples. Near Constanza is the Valle Nuevo, which is a plateau upon which alpine-like vegetation can be found. A beautiful waterfall called the Salto de Aguas Blancas is located nearby. The Peravia Valley and the Neiba Valley, in the south, close to Lake Enriquillo, are also notable for their beauty.

The long Dominican coastline boasts sixteen bays, some of which have had great historical importance, most notably the beautiful Samaná Bay which separates the peninsula of Samaná from the eastern mainland. This bay was for centuries considered to be a strategic harbor, a vital center from which to control the Caribbean. In various points of its history the bay was disputed by the British, the French, and the United States. Other bays of interest include the Bay of La Isabela, along the northern shore, where Columbus first made landfall; Montecristi Bay, in the far northwest corner of the island, from which most banana exporting was channelled in the nine-

The Constanza Valley. Courtesy of *Listín Diario*.

teenth century; and Calderas Bay, which houses the Dominican Navy. To-day's most important ports include the capital itself, Santo Domingo, which hosts cruise ships; Haina, to the west of Santo Domingo, which serves as the main port for cargo ships; Puerto Plata, along the north coast, which also serves cruise ships; and Barahona, on Neiba Bay, which is an important venue today for the export of bananas and banana products such as plantain chips. Of related interest are the beaches, which according to a recent United Nations Educational, Science, and Cultural Organization (UNESCO) report are among the best in the world (Cambeira 19).

Three islands off the Dominican Republic's shore include Saona, Catalina, and Catalinita. The main seaways of the country include the Mona Passage, the Beata, and the Catalina. The Mona Passage separates the Dominican Republic from Puerto Rico and is one of the most important seaways as it offers access to the Caribbean region. There are several keys, or small islands, in the Mona Passage, among them the Mona, Monito, and Desecho keys.

The waters off the coast of the Dominican Republic hold the remains of sunken galleons that today constitute a point of interest for divers. Some of these include the *Nuestra Señora de la Concepción* sunk in 1641; *Conde de Yolosa* (1724); *Nuestra Señora de Guadalupe* (1724); *Scipión* (1752); and *Diómedes Imperial* (1806). These waters also contain a rich barrier reef off the north coast between La Isabela and Cabarete, Oviedo and Pedernales,

Northwest coastline view. Courtesy of *Listín Diario*.

and Neiba. It is thought that the terrain as such would not exist if it were not for the barriers formed by the coral reefs.

There are seven national parks in the Dominican Republic. At the southwest corner of the island, in the most remote area, is the Jaragua National Park. The magnificent Bahía las Aguilas ("Eagles' Bay") beach includes a coastal strip behind Oviedo lagoon where sea turtles lay eggs. A bit north from it is the Sierra Bahoruco National Park. Just north of this park lies Lake Enriquillo, which is 112 square miles (180 square kilometers). The island of Cabritos ("little goats") in the middle of Lake Enriquillo is a designated national park. Its attractions include large colonies of flamingos, herons, spoonbills, parrots, and what is considered to be the most important colony of American crocodiles in the hemisphere. Two iguana species inhabit the southwest area. One is the rhinoceros iguana (which is also found in other dry areas of the country) and the other is the ricordi iguana characterized by its fierce red eyes, found exclusively in the Jaragua Park area. Two national parks established along the Cordillera Central include the José del Carmen Ramírez National Park, and to the north, the Armando Bermúdez National Park. Both of these parks have many rivers running through them and bathing areas adjacent to waterfalls. Pico Duarte is located in José del Carmen Ramírez National Park. Besides providing for the opportunity of enjoying impressive views, hiking up Pico Duarte allows for birdwatching, particularly parrots. The hike takes about three days. The national park of Montecristi extends along the northwest corner of the island, and to the east is the national park of the Haitises, located along the southern edge of Samaná Bay. It is regarded as one of the most beautiful regions of the island given its knolls and limestone hills covered with thick tropical forest. The Parque Nacional del Este ("National Park of the East") is located at the extreme southeastern corner of the island, next to La Romana province. This park includes beautiful beaches such as that of Puerto Laguna and those adjacent to the towns of Mano Juan and Adamaday on Saona island, which is part of the park. Many caves are accessible for exploration, such as Cueva La Lechuza ("The Owl's Cave").

The Dominican Republic is prone to two types of natural disasters: hurricanes and earthquakes. The term "hurricane" comes from the Taíno *huracán, meaning big wind*. The hurricane season extends from June through November. During the history of the Dominican Republic, some hurricanes have had devastating effects, resulting in the complete destruction of certain areas of the country. Spanish colonists first dealt with the capricious forces of hurricane winds in 1494 when the port of La Isabela was buffeted by hurricane winds, which also sank several ships during Columbus' second voyage. Perhaps the most notorious storms include the one in 1502 which destroyed the original settlement of Santo Domingo. Twenty ships en route to Spain sank somewhere between the islands of Saona and Mona. Their cargo included captured Indians that were to become slaves in Spain. The hurricanes of 1508 and 1509 have been recorded as the worst of colonial times. Saint Xenón, a hurricane in 1930, leveled the capital, Santo Domingo, killing 2,000 inhabitants of the 60,000 recorded at the time and destroying 4,000 residences of the 7,000 registered (Franco Pichardo, *Historia* 506). In 1979, Hurricane David was responsible for serious damage to the infrastructure of the capital city and indirectly contributed to the overall economic decline experienced by the nation during the 1980s. Hurricane Georges hit the island in 1998 and did most damage to the resort areas in the southeast and to the banana, coffee, rice, and tobacco crops.

The Dominican Republic lies on a fault zone of earth crustal fractures which occasionally shifts, causing earthquakes. One devastating earthquake occurred in the area of La Vega in 1562, completely destroying it. The city was rebuilt in 1563 and moved to the shores of the Camú river. Other historical earthquakes include the one in 1673 in Santo Domingo, which "did not leave a house standing" (Moya Pons, "Terremotos" 10), and one in 1751 that levelled the town of Azua and in Santo Domingo, destroyed the San Franciscan convent, whose ruins still stand. Another earthquake in 1842 damaged Santiago, killing about 200 people. The last recorded major earthquake occurred in 1946. It initiated a tidal wave that wiped out the communities of Nagua and Matanzas and other small fishing villages on the northern part of the Samaná peninsula.

MAJOR CITIES AND TOWNS OF THE DOMINICAN REPUBLIC

Santo Domingo

The capital city of the Dominican Republic is Santo Domingo. Legend has it that a colonist named Miguel Díaz, living along the north coast in the first town to be settled on the island, La Isabela, fled to the south to escape the wrath of a companion whom Díaz had stabbed. He settled along the shores of the Ozama river, which today splits the capital in two. That part of the island was ruled by a female chieftain named Catalina. (Catalina is a Christian name. Her Taíno name has been forgotten.) Catalina, in love with Díaz, showed him gold deposits along the Haina river, which is located to the west of Santo Domingo, right at its outskirts. Díaz returned to the north coast to inform Bartolomé Colón (Columbus), Christopher Columbus' brother about the gold mine. Bartolomé Colón then resolved to establish a town along the southern coast. On August 4, 1496, Bartolomé Colón and his men founded the town of La Nueva Isabela Santo Domingo del Puerto de la Isla de la Española ("The New Isabela, Holy Sunday Port of the Island of Hispaniola"). The town was destroyed by a hurricane in 1502, and was refounded the same year on the western shore of the Ozama river by Nicolás de Ovando. Ovando is credited with what was considered at the time to be the modern, urban design of the city that would then serve as the model for all future cities founded by the Spaniards as they explored the hemisphere.[1]

Santo Domingo is a city of many firsts. It was the first European city in the Americas; the first American archdiocese for the Roman Catholic church (founded in 1503); and the first municipality in the New World to be assigned its own coat of arms by royal decree (1507). The first University of the Western Hemisphere was founded in Santo Domingo in 1538, the Universidad de Santo Tomás de Aquino ("St. Thomas Aquinas University"). Santo Domingo is also one of three sites that claims to be the burial place of Christopher Columbus along with Spain and Italy.

In 1936, the capital city's name was changed to Ciudad Trujillo, named after the ruthless dictator Rafael Leonidas Trujillo who then ruled the country. In 1961, shortly after Trujillo's assassination, the original name was restored. The Organization of American States (OAS) has recently designated the city as the "Cradle of the Americas."

Today, Santo Domingo stretches over 249 square miles. It is dotted with significant historical monuments, structures, and buildings that commemorate its rich history. The colonial center of the city, restored within the past decade, accurately reflects the distribution of streets, public buildings, and residences much as they would have been during colonial times. The rest of the city is modern, but its surrounding areas are constituted by numerous shanty towns whose flimsy constructions and sheer numbers are testament to the poverty that coexists with the active modern urban city. Typical of a late-twentieth-century overcrowded metropolis, Santo Domingo suffers from extreme noise and environmental pollution. Common problems include a serious lack of adequate water and electrical supply, proper means of disposal of garbage and sewage, and a high crime rate. Vociferous critics denounce the lack of planning in a city suffering from an apparently chronic case of urban sprawl.

The city's rapid and, for the most part, unplanned and uncontrolled growth has been spurred by industry and the proliferation of the so-called free-trade zone enterprises. In other words, the city sacrifices common sense in its development to the business potential represented by factories. Specializing in the garment industry, foreign-owned factories are major employers with some of the lowest wage levels in the Caribbean. As part of the Caribbean Basin Initiative, which included tariff benefits to "offshore garment producers" (Safa 32), the creation of the many free-trade zones, as much in the city of Santo Domingo itself as throughout the country, has insured that clothing is the Dominican Republic's main export by far displacing sugar, tobacco, produce, and other traditional products.

Far from the industrial centers are two large parks, the Mirador del Norte and the Mirador del Sur, which provide a place for recreational activities. The Mirador del Sur, the older of the two parks, extends over three and a half miles. It has an artificial lake, fountains, sculptures, bicycle and rollerblading paths, restaurants, and jogging trails. There are also caverns and caves that have been turned into popular night clubs and restaurants. The private residences for the ambassadors of various countries, for United Nations representatives, and other important international organizations are located close to this park. The Mirador del Norte park was built more recently with the idea of providing some of the same facilities to the inhabitants of the northern part of the sprawling city. Another park lies to the east of the Ozama river. It is called the Mirador del Este Park and features the Columbus lighthouse. This monument, in the shape of a large cross, was built in 1992 to commemorate the 500-year anniversary of the Discovery. Occasionally, at night, the beam from the lighthouse projects a gigantic cross into the night sky.

Also on the eastern shore of the city is a large, modern aquarium where tropical fish are exhibited. A little farther eastward is another popular tourist attraction, Los tres ojos ("The Three Eyes"), an enormous natural cavern which encloses three perfectly round spring water lakes and then, deeper inside the caverns, a fourth lake containing sulphur. The lakes are renowned for the clarity of their waters. Along one of the paths of these lakes is the largest of the interior rooms, which is actually the crater of an extinct volcano. The depth of this particular lake is not known.

A botanical garden and a zoo are located in the northern part of the city. The botanical garden is named after the first Dominican botanist to write about this subject, Dr. Rafael M. Moscoso. It is considered to be the largest in the world in area; it includes a forestal reserve of 1.35 square miles (2.186 square kilometers). The world's largest clock made of flowers can be found in these gardens. The Santo Domingo Zoo is conceived along modern precepts that dictate that animals should not be caged but rather confined to specific areas by natural boundaries. It includes a replica of an African plain and an aviary that measures 3.1 acres.

The Cibao Valley

The extensive Cibao Valley is considered to be the most fertile region of the country. For centuries it has been the center for cattle ranches, tobacco farms, and rum factories.

Santiago de los Treinta Caballeros ("The Town of Thirty Gentlemen"), commonly referred to simply as Santiago, was initially founded in 1498 by Columbus who built a fort on a hill bordering the Yaque River. Later, Nicolás de Ovando converted it to a summer vacation area. Destroyed by the 1562 earthquake, the city was definitively founded shortly thereafter by the legendary thirty gentlemen in 1563 and has since been considered the heart of the nation, located in the middle of the Cordillera Central. It has been at the center of most of the important historical events such as the initial retreat of Haitian forces in 1804, the War of Independence in 1844, and the War of Restoration between 1861 and 1865. Most of the presidents of the Dominican Republic have come from Santiago. The city is famous for its carnivals, which are celebrated in February and August. In fact, the city is primarily an industrial vortex, manufacturing rums, liqueurs, cigars, and articles made of rubber, aluminum, and plastics. Santiago differs from Santo Domingo in that it has not suffered from the pains of uncontrolled growth. Learning, perhaps, from the mistakes that occurred in the capital with regard to explosive growth, Santiago, whose architecture also ranges from colonial

Cathedral in La Vega. Courtesy of *Listín Diario*.

to contemporary, has been able to manage its growth. The most important university of the country nowadays is the Universidad Católica Madre y Maestra, located on the outskirts of the city. It has become a significant research center and has developed a popular year-round study-abroad program coordinated with various universities in the United States.

The former La Vega named by Columbus and located at the foot of Santo Cerro became the first official European town during colonial times. It was in La Vega that sugarcane was first planted in the Americas, where the first American papalcy was established, and where the king of Spain authorized the first brothel of the New World to be built. La Vega also became an archdiocese, rivaling that of Santo Domingo. It was the summer home for the Viceroy Diego Colón and his wife María de Toledo. The San Francisco monastery in La Vega was the place where Bartolomé de Las Casas lived for many years. Las Casas is the author of two important works, among others, about the indians: *Historia de las Indias* and *Brerísima relación de la destrucción de las Indias*. In 1562 an earthquake left the city in ruins. The new La Vega was founded on the banks of the Camú river in 1563. Today, the town is best known for its carnival and because of its location in the most fertile valley of the country, La Vega Real. It is also a stopover for visitors to the popular weekend mountain resorts of Jarabacoa and Constanza.

Montecristi, in the farthest northwestern corner of the country, is a town

noted for the predominance of Victorian architecture throughout the downtown area. It was first founded in the sixteenth century, only to be destroyed
by the so-called government-ordered devastations that occurred between the
years 1605 and 1606 in an attempt to curb all smuggling activity along the
northern coast. The town reached its apogee in terms of global economic
significance towards the end of the nineteenth century and the beginning of
the twentieth when it became the main port venue for shipments of mahogany and agricultural products to Europe. Immigrants from Germany, Italy,
Spain, and Great Britain settled here, which explains the Victorian-style
buildings. Legend has it that French author Alexandre Dumas wrote his
famous novel *The Count of Monte Cristo* while vacationing at the Yacht Club
of Cabrito Key. Dutch and French galleons from the sixteenth, seventeenth,
and eighteenth centuries lie sunken in the vicinity of the key. An area referred
to as the Caños is made up of marine canals formed through the mangroves
of the coast, a natural habitat for all kinds of marine species, a large variety
of birds, and sea turtles.

A little town of firsts is La Isabela, which was the site of the first town
founded in the Western Hemisphere. It was historically divided into two
main sections: the military and the civilian. Today those distinctions remain.
One can still visit the observation tower, the fort, the first church, the first
port, storage areas, ovens for melting and forging metals, and the first Christian cemetery of the Western Hemisphere.

The city of Puerto Plata, on the north coast, is the city with considerable
development for tourism in the Dominican Republic, second only to La
Romana. It was founded in 1496 by Bartolomé Colón. Puerto Plata also fell
victim to the devastations of 1605 and 1606 and was not reestablished until
1742, by families from the Canary Islands. This city became the main export
center for agricultural products of the Cibao region during the eighteenth
and nineteenth centuries and even enjoyed a short stint as the capital of the
Republic during the presidency of Gregorio Luperón in 1870. Today the
seventy-five miles of coast that surround Puerto Plata have been nicknamed
the "Amber Coast" after the rich deposits of the fossil resin that is found
there. The beach itself has gained worldwide fame for its pristine beauty.
Some points of interest in Puerto Plata include the Isabel de Torre Hill, upon
which there is a gigantic statue of Christ with outspread arms, similar to the
one found in Rio de Janeiro, Brazil. A cable car (the only one in the country)
takes sightseers up to the foot of the statue.

Sosúa, a little town about nine miles to the east of Puerto Plata on the
Amber Coast, has always been associated with the bigger city given its proximity. Most Dominicans will speak about both in the same breath and not

draw a distinction between the two. The history of Sosúa is unique in that it is a Jewish colony established in 1940 as part of Trujillo's project for "whitening" the primarily mulatto Dominican populace. Some of the best Dominican cheeses come from Sosúa.

West of the Capital

To the west of Santo Domingo is the city of San Cristóbal. The colonists built a fortress tower to warehouse gold and then placed it under the protection of the patron saint of travellers, whom the city is named after. San Cristóbal ("Saint Christopher"), is actually most associated with Trujillo, the dictator who ruled the Dominican Republic from 1930 to 1961. He was born in this town and maintained two luxurious residences there. One of them, called El Castillo del Cerro ("The Castle of the Hill"), is six stories tall, and the other one is named the Casa de Caoba ("The Mahogany House"). Both are museums today, and the latter exhibits all of Trujillo's many uniforms. Although there is a tomb there with his name engraved, Trujillo is actually buried in Spain.

Close to San Cristóbal lies a network of caves called El Pomier. Discovered in 1849 by the British consul to the Dominican Republic and explorer Robert Schomburg, the caves house a rich exhibit of over 590 pre-Columbian cave drawings, some dating as far back as 2,000 years. The area has been declared a World Heritage for Humanity Zone by UNESCO.

Barahona and Cabral

The town of Barahona is located toward the southwestern part of the island. This is the area that is least developed, least spoiled by tourism, and that offers some of the most enchanting experiences for the visitor. The area immediately surrounding Barahona has become important for the production and export of agricultural products, particularly plantains. Barahona is also a great point of departure for visiting some of the most pristine beaches of the island, Lake Enriquillo, and the town of Cabral. This town is famous for its *cachuas*, costumed devils, that appear only from Good Friday through the Monday after Easter.

The Southeastern Provinces

Traditionally this part of the country is known for its sugarcane production. Although this activity still continues in this area, the southeastern part of the Dominican Republic is also the area most developed for purposes of

Sugarcane cutter in La Romana. Courtesy
of *Listín Diario.*

tourism. Some of the largest tourism compounds there are self-contained so
that international tourists can spend their time golfing, playing tennis, fishing, diving, horseback riding, and so on without ever leaving the premises.
Some of these developments include the Bávaro compound and the Casa de
Campo that are located near the town of La Romana. Another "claim to
fame" of the southeastern provinces is that this is where many formidable
professional baseball players have originated, specifically from the town of
San Pedro de Macorís.

Apart from La Romana, the most important town of the southeast is San
Pedro de Macorís. It was founded in the 1870s by Spanish immigrants fleeing
Cuba's war for independence. The town enjoyed its height of prosperity and
fame during the first decades of the twentieth century, given the economical
success of the sugar industry at that time, resulting from the high demand
for sugar during and after World War I. San Pedro de Macorís was also
settled by Cocolos, the name given to cheap labor brought in from Tortola

Hauling the sugarcane in La Romana. Courtesy of *Listín Diario*.

in the Virgin Islands to work in the sugarcane fields and mills. The town was, during its best days, a cultural center of international importance. Most Dominican sugar passed through its custom house and docks. It had the first telephone and electrical plants of the country. The beloved Swedish singer Jenny Lind and the opera star Enrico Caruso sang in its opera house in the late 1800s and early 1900s respectively. All that remains today of its past splendor is conserved in the beautiful architecture of the town.

La Romana, one of the country's youngest cities is, paradoxically, the best known internationally, mainly due to its being the port of access to the many tourist resorts. La Romana was founded in the beginning of the twentieth century with the establishment of the country's largest privately owned sugar mill, the Puerto Rico Sugar Company. The town was populated by a diverse group of nationalities, most of whom came to work at the mills. These included Puerto Ricans, Corsicans, Haitians, and people from the nearby English-speaking islands. The town's name refers to the Roman scale that was used to weigh products for export when the town was simply a commercial port.

The town of Higüey is the most important religious center of the Dominican Republic. It was founded in 1650 by the prosperous Trejo brothers from Extremadura, Spain, who were among the first to build a sugarcane mill in the country. They brought with them a small sixteenth-century oil painting of Our Lady of Altagracia. This painting has had miracles attributed to it, related to the second local industry, that of orange cultivation. Folklore maintains that the painting once disappeared from the hands of a child only to appear in the branches of an orange tree that ever since flowers out of season. These miracles are celebrated annually with parades and other ceremonies. Juan Ponce de León, the explorer who searched for the fountain of youth in Florida, once lived close to Higüey in a house which has been restored as a monument to the famous Spaniard.

Last, but by measure of beauty certainly not least, is the town of Samaná and the incomparable Samaná Bay—a natural harbor, where Columbus killed the first Indian. In the seventeenth century this harbor was used by buccaneers and pirates and, in the nineteenth century it played a role in the strategic maquinations of the great powers of the time, alternately, Britain, France, and the United States. Alastair Reid calls Samaná a "geographical oddity," noting that on some ancient maps the area is depicted as an island, which reflects a pervasive sense about Samaná: it is somehow marginalized from the rest of the Republic. "The place survives . . . on rumors of imminent prosperity" (74). It has a long way to go, according to Reid, who describes the local market as a place "where goats' throats are often cut in public . . . where the only hardware store [is] like an Aladdin's cave . . . [where] there are vendors of hats made of varnished palm leaves and . . . three shoeshine boys who stare gloomily at tourist sandals . . . and not much more except for the roar of motorcycles, the main attainable dream of young Dominicans" (74). Prospects for the future of Samaná include the construction of luxury hotels, oil exploration, and the creation of a Biosphere Reserve "to maintain the native species, including the manatee, to prevent pollution of the bay, and to protect the habitat of the humpback whales that spend their breeding time in the bay from late January until early March every year" (Reid 74).

History

The most common way of introducing Dominican history involves quoting Christopher Columbus' diary in which he relates his first encounter with the island he named Hispaniola. (The spelling of Hispaniola is an archaic representation of "La Española," the Spanish one.) In 1992 the Dominican Republic celebrated the 500th anniversary of the Discovery. The preparations that led to the commemoration allowed Dominicans in all walks of life to reflect upon their country and its development to date. The issue of Columbus himself, and many other explorers and colonists, became controversial as Dominicans revisited their ancient and more recent history, and explored, for the first time collectively, aspects of their past that for many years had been concealed by official rhetorical history.

Only during the last quarter-century have Dominicans dealt directly with their true ethnic origin, which mainly combines the Spanish and the African. For centuries they preferred not to admit to their African heritage, referring to the darker members of the populace as *indios* ("Indians"). Actually, there really is little or no discernible trace of Indian heritage, despite the interracial conjugal activities during colonial times which led to numerous mixed offspring. Today the general population of the Dominican Republic is officially classified as mulatto.[2]

Nonetheless, the presence of the Taíno people on the island has always been a source of great pride for Dominicans. To Dominicans, the hero of Bartolomé de Las Casas' *Historia de las Indias* (*Story of the Indies*), Enriquillo, a Taíno Indian, is a great romantic and national symbol. This young, handsome, Christian Indian, as he is depicted in the Las Casas chronicles, stood up to the Spanish colonialists defending the rights of his people. Despite Las Casas' and others' impassioned battle with the Spanish crown on behalf of the Indians, by 1550 there were none left in Hispaniola. They died as a result of abuse, overwork, diseases brought by the Spanish, and starvation that occurred when fleeing from the Spanish into the hinterland, where they were not able to continue traditional agricultural and social practices.

The Taíno Indians

The Taíno Indians were members of the larger Arawak group, who originated in the Orinoco-Amazon basin. Over centuries they had migrated north and settled, among other Caribbean islands, in Hispaniola. The social and economic evolution of the Taínos was uneven, given that on the one hand, they barely clothed themselves, but on the other hand their use of stone was as refined as that of the most advanced cultures of the American mainland, especially in the art of crafting figures from stone and jewelry from gold. They were also well advanced in the art of ceramics. There is much evidence that in terms of spiritual, economic, and social development at the time of the arrival of the Spaniards, the Taínos, who numbered millions, were well on the way to becoming an organized civilization in the fashion of the Mayas of the Yucatán peninsula.

One indicator of the degree of advancement of a civilization is when agricultural labor is separated from cultural labor. The Taínos were approaching this degree of civilization at the time of the arrival of the Spaniards. For the most part though, all members of any given Taíno community worked the fields, fished, hunted, made their own tools and artifacts, and built houses and plazas. The women dedicated their time to cooking, basket-weaving, and weaving and dyeing cotton. The community was headed by a *cacique* (chief) who decided how the gathered foods were to be distributed. In the case of a larger community, the *cacique* was counseled by the *behique*, or witch doctor, and other advisors. The role of these people was exclusively that of directing and controlling. Children had the job of watching after the *conuco* (a tract of land shaped into a mound and prepared for growing Yucca) making sure it was safe from predators, and the old, if infirm and unable to contribute to the community, were either abandoned with some provisions to last them a few days, or strangled. As a result, not many Taínos grew to be very old.

The study of Taíno customs and culture was begun by the chroniclers during the conquest of Hispaniola. It was then interrupted for almost 500 years whereupon it has resumed as part of the exploration of Dominican identity. Anthropological digs and the rereading of the chronicles written by the earliest Spanish settlers are two ways in which this ancient world is being reconstructed. The Taínos live on in the imagination of artists, in the practice of *gagá*, and by coloring and enriching the Dominican-Spanish vocabulary.

Colonial Times (1492–1864)

The colonial history of the Dominican Republic begins with accounts of Columbus' settlements in Hispaniola, the exploitation and extermination of the Taínos, the importation of African slaves, the rise of buccaneers, and the corresponding defensive strategies of the island governors. Later the colonial government had to deal with French infiltration of the western half of the island, that half's lucrative economy, and its slave plantations. The French Revolution and its ideals of equality, liberty, and freedom for all divided the French half of the island into royalists and republicans. The blacks and mulattos on the French side began fighting for their rights. The entire island became French, and the Dominican Republic eventually earned the distinction of being the only Hispanic-American country to obtain its independence not from Spain, but rather from Haiti.

On December 5, 1492, Columbus first saw the island that he was to name Hispaniola after Spain. He had sailed eastward after leaving the Bahamas, and upon arriving on the north coast of Hispaniola, made frequent stops to inquire about the existence of gold. On December 21, Columbus encountered an indigenous tribe that did not run and escape like previous groups had upon seeing the sailing ships. He met the tribe's *cacique*, Guacanagarix, who informed Columbus that there was gold in the area known as the Cibao, which Columbus confused with the word Cipango, an old Spanish word for Japan. On December 24, Columbus set sail once more to continue his exploration of the island. One of his ships, the *Santa María*, ran aground and was almost completely destroyed. The Indians as well as the Spanish sailors on the second ship, *La Niña*, helped in the rescue. (The third ship, *La Pinta*, under the command of Martín Alonso Pinzón, had separated from Columbus while they were still exploring Cuba.) Columbus decided to construct a fort with the remains of the *Santa María*. La Navidad, which means Christmas Day in Spanish, became the first settlement of the New World.

Columbus' second expedition in 1493 was very different from the first. Seventeen ships were readied for the trip with workmen, carpenters, bricklayers, and six clerics as part of the crew. Horses, pigs, various seeds, grapevines, sugarcane, medicine, war munitions, tools, and merchandise for exchange such as mirrors, jingle bells, cloth, and costume jewelry made up the cargo. Juan Ponce de León, the Spanish explorer who is credited with exploring Florida, was among the members of this expedition.

This group arrived on November 22, 1493, finding La Navidad in ruins and all its people gone. Various interpretations of what might have happened to the group exist, but what is most likely is that the men who had stayed at La Navidad began to fight among each other. Some probably decided to abandon the fort and head inland to the Cibao region. The *cacique* Caonabo killed these intruders and then went to the fort and set it and its occupants on fire. Guacanagarix supposedly defended the Spaniards and was injured by Caonabo during the attack.

Columbus then founded the settlement of La Isabela after Queen Isabel of Spain and headed for the Cibao region. He crossed a valley that to him was so beautiful that he could only compare it to paradise. He named it *La Vega Real* or Royal Valley. Columbus' descriptions of the land he explored and his depiction of the gentility of the Taíno inspired the collective imagination of all western Europeans with regard to forging an image of America—the image of an Edenic paradise populated by innocent, simple peoples. This image would eventually influence the work of two nineteenth-century philosophers, Thomas More's *Utopia* and Jean-Jacques Rousseau's concept of the good savage.

Colonial economy in Hispaniola shifted gradually from the exploitation of gold to the production of sugarcane and raising cattle. By 1520 there were twenty-four sugar mills and four sugar processing plants on the island. Columbus had brought a few sugarcane plants on his second trip to the island, and initially the plant was raised for its syrup. Ten years of experimenting by two different scientists ultimately produced sugar.

By 1530 there were more pure African blacks than any other race on the island. The first record of African slaves on the island dates back to 1501. Santo Domingo was increasingly becoming a port of transition. The settled colonists refused to do any manual labor and left it all for the slaves to do. Each mill needed eighty or more slaves to work it, and the processing plants needed between thirty and forty. More and more whites were leaving the island, in part to explore the newly discovered lands to the west that promised many more riches, such as Mexico and Peru. Some also felt unsafe staying on Hispaniola, given the continued attacks by *cimarrones*, African slaves who had escaped from the plantations.

On the northern coast of the country, far away from the watchful representatives of the Spanish crown, merchants were freely engaging in contraband, trading with British, Dutch, and French privateers. Catholic church officials on the island became edgy because the Reformation movement, which was taking place in Europe, resulted in the introduction of numerous Protestant bibles along those same northern shores. Archbishop Dávila Padilla, in a conciliatory move, suggested that the northern inhabitants be allowed to trade freely with their neighbors. Furthermore, he felt that ships from Spain should make port calls along the northern coast instead of limiting their destination to Santo Domingo exclusively. Stopping at ports along the northern coastline would ensure that goods from Hispaniola, especially cow hides, were making it to Spain legally. Conversely, direct supplies from Spain would circumvent the need to purchase from pirates. The archbishop's advice was ignored, and instead an ill-conceived policy of depopulation of the northern coast, known as the *devastaciones*, was instituted. Opposition to this move was organized in 1605 by Hernando Montoro. Armed with munitions purchased from ransacking pirates, the inhabitants of the north coast fought the Spanish Royal forces sent from Santo Domingo. The struggle lasted several months, and the Royal forces, who set fires to entire settlements, eventually triumphed. The depopulation and the fires spelled economic disaster for the northern portion of the island, as cattle were left behind and quite a few sugar mills were abandoned. The once thriving and well-populated colony was reduced to a few towns along the southeastern coast. Escaped slaves thrived along the northern coast where buccaneerism became the accepted form of survival.[3]

By the mid-1700s towns that had been depopulated a century earlier along the northern coast were settled again. Towns along the border between the

French and Spanish sides of the island received the most reinforcement, in military terms, but also in terms of the amount of people settling those areas.

Economic development in the eighteenth century primarily consisted of cattle-raising, and to a lesser degree the pork and horse industries on the 1525 -1600 eastern side of the island. The animals were raised on extensive pieces of land called *hatos.* Slaves did not work these farms as the slave industry on the island was basically limited to the growth and production of sugarcane, sugar, and rum. The proprietors of the *hato* and what is referred to as "slave plantations" were civilian and military colonial officials. There were also all sizes of farms on which coffee, cotton, cocoa, tobacco, fruits, and vegetables were cultivated for consumption by the inhabitants of the island. The main source of labor for these was the slave who by 1780 was numbered in the thirty-thousands.

The French Revolution in 1789 and the consequent declaration of the Rights of Man were met with indignation by the French proprietors in Sainte Domingue. The mulattos received the news happily, anticipating long-awaited vindication. Almost simultaneously there were mulatto delegations in Paris as well as in Port au Prince fighting for the institution of these rights and, at the foremost, demanding the freedom of slaves. Armed rebellion followed shortly, and by a peculiar twist of political strategy to aggravate the Republic of France, the governor of the Spanish side of the island, an avowed royalist, decided to support the insurgent slaves with arms and provisions. Such a move on the part of Governor Joaquín García was deemed outright intervention. García's ultimate goal was to create such havoc on the western side of the island so as to be able to invade it and reposses it for Spain. On August 27, 1793, slavery was officially abolished on the French side. Meanwhile, Spain's loss to the French Republic and the Treaty of Basilea (1795) handed over control of the Spanish side of the island to the French. In the bitter struggle to defend the island several mulattos stood out; names that would become significant in Haitian history were Toussaint Louverture, Henri Cristophe, and Jean Jacques Dessalines.

On January 1, 1804, the Republic of Haiti was born. The governor of the eastern part of the island, which was still French, was General Ferrand. He fully intended to reestablish French control over the entire island. Although trade with the United States was encouraged, including the export of mahogany, logwood, and hardwood, Ferrand prohibited trade with Haiti. This policy angered the cattle owners and the tradesmen of the Cibao region and the border area, and bitterness toward the French grew among the Spanish on the eastern half of the island.

As King Ferdinand VII of Spain was removed from the Spanish throne by Napoleon's forces and the emperor's brother was put in the king's place in 1808, a spirit of independence invaded most Spanish colonies. In the western half of Sainte Domingue, as the island was now called, the pervasive sentiment was to get independence from the French in the name of the restitution of Ferdinand VII to the throne of Spain.

The changes in Spain were the last straw for the colonists who wanted independence. On December 1, 1821, under the leadership of José Núñez de Cáceres, the eastern half of the island was declared independent and named Haití Español. The idea was to become part of Simón Bolívar's Grand Colombia which was to include French Haiti and the countries that are today known as Venezuela, Colombia, and Ecuador. Just as Bolívar's project was doomed to failure, so was Núñez de Cáceres' government. He lacked popular support because the mulattos and freed slaves, which constituted the majority of the population, were suspicious of Núñez de Cáceres. He was a member of the elite and as such was not expected to represent the lower classes. For many people the idea of two independent republics on the same island made no sense. Juan Pedro Boyer, the president of the French side, articulated the notion that the island was meant to be one country. With the support of many of the interior provinces of Haití Español, who were used to many years of trade and good relations with the French half, Boyer peacefully overtook the Spanish half of the island on February 9, 1822. His first mandate was the abolishment of slavery. Blacks, mulattos, and whites were given positions in both the municipal and federal government.

The white minority upper classes panicked and fled to Cuba, Puerto Rico, and Venezuela where they began to plot takeovers. Boyer's biggest enemy, however, was the Church, which had initially not taken sides with regard to the French Haitian takeover. Boyer promulgated laws according to the Haitian constitution, based largely on the French constitution, which included the appropriation of much of the Church's real estate possessions and the institution of a tax for all church services. Thus nuns and priests, who were for the most part white and Spanish, led the resistance movement against Boyer's government.

Haiti experienced great difficulty in receiving world recognition as an independent country. Requests for diplomatic relations to John Quincy Adams, president of the United States, were turned down, presumably because of the abolishment of slavery on the island nation. Boyer also extended an invitation to freed slaves from the United States to establish themselves on the island, guaranteeing them full rights of citizenship. A few freed slaves from the United States did settle in Samaná, on the Spanish side of the island.

Although most were not able to adjust to conditions on the island, the descendants of some of these English-speaking blacks can still be found in Samaná. Meanwhile, Boyer agreed to a nefarious arrangement with the French whereupon Haiti would be granted political recognition in return for a very high indemnization fee for damages suffered by the French in their war against the Haitian freed slaves.

On July 16, 1838, on the eastern side of the island a group of lower-middle-class tradesmen got together under the leadership of Juan Pablo Duarte, and formed a secret society they called La Trinitaria.[4] This society's main objective was to definitively separate the eastern two-thirds of the island from the government of Haiti, and to create a "Republic that would be free, sovereign, and independent from all foreign domination and that will be named the Dominican Republic" (Franco 190).

Duarte was born in Santo Domingo to a Spanish father and a *criolla* mother (one who had been born on the island). As a young adult, Duarte traveled for several years through the United States, England, France, and Spain. He thus came in contact with the most recent political thinking on the continent: liberalism and romanticism. By 1842 La Trinitaria was a well-ingrained organization with members in various towns of the eastern half. The movement was, for the most part, composed of middle-class whites with a few mulattos integrated therein. Another group, headed by Buenaventura Báez, sought independence from the western half of the island not as an independent country, but rather as a protectorate of a powerful nation. Meanwhile, on the western half of the island, Boyer, who had suspended the payments due to France and who had, by numerous accounts, become a tyrant, was facing dire opposition of his own and was ultimately forced to flee the island in 1843. He was replaced by an eight-person provisional government headed by Charles Hérard Aine. The tumultuous situation in the west only served as incentive for the eastern half to separate. Duarte organized an armed rebellion and the government of Governor Carrie, the Haitian representative to Santo Domingo, capitulated. Duarte and his people took over the government by distributing power throughout the eastern half in the form of small groups of governing bodies or *juntas* made up of townspeople. This initial triumph was short-lived and Hérard personally took over the country and had many of the people involved in the movement for independence arrested. Duarte fled to Venezuela where he hoped to obtain reinforcements for his struggle.

Hérard instituted a new constitution that decreed, among other postulates, that no whites could ever hold governing positions. This angered the eastern half once more and spurned Báez on to making a deal with France whereupon it would help the eastern half of the island gain its independence. The province of Samaná went so far as to secede to France.

The actual rebellion, that today is commemorated as Independence Day, took place on February 27, 1844, and was amazingly small. Duarte was still out of the country, so Ramón Mella staged a small uprising in the middle of the night with shots in the air that brought out the Haitian authorities in Santo Domingo, who decided that whatever was happening was too big for them to handle. They retreated and waited for assistance from the west. The next day, negotiations between the two sides, headed by Francisco del Rosario Sánchez, the third party of the original La Trinitaria (Duarte, Mella, and Sánchez), led to a peaceful agreement between the two sides, granting sovereignty to the eastern side.

Independence—The First Republic

The years of 1844 to 1852 were abysmally ruinous for the economy of the young republic. Since most of the men were engaged by the army in constant defense of the country, from the ever-present threat of a Haitian invasion, there were few available for agricultural work, cattle tending, and manufacturing. There were only two public schools with just a few students enrolled, and no libraries or hospitals. The roads were virtually impassible. The children of the lower classes, age eight and under, wandered about naked, and few in the populace could afford shoes. Exported goods included mahogany, logwood, cow skins, and tobacco. Many goods including flour, salted meat, cod, herring, cheese, bacon, butter, soap, candles, cloth, and agricultural implements were imported mainly from the United States. Commerce was handled by foreign-owned companies. Given the fact that there were no interior roads or bridges connecting the port cities with their interior counterparts (a trip to Santo Domingo, from the second largest city, Santiago took one week on horseback), the Dominican Republic found itself in the paradoxical situation of being involved in international trade rather than national. This led to a fundamental change in government: annexation.

The Dominican Republic was annexed to Spain on March 18, 1861. During annexation all important government offices were occupied by Spaniards, as were many ecclesiastic jobs, and most soldiers in the armed forces were Spanish.

The War of Restoration

Popular sentiment against the neocolonial status of annexation grew rapidly, and the revolution for restoration (La guerra de la Restauración) of the republic began. The battles that were fought between nationalist forces (assisted to a small degree by Haiti) and the Spaniards dragged out over months. The hero of this insurrection was Gregorio Luperón. The country was divided into north and south, with the northern forces being those of the Spaniards and the southern those of the opposition.

The Second Republic

In May 1865, the Spanish court resolved to annul the annexation of the Dominican Republic, and thus the Second Republic was born. Pedro Antonio Pimentel became the first president, and he governed from Santiago. Given his popular-based political sentiment, Pimentel ostracized people with business interests. Business supported José María Cabral for president of the Republic, and with that endorsement, Cabral staged a successful coup against Pimentel. Actually Cabral's role was simply a venue for Báez, a long-time friend and supporter of Cabral, who used the opportunity to return from exile. In a short time, Báez assumed the presidency of the Republic, albeit for a limited time, after which he was sent into exile in Curaçao.

Luperón, the hero of the War of the Restoration, became president. His main goals were to stabilize the country economically, and to promote education and culture. Since he had never aspired to the presidency, he only agreed to take charge for a year until elections could be held. Luperón was succeeded by Catholic prelate Fernando Arturo de Meriño who basically continued Luperón's policies. After the conclusion of his designated two years in the presidency, Meriño handed over power to Ulíses Heureux who was elected in 1882.

Ulíses Heureux's Dictatorship

Heureux's tenure saw a change in the basic agrarian economic infrastructure of the country. An increase in sugarcane mills meant the elimination of the communal farmer. This translated into somewhat more income for the government, but also into the elimination of multi-faceted farming. Rich businessmen, who wished to establish sugar factories, purchased plots of land from poor *campesinos* (farmers), taking away their sole means of support.

Those same *campesinos* ended up working for the entrepreneurial sugar producers, and agriculture production saw its shift to the monoculture of sugarcane.

Heureux (referred to popularly as Lilís) negotiated a loan with a Dutch bank that saw the country out of immediate financial bankruptcy. The fact that a European government had faith in the Heureux government elevated his prestige in the country. He used the money to pay debts and salaries, to reinforce the spy network he had established throughout the country, and to finance his next elections. His wheeling and dealing betrayed the fact that Heureux did not distinguish public finances from his own and used the money from the loans he was securing for personal advancement. He became a great landowner as well, with property all over the Republic and also in Curaçao.

Many public works were accomplished during the Heureux dictatorship, most importantly the electrification of Santo Domingo which was begun in 1890. Heureux also finished the construction of the bridge over the Ozama river, inaugurated rail service inland, and had the aqueduct of Santiago completed. More elementary schools were built and attendance to these increased; renewed attention was paid toward the betterment of high schools as well.

The main reason Heureux found it so easy to stay in power was the fact that his regime saw an end to the civil war that the country had endured, in one way or another, since its independence in 1844. The peace he maintained was at the price of bribery, favoritism, buying out individuals, repression, and assassinations. Heureux's unrestrained borrowing from the United States led the country to virtual bankruptcy. Heureux was assassinated in Moca in 1899, and the country descended, once again, into an anarchy that would eventually lead to a U.S. occupation.

Years of Anarchy (1899–1916)

Four revolutions occurred and five presidents gained office in the six years following Heureux's assassination (1899–1905). A provisional government was formed by Horacio Vásquez. Elections were held, and Juan Isidro Jimenes, an extremely wealthy businessman, was elected president with Vásquez as his vice president. In 1900 the San Domingo Improvement Company was given virtual control of Dominican customs receipts. This unpopular move resulted in the overthrow of Jimenes by Vásquez, who in turn made his own agreement with the U.S. government, which agreed to take over and settle the debt to San Domingo Improvement. Vásquez was overthrown by General Woss y Gil, and this presidency was overturned by General Carlos

Morales who was officially elected president with General Ramón Cáceres as vice president.

Cáceres known familiarly as "Mon," had the potential of being a good president for the country. He initiated public works, and the country enjoyed a brief interlude of economic prosperity under his rule. But Cáceres took unusually harsh measures to deal with the nationalist rebellion led by the leader of a peasant revolt, Desidero Arias. He began by relocating the inhabitants of the northwest (one of Arias' strongholds) to other parts of the country and by ordering the slaughter of all local cattle. These moves had the immediate and long-lasting effects of impoverishing that part of the country. Cáceres allowed foreign investors to buy up large tracts of land for the purposes of growing and exporting their own agricultural goods. These foreign investors were given considerable leeway in their business dealings.

During Jimenes' second term, which began at the end of 1914, the United States tightened its control over the Dominican Republic, going beyond demanding the right to oversee all expenses incurred by the government, to complete control of customs receipts. They suggested that the Dominican Republic eliminate its army and rural guard forces, and install a national guard instead, which the United States was prepared to train. The Dominican government responded to the United States, stating that it viewed civil peace as its primary objective, and that as long as the United States dictated how it was to handle its finances and its forces, there could not be peace. For its part, the U.S. government was particularly fearful of Arias whom they branded as a robber and bandit. Jimenes retired to a country house for reasons of bad health, but continued to rule the country. Seeing the virtual vacancy in the presidential palace, Arias took over. This was all the pretext the United States needed to send in the Marines, who landed in the first days of May 1916.

The U.S. occupation lasted eight years, during which time the United States tried to install a puppet president, but no Dominican was willing to assume such a role. The actual occupation was peaceful, and the protest of the Dominican nation was manifested only by silence and a general state of mourning. A columnist described the event as an "occupation of a cemetery" and not of a country (Franco 425). Dr. Francisco Henríquez y Carvajal, a medical doctor residing in Santiago, Cuba, was brought in to head a provisional government with no power. There were reports of brutality on the part of the U.S. Marines who would arbitrarily assault and arrest Dominican citizens. The United States censored all Dominican publications and prohibited the ownership of all arms and ammunitions.

The apparent tranquility that ruled over the island was to be shortlived as bands of *campesinos* from the eastern part of the country, with no prior affiliation to any previous political group, began to protest the occupation. They objected to the politics of divestment propagated against the small farm owners by the giant, U.S.-owned sugar plantations, and to the racism perpetuated by occupation forces who were mostly from the southern part of the United States (Calder 182). The first leader, Vicente Evangelista, was tricked into a meeting to sign a peace treaty with U.S. forces who then shot him. His martyrdom ensured the rise of forces known henceforth as *gavilleros.* These guerrilla forces quickly captured the local imagination, and their actions attained heroic proportions. They counted on the full support of all peasant farmers. The U.S. forces were desperate to liquidate the guerrillas and for this purpose endorsed measures of extreme cruelty, subjecting entire villages to pillaging, looting, and burning with complete disregard to the inhabitants. The United States Air Force ultimately resorted to bombing the villages, which goes down in history as the first time the United States used air power in a Latin American country.

The brutality of the U.S. military became notorious. Supported by wealthy Dominican landowners who provided the occupying forces with provisions and spies, woe befell the *gavillero* who was captured. The majority of them were beheaded or shot on the spot. The few who were captured were immediately imprisoned and forced into hard labor. Conditions became so bad that other Latin American countries declared their allegiance to the *gavillero* cause and clamored for the U.S. Senate to send in investigators. These investigators found that horrendous abuses had been committed against many innocent citizens.

Between 1916 and 1919 the only real opposition forces to the invasion, or intervention, as it is referred to in American history books, besides the *gavilleros* was recorded by the provisional president Henríquez y Carvajal, his son, Max Henríquez Ureña, and poet Tulio M. Cestero. The first nationalist movements against the occupation were thus initiated in Cuba where Henríquez y Carvajal had settled in exile.

The formation of the National Dominican Union assured that a solid opposition front had been formed. The partial lifting of general censure allowed for the publication of essays, reports, and poetry that railed against U.S. forces. This resulted in the frequent arrest of the perpetrators, most notably that of poet Fabio Fiallo whose patriotic poems and essays were known and admired throughout Europe and the Americas.

Historically there had been very little communication between farmers and urban dwellers in the Dominican Republic. The poor conditions of communication throughout the country, but most particularly in the case of farmers attached to very old traditions, some passed right down from the Taínos, created a cultural schism between the *campesinos* and the city dwellers. As a result, the *gavillero* movement and the city-based nationalist movement did not work together.

President Francisco Henríquez Carvajal had disbanded the Dominican Armed Forces due to lack of capital to sustain them. The United States decided to form its own armed forces for the Dominicans which was made very difficult by the fact that only a scarce number of what would have to be amoral Dominicans would even consider enlisting in such forces. The first task of this new Dominican National Guard was to fight the *gavilleros*. One of the first officers to really stand out was twenty-seven-year-old Rafael Leonidas Trujillo. Since there were few volunteers, the ranks were also filled by U.S. Marine sergeants and corporals who, upon entering the Dominican National Guard were immediately promoted to the ranks of captain and major. In 1921 the Dominican National Guard became the National Police Force. Salaries were attractive, and the force was made in the semblance and image of the United States Marine Corps, down to the emblems and the insignia of the uniforms.

Horacio Vásquez, now sixty-four years old, began his third term as president amidst great joy and jubilation by the populace, who celebrated the lowering of the foreign flag and the retreat of the occupational forces. Vásquez's term started in dire economic straits and obtained bonds issued by a Chicago-based firm to continue some of the public works projects initiated by the Americans and to buy out the American-owned power company. He was criticized for paying the asking price of $40,000, which was considered exorbitant given the state of decay and disrepair of the power company building. Toward the end of his presidency Vásquez's government was accused of corruption. Having secured healthy loans for the completion of numerous public works projects, Vásquez's government allegedly hired friends of the party to complete these projects. These engineers and architects proceeded to work without plans and, more significant, without a budget, so that enormous amounts of money were unnecessarily wasted, when not lining the pockets of those favored by Vásquez.

Trujillo, meanwhile had ascended to the position of brigadier general in what was now referred to as the National Armed Forces. The degree of corruption occurring within the military matched that of the Public Works faction of the government. Observers of the era comment that Trujillo was simply given a license to steal, thus quickly amassing a personal fortune. Despite warnings as to the dangers of Trujillo's character and corruptive activities, Vásquez, convinced of the general's loyalty to him and his government, did not listen.

Vásquez prepared to run for reelection in 1930, but prior to fully realizing his campaign, he became ill and had to leave for the United States for a kidney operation. Trujillo, counting on the support of his old friends in the United States Marine Corps who were still stationed in Haiti, planned a takeover. Although he got acknowledgment from some, he was ultimately severely chastised by Minister Young who stated that as long as Trujillo wore a military uniform he was to serve his nation and constitution and not plot overthrows. Trujillo pledged to follow this advice in a dramatic move whereby he knelt before Young. Vásquez returned sooner than his convalescence should have allowed, and when confronting Trujillo about the allegations, Trujillo genuflected once again, pledging loyalty to the president.

The Trujillo Era (1930–1961)

The forces of Desiderio Arias, Estrella Ureña, and Elías Brache staged an uprising in Santiago which Trujillo quickly suffocated without bloodshed on February 23, 1930. American naval forces went on alert in the waters surrounding the island, all the while maintaining a distance. The insurrectionists demanded that Vásquez be withdrawn from presidential candidacy. U.S. diplomatic envoys, including John Moors Cabot and Charles Curtis, functioned as intermediaries between Vásquez and the opposing forces. Trujillo, taking advantage of Vásquez's failing health, allowed the insurrectionist forces to take over the capital without ordering any of his soldiers to act at all. Consequently, Rafael Estrella Ureña, a presidential candidate in the upcoming elections of 1930, was appointed provisional president in March 1930. His cabinet, according to the recommendations of the U.S. envoys, was composed of different parties.

American envoy Curtis in a moment of clairvoyance writes about his misgivings regarding the immediate future of Trujillo, the minister of the Armed Forces. Trujillo had made his intentions of running for the presidency in the upcoming elections widely known. As Trujillo was not really known or liked outside the military, Curtis surmised that the only way he could be elected was by using the military to inflict terror upon the populace. Curtis forecast a long and tyrannical dictatorship should Trujillo be elected (Franco Pichardo, *Historia* 490). By exerting terror and systematically eliminating all opposing forces and having confiscated all arms from all households on the island, Trujillo declared himself winner of the elections and was sworn in on August 16, 1930.

Recession.

The economy of the island completely deteriorated as a direct result of the stock market crash in the United States in October 1929. The price of and need for raw materials plummeted on the world market. The exterior debt of the country was estimated at $20 million. There was also a floating interior loan of $3 million that had come due. To make matters worse, the capital was besieged by hurricane Xenon, which leveled the capital city and severely hurt agriculture in the eastern and southern parts of the country.

By 1932 Trujillo had wheeled and dealed his own personal wealth to incomparable amounts. Because he regularly met the monthly payments and because of the devastation of the hurricane, the United States had agreed to extend one more loan to the country, the income from which was enough to generate operational cash for the regime. Trujillo purchased industries, factories, and production plants for nominal sums for the purpose of holding exclusive rights to, for example, the milk industry, the meat industry, the salt industry, and so forth. By 1939 it was calculated that either he or his family members owned more than half of the industries in the Dominican Republic.

Trujillo fomented the cultivation of agricultural products that up to that time had been imported and yet formed the staple of the Dominican diet: rice, beans, corn, and peanuts. He also promoted small business industries by facilitating the production of clothing, furniture, butter, and cheese, rather than importing all of these.

The cult of adulation, carefully orchestrated by Trujillo, began with his naming himself the Benefactor of the Nation. Later he added the title of *Generalísimo* to his name. He also changed the name of the capital city to Ciudad Trujillo. He had the University of Santo Domingo award him an Honorary Doctorate, and his five-year-old son Ramfis was given the title of Honorary Colonel of the Army.

Trujillo had prisons set up throughout the island with torture cells that became infamous for the horrors that occured within. Opponents to his regime were dealt with swiftly and brutally, usually succumbing to death from the effects of torture or disease, if not assassinated. Trujillo's dictatorship is ill-famed for its sanguinary brutality. His ways of disposing of opposition forces varied from simply throwing the bodies to the sharks to publicly displaying carcasses with signs attached. The signs would crudely remind the passerby the reason the person was dead or, more appropriately, eliminated. If the opponent had demanded a pay raise the sign would read: "Here is the pay raise you asked for" (Franco Pichardo, *Historia* 549). Trujillo's wrath was not limited to Dominicans. He incarcerated a rich Italian entrepreneur and Honorary Consul named Amadeo Barletta as he, along with some Dominican co-conspirators, threatened the overthrow of the government. It took the Italian dictator Benito Mussolini to threaten the Dominican coastline with Italian warships to convince Trujillo to release Barletta.

One of the most notorious incidents of the thousands that are recorded during the Trujillo Era is that of the massacre of Haitians in 1937. This event, as no other, "revealed to the face of the world, the bloody and savage character of the dictatorship that governed the Dominican Republic" (Franco Pichardo, *Historia* 521). The actual number of the people massacred is not known. Franco cites 17 million (522), Bell states that the figure could be as high as 25,000 (68), and Robert Crassweller estimates between 15,000 and 20,000 (156). The Haitians were massacred by common thugs and violent criminals released from prison for the specific purpose of committing these murderous acts.

The reasons for the massacre ostensibly date back a century and are directly related to the lack of a well-defined border between the two countries, but they more acutely reflect the pervasive racism that rocked the Western Hemisphere as a direct result of fascism in Europe. In fact, most of the men surrounding Trujillo espoused the theories of Arian superiority over blacks and Indians. Trujillo even entertained a policy for "whitening" the border area by encouraging the settlement of Europeans of Spanish, Polish, and Jewish descent. A definitive border had been established in 1929 during the Vásquez administration, and was reconfirmed in 1934 during a highly publicized and cordial meeting of the heads of state of the two countries, Trujillo and Stenio Vincent, then president of Haiti. Matters reached a boiling point when Dominican landowners at the border were angered by the continuous presence of Haitians who poured in looking for employment. Compounding the gravity of the situation, Cuba's president at the time, Domingo Faustino Batista, had expelled over 20,000 Haitians, sending them home. The small nation of Haiti, with a population almost double that of its neighbor and with nonarable land, faced a crisis resolved, in part, by the migration of Haitians to the Dominican Republic.

His international image tarnished by the massacre, Trujillo realized that he would be better off not running for reelection and instead postulated Jacinto Peynado as president. The Dominican Republic's economic situation was greatly improved by 1938. Trujillo and his family had the monopoly over most national industries to the point of becoming a mega corporation. He initiated many public works projects, among them the completion of roads throughout the country, which led to much better national trade. Small businesses were doing well, and as has been noted, the coffin-building trade was third only to the production of sugar and furniture (Franco 529). General poverty, though, was as prevalent as ever, as the only ones to benefit from

Trujillo's wealth and the country's economic stability were his own family and the middle class. At the end of 1940 Trujillo signed an agreement with the United States that annulled the Conventions of 1907 and 1924 which had authorized U.S. control over customs receipts.

Over a decade into his dictatorship, the extent of Trujillo's manipulative power was so ingrained and widespread that no one dared challenge it. Each Dominican household had to prominently display a plaque which read: "In this home Trujillo is the Boss." For assassinations ordered by him, the perpetrators were tried in court and convicted and then secretly released. Trujillo was on great terms with the government in Washington, which tended to overlook rumored problems when the situation apparently was good, as there was peace and democracy, and loans were being remunerated. The peace that existed in the Dominican Republic was at the price of indescribable repression maintained by a continuous enforcement of terror and indoctrination. Adulation of Trujillo was required and the prevailing democracy was a well-orchestrated sham. Trujillo satisfied Washington's demands by scheduling elections, at first every four years, then every five. The changes that the dictator made to the 1942 constitution included granting women suffrage and extending the presidential term to five years. For each of those elections there was only one well-supported candidate.

On the list of positive outcomes of Trujillo's tenure, the most salient are the fact that the country's foreign debt was completely liquidated and many *(pros)* construction projects in the area of public works were completed, especially the massive construction of schools.

A curious development during what has become known as the Era of Trujillo is the government's invitation to Jewish and Spanish war refugees to settle in the Dominican Republic. The first 750 Jewish refugees came in 1940 and settled along the northern coast, and about 4,000 or 5,000 Spanish refugees fled the Spanish Civil War. The Jewish refugees did not immediately try to integrate themselves into Dominican culture. The Spaniards, whose assimilation was facilitated by the common language and many common cultural practices, were for the most part progressive in terms of political thinking, including anarchists, liberals, communists, and socialists. Many of them left the Dominican Republic almost immediately upon gauging the degree of repression suffered by the masses. Ultimately, less than a thousand remained, but this was enough to make a difference in the political arena.

The Spaniards ensured that the quiet and greatly diffused voices of the opposition cohered, and by 1943 a clandestine political party was formed: the *Partido Democrático Revolucionario Dominicano* (PDRD) ("The Revolutionary and Democratic Dominican Party"). By 1945, when the PDRD publicly declared its opposition to Trujillo, the United States was also beginning to show dissatisfaction with his leadership, responding to a general antifascist feeling generated by the effects of World War II.

Another slowly gathering opposition force was registered in the eastern part of the country where the majority of the sugar plantations were located. The opposition took the form of unionized laborers protesting the utter misery of their working conditions, the unconscionably low wages, and the coupon system redeemable only at the company store. For Trujillo the existence of the sugarcane mills was a thorn in his corporate machine as he was not able to appropriate them. He raised export taxes on sugar to aggravate the plantation owners, but it also had the effect of alienating him even further from the United States.

There were hundreds of Dominicans in exile residing mainly in Cuba and Venezuela. Directed by Juan Bosch, Angel Miolán, and Juan Isidro Jimenes Grullón the *Partido Revolucionario Dominicano* (PRD) ("The Dominican Revolutionary Party") was founded in 1939. This group was planning an armed invasion for which Trujillo prepared himself by purchasing arms from Brazil, having been turned down by the United States. On the other hand, in an effort to improve his own and his regime's public image, Trujillo took a gamble. He invited the leftists in exile to return to the Dominican Republic where he promised freedom of speech, action, and so forth. Some of the exilees took him up on it and returned to form political parties and platforms that called for better conditions for the worker, equal educational opportunities for men and women, women's rights, and the development of national industries. Trujillo underestimated the popularity of the movements' leaders and their ideas. He found himself having to send in troops to break up enormous manifestations that protested the government. The troops were ruthless with the protesters who were, for the most part, university students, clubbing them brutally. Trujillo staged a sucessful anticommunist protest in the presses and increased the repression against the groups, chiefly by assassinations.

The president of Venezuela, Rómulo Betancourt, and the president of Guatemala, Juan José Arévalo, were instrumental in organizing an armed incursion into the Dominican Republic from Cuba with the purpose of toppling the regime. Trujillo purchased weapons illegally from the United States, Canada, and Hungary, and opened a machine-gun and rocket-producing factory in the Dominican Republic. Luckily for Trujillo, U.S. politics also turned tough against communism under the notorious influence of J. Edgar Hoover, the director of the FBI, so Trujillo could count on U.S. support.

The invasionary expedition organized in 1947, whose members included Fidel Castro, failed before it got started as it was stopped in its tracks by Cuban patrol boats. A second expedition, proceeding from Guatemala and integrated by Guatemalan, Nicaraguan, and Costa Rican citizens, attempted an invasion in 1949. They were stopped by the Dominican Coast Guard, and the retribution for those that made landfall but were later captured was harsh.

For the 1952 elections Trujillo had his brother Héctor Bienvenido Trujillo Molina elected president and used the time away from the office of president to travel and garner positive public opinion abroad. Trujillo spent some time in Washington where, among others, he was celebrated as "one of the few men in the world who have the privilege of lighting the torch of civilization, like [George] Washington did for the United States, for the purpose of fostering good, progress and prosperity for its people" (Fred N. Vinson, Supreme Court Justice, quoted in Franco 567). In Spain, Trujillo was splendidly received by the dictator Generalísimo Francisco Franco, and in the Vatican Pope Pius XII received him with celestial blessings. By 1955 Trujillo was celebrating a quarter of a century in power during which many changes had taken place in his country, primarily in the growth of the population, the growth of urban centers, the sharply increased military and police forces, and the institution of an immensely feared Secret Service, referred to popularly as the SIM, headed by the notoriously evil Johnny Abbes García.

A change in the constitution by Trujillo in 1957, reopening the position of vice president, allowed for the arrival of a lasting presence on the scene. Dr. Joaquín Balaguer Ricardo, a historian and literary critic, was appointed to the first vice presidency of the Trujillo dictatorship.

Any apogee is followed necessarily by a downfall. A World's Fair was organized by Trujillo in 1957 for which millions of dollars were spent, characterized by a boom in construction, with visitors from around the world. This marked the beginning of the end. The strong economy of the previous decade began to experience a serious decline as Trujillo was borrowing large sums of money to finance the projects for the World's Fair. The situation of the poor, particularly the rural farmer, grew worse as his salary remained unchanged and yet the prices of goods spiralled.

But it was the practice of assassinating opponents that finally caught up with Trujillo. Spaniard Jesús de Galíndez, a student at Columbia University in New York City, was writing a dissertation about the Trujillo dictatorship when he was kidnapped, brought back to the island by an American pilot named Gerald L. Murphy, and shot. Murphy disappeared and the man accused of Murphy's death "committed suicide" in jail. This chain of events, which took place in 1956, was followed by other allegations and horrendous crimes, the most wicked of which was the assassination of the Mirabal sisters.

These unlikely revolutionaries were daughters of a wealthy landowner from the Cibao region. Minerva was a lawyer; Bélgica (nicknamed Dedé) ran the family business after their father's untimely death; Patria had married young and became deeply involved in the Catholic Church; and María Teresa intended to follow in her sister Minerva's footsteps and earn a law degree. While at the university Minerva met and was attracted to leaders of a swelling underground movement whose goal it was to overthrow Trujillo. She was elected to head the J14 (the name of the group commemorates the June 14, 1959, attempted invasion of the island), but she declined in favor of her husband, Manuel Tavárez. Minerva eventually enlisted Patria's support in her fight against Trujillo. Patria took the movement's message to the church and started a grass roots effort to shake the Church's foundation and its dreaded fear of Trujillo. María Teresa assisted Minerva directly in plotting the overthrow. Dedé, while all the time supporting her sisters' activities, managed the family business.

Trujillo had Patria, Minerva, and María Teresa killed in an ambush made to appear as a car accident on November 25, 1960. The ruse did not fool anybody and caused an immediate international furor. This tragic incident, along with an attempt on Venezuela's President Rómulo Betancourt's life, sealed Trujillo's fate. Trujillo was assassinated on May 30, 1961, by a group of conspirators, and the Mirabal name became synonymous with patriotism for the Dominican Republic.

History remembers 1960 as the year when Trujillo's downfall was a certainty. Conditions had deteriorated in all sectors. The government, in order to finance its repression, instituted new and steep taxes including the requirement that each citizen be issued and carry an identification card on his person. The economy was doing badly and the foreign debt began to rise again as Trujillo was granted loans from the International Monetary Fund (IMF).

Direct CIA involvement in Trujillo's death was ultimately limited to supplying arms to the conspirators. The agency, as well as President John F. Kennedy and other high-ranking U.S. officials, were very much aware of the assassination plot. The details of the assassination and its aftermath take on Hollywood proportions. Trujillo was fatally shot on his way to his country residence in San Cristóbal on May 30, 1961. Although always accompanied by bodyguards and look-out men, he sporadically decided to be taken to San Cristóbal, and at those times, only his chauffeur accompanied him. The conspirators had practiced for months and were ready the night that the car took off down the highway that skirts the Caribbean shore from the capital to San Cristóbal. Antonio de la Maza is credited for actually shooting the dictator from a passing car while another car blocked the progress of Trujillo's car from the front.

Vice president Balaguer wrote and read the panegyric for Trujillo's funeral. Its content and words were later undermined in a novel by Marcio Veloz Maggiolo, *La biografía difusa de Sombra Castañeda* (*The Diffuse Biography of Sombra Castañeda*). Balaguer went to great lengths to extol the virtues of the tyrant, to the point of ridicule, given the evasiveness of the truth of the fallen dictator.

The Aftermath

What followed was chaos. While an immediate *coup d'état* had been planned, ousting then-president Joaquín Balaguer, the conspirators were faced instead with insubordination, particularly from the Armed Forces and the dreaded secret intelligence forces. Johnny Abbes Garcia, head of the Secret Service (SIM), took it upon himself to hunt down all those involved in Trujillo's assassination, to round up all family members of the accused, and to submit them to tortures of "dantean" proportions (Franco Pichardo, *Historia* 592). Suicides were widespread in the days following the tyrannicide as the only means to avoid being captured by the Secret Service.

Rafael Trujillo (Ramfis), the dictator's son, decided to extend his father's regime with himself in the seat of power. He couldn't stop the masses though, and the country erupted in a collective protest, vehemently expressing its anger and indignation with anyone that in any way represented the dictator. These masses called for the immediate exile of every member of the dictator's family.

Balaguer's first rule of order was to give the appearance of the establishment of a democracy. He was intent on having the sanctions previously imposed by the Organization of American States (OAS) lifted. At the instigation of the United States he clamped down on communists, primarily by not letting many liberal thinkers, long-since exiled, back into the country. The situation became truly precarious in October 1961, and the tension was only relieved by the departure of the entire Trujillo clan and Balaguer's taking refuge in the Papal Nunciate.

A council composed of three men, Rafael F. Bonnelly, Dr. Fernández Caminero, and Dr. Donald Reid Cabral took power in 1962 calling themselves the State Council. This group promised to lead the country until elections could be held. They received support from the United States and the Civic Union Party. Their first order of business was to expropriate Trujillo's and his family's wealth both in cash and properties. The government was suddenly immensely rich. It was soon evident that those who would benefit from the rule of this government were the rich and the Americans, so mass protests ensued again. The protesters demanded punishment for the perpetrators of the dictatorship; they demanded respect for national interests and respect for democratic rights.

As the 1962 elections approached, three parties emerged. On the left was the J14 party, represented primarily by university students encouraged by the concomitant success of the Communist Party in Cuba. Rather than participate in elections, this group prepared for an armed insurrection. On the right was the *Union Cívica party* (UC), whose propaganda tried to distance itself from the ruling council, but who nevertheless was associated with the upper middle classes and the oligarchy. Their propaganda concetrated on anti-Trujillo rhetoric and tended to ignore the plight of the masses, most particularly the reigning poverty of the rural population. The PRD, headed by Juan Bosch, directed its message to the rural poor and concentrated on issues such as agrarian reform and the redistribution of wealth. Bosch completely avoided the anti-Trujillo barrage, which paradoxically resulted in many soldiers and former government employees enrolling in Bosch's socialist party. As it became obvious that the PRD was most probably going to be victorious in the elections, the UC accused its leader of being a communist and enlisted the help of the Church. A leading prelate then accused Bosch publicly of being a communist. Bosch asked to be allowed to defend himself publicly on television in a debate with the priest. The debate that ensued lasted well into the night and was watched closely by a large percentage of Dominicans. The priest finally had to concede that Bosch was not a communist, but Bosch did not feel triumphant at the end of the night, even though his supporters did. He prophetically announced that his presidency would be doomed because of the onus of communism. Bosch won the election with 60 percent of the votes while the UC received 30 percent. Bosch's presidency, which lasted only seven months, was singular in the history of the Dominican Republic for the reason that it is indisputably the first and only truly democratically elected government, with the exception of the current presidency of Leonel Fernández Reyna. Upon his election, Bosch enjoyed fairly enthusiastic support from the United States, particularly from President Kennedy. It wasn't long, though, before Bosch and his cabinet took a series of measures that angered the United States, the middle class, and the oligarchy. The first of these was to secure loans from Switzerland and Great Britain and to contract important construction projects with them.

For example the British General Electric Company was contracted for the construction of a hydroelectric dam at Tavera. This unlikely and untimely procedure was Bosch's way of seeking economic independence from the United States. It was widely misinterpreted, however, as a maneuver to politically distance himself from the United States. The allegations of his communism surged forth again, launched by critics as a way to weaken him politically. Bosch has been regarded by some as unsuited for ruling his country since in some ways he was "greater" than his country (Bell 82). Bosch had spent most of his life in exile and was thus as much a citizen of the world as he was a Dominican. History regards the Bosch presidency as tragically flawed especially when considering the potential it had for overcoming the past and setting the nation on a definitive path toward democracy, relative economic independence, and even prosperity. The flaw was circumstantial, as much as it was the nature of Bosch's character, which has been described as arrogant and moody. The constitution he drafted in April 1963 angered four major areas that, in retrospect, he could have at least humored. As a result of the constitution, landowners, both big and modest, feared expropriation, since Bosch proclaimed the right of the poor to own land. The constitution was "essentially secular" and omitted any reference to the concordat (Bell 84). Workers' rights were favored over employers', and the military was offended by the implication of civilian involvement in court martials of military personnel for "offences committed on duty" (Bell 84).

A dangerous confrontation with Haiti also contributed to Bosch's appearance as a weak president. François Duvalier, Haiti's dictator since 1957, was planning, along with members of Trujillo's family, to overthrow Bosch. As Bosch got wind of this he planned a bogus attack on Haiti, naively hoping to scare the Haitians into overthrowing Duvalier whom Bosch saw strictly as "a thoroughly evil man who had no business governing anybody" (Bell 86). At this point Bosch made two crucial mistakes. The first was underestimating Duvalier's "hypnotic spell" over the Haitian people, and the second was to fail to let the Dominican Armed Forces fully in on his intentions with regard to the Haitian dictator. As far as they understood, they were to invade Haiti with the ojective of overtaking the capital, Port-au-Prince. After assessing the forces, Colonel Elías Wessín y Wessín became convinced that the operation was doomed to failure because he lacked adequate armaments—not ever realizing that what Bosch was planning was simply a bluff. This public humiliation and his passionate sense of divine mission to overthrow communism, which he saw personified in the Haitian president, inspired Wessín y Wessín to stage a coup.

The coup transpired on September 25, 1963. Bosch was sent to exile in

Puerto Rico, his constitution was abolished, and the appointed government was a triumverate including Emilio de los Santos, Manuel Enrique Tavares, and Ramón Tapia Espinal with Donald Reid Cabral as the minister of foreign affairs. One of the immediate casualties of the opposition occurred in a clash with the banned J14 movement. Its leader, Manuel Tavares Justo, Minerva Mirabal's widower, was killed along with fourteen others. The original members of the triumverate resigned, and Reid Cabral stepped into power accompanied by Ramón Cáceres Troncoso. Although it called itself a triumverate it only consisted of two members, which Bell metaphorizes as "an ungainly tricycle with one wheel missing and the other two of different sizes and incapable of any movement except in a circle or of remaining upright without the prop provided by the armed forces and, in particular, . . . by General Wessín y Wessín" (Bell 90).

Befallen by excessive corruption, the armed forces were having troubles of their own. Members of the military were deeply involved in contraband, using military ships and planes to illegally transport cigarettes, alcohol, perfumes, watches, electrical appliances, shoes, and even clothes. These illicit activities had devastating consequences on the nation's economy, which depended in part on import duties, not to mention the national morale. The government of Reid Cabral began using repressive measures to quell opposition, and this, along with rapidly rising unemployment and the open abuse of human rights, led to the consolidation of several opposition groups. One was made up of university students who demanded the upholding of the constitution, meaning the institution of elections and a democratically elected government. Another group, the neo-Trujillo forces, who backed Balaguer, had its own ideas for overthrowing the so-called triumverate. The latter group called itself the San Cristóbal group and was led by Colonel Ney Nivar Sejias.

April 24, 1965, marked the beginning of a sad, albeit short, period for Dominican history, and one that still haunts the collective unconscious of Dominicans who lived through it. In fact, all events from the Trujillo era henceforth have remained alive in people's memories and serve as a continuous and powerful inspiration for cultural expression. A vicious civil war broke out in the middle of the streets of Santo Domingo, splitting the capital in two. U.S. President Lyndon B. Johnson ordered the Marines to land in the Dominican Republic once again.

The man who actually began the civil war was José Francisco Peña Gómez. A member of the PRD, Gómez grabbed control of Radio Comercial and announced the fall of the triumverate. The goal of the constitutionalists, headed by Francisco Caamaño Denó, was to bring Bosch back. General Wessín y Wessín, for his part, wanted to assume control and ordered that the

National Palace be bombed while the chief of the navy, Commodore Francisco Rivera Caminero, bombed the capital from the sea. The way the U.S. assessed the situation was that the constitutionalist revolt was being supported by communist sympathizers, and if it was allowed to win, the Dominican Republic would turn into another Cuba. By April 28 the U.S. 82nd Airborne Division had replaced the Marines and was able to maintain relative peace. The OAS was called upon to establish an Inter-American Peace Force with troops from Costa Rica, Guatemala, Honduras, Paraguay, and a large contingency force from Brazil. The civil war is immortalized in Marcio Veloz Maggiolo's novel *De abril en adelante* (*From April On*), which describes the events from a constitutionalist point of view. The constitutionalists were holed up inside Santo Domingo and refused to surrender. They were continuously bombarded by the Air Force who aimed their bombs at the television stations and radio stations, particularly Radio Santo Domingo, and the National Palace. The military's intention was to set up a military junta, an idea supported by the United States. Finally, in September, a peace accord was written in which a head for a provisional government would be found, followed by elections nine months later. Antonio Guzmán, minister of agriculture under Bosch and future president, was asked to preside, but he declined. Héctor García Godoy became the president.

García Godoy turned out to be a good choice as he gradually moved the country toward reconciliation and toward peaceful elections that were closely supervised by the OAS. Joaquín Balaguer won the promised election in 1966 and ruled the country for the following twelve years—surreptitiously manipulating elections, along the way, so as to guarantee his victory (Cassá, *Historia* 331). History remembers this period as the "twelve years."

It is held that Balaguer "maintained himself at the head of government through a combination of procedures that involved electoral fraud, the exercise of extralegal violence, the repression of social protests, bribery, corruption of the highest spheres of government and, in general, the refusal to observe the canons of the law" (Cassá, "Negotiated" 20). Balaguer governed from 1966 to 1978. He was reelected again in 1986, 1990, and finally 1994—always amidst stringent charges of fraud. The charges of fraud in 1994, when he ran against Peña Gómez, were so acute that the Dominican government called for new elections in 1996 whereupon the current president of the Dominican Republic, a young, U.S.-educated candidate, Leonel Fernández Reyna, assumed the presidency.

Balaguer's rule was contradictory at best. His regime was characterized by repressive tactics that he was able to camouflage from the scrutiny of interested organizations such as the OAS. He launched a building boom and prepared the country to become what it is today, a tourist attraction. The restoration of the downtown colonial center, which has stirred a sense of identity and continuity among Dominicans with regard to their history, can be attributed to him.

Many people could never entirely forget Balaguer's participation in Trujillo's regime and felt he was accountable, at least indirectly, for the infamy of that era. Balaguer's first term, 1966–1970, was essentially uneventful except for the austere measures he imposed upon government employees. He got into trouble when he decided to run in the 1970 elections because it gave the impression of the potential for a new dictatorship. Bosch, still head of the PRD, declined to even participate in the elections. Between 1970 and 1974 Balaguer's repressive hand was better felt as, among other events, he had Caamaño, who had landed on Caracoles beach as head of a guerrilla group, killed. This action soured Balaguer's image, given the fact that Caamaño's heroism during the 1965 civil war was still fresh in people's memories. Balaguer would manage reelection by weakening his opponents' parties through intrigue and innuendo. Time and time again, when it was time for an election, the opposing parties simply withdrew their candidacy.

The 1978 election was won by the candidate for the PRD, Silvestre Antonio Guzmán. Balaguer accepted his defeat, but the status of the vote count for congressional seats remained shrouded under a cloud of allegations of conspiracy. Guzmán committed suicide in office, and Jorge Blanco, his successor, also of the PRD, allowed corruption to reach scandalous proportions. He wound up fleeing the country in disgrace. In the 1986 elections Balaguer was triumphant once again, as if to prove that the PRD could not rule the country. The two PRD presidencies proved to be economically detrimental to the country. Public works projects came to a halt, and the continuous squabble of dissent did much to demoralize all levels of the country's industry and production capabilities.

The Political Situation in the Late Twentieth Century

Juan Bosch, head of the recently formed Dominican Liberation Party (PLD); Francisco Peña Gómez, head of the PRD; and Joaquín Balaguer, head of the Partido Revolucionario Social Cristiano (PRSC) have dominated Dominican politics since 1963. Bosch and Peña Gómez, once political allies, split apart as Peña Gómez's ideals became too leftist for Bosch's taste, or one can also see it as a power struggle between the two political giants.

In the 1994 elections Peña Gómez received the most votes in the capital city, but Balaguer just barely won overall. The allegations of fraud were so strident that President Bill Clinton sent U.S. State Department functionaries to draw up a pact that would limit Balaguer's term to two years and allow for new elections in 1996, ostensibly making room for Peña Gómez to take over in 1996. The 1996 elections, however, introduced a new figure, that of Leonel Fernández Reyna, a candidate of Bosch's party, the PLD. Amazingly the PLD and PRSC, Balaguer's party, united to defeat the PRD. Amidst allegations of racist remarks by the PLD, who under no circumstances wanted to see Peña Gómez in power, they saw their only opportunity being that of uniting with their archenemy over the years, the PRSC, to defeat the common enemy. For Balaguer, too, anything was preferable to a Peña Gómez presidency.

Leonel Fernández Reyna was forty-two years old at the time of the election. The vice president is Jaime David Fernández Mirabal, son of Bélgica Mirabal, the only surviving sister of the Mirabal group martyred by Trujillo's henchmen. Minou Tavárez Mirabal, Minerva Mirabal's daughter, occupies the position of undersecretary of foreign affairs in Fernández's government.

Early indications are that Fernández Reyna's presidency will increasingly focus on foreign policy with the objective of inserting the Dominican Republic in a global consideration. On the domestic front Fernández Reyna sees his presidency as a necessary rupture with the past:

Dominican post-Trujillo democracy, that experiment that we have had for the past thirty-five to thirty-six years has rested initially on two great people: Dr. Joaquín Balaguer, who has been in power for a long time, and on the other side, Professor Juan Bosch. Later, one sees the emergence of yet another figure, in the seventies: Doctor José Francisco Peña Gómez. The transitional democratic process in our country has rested fundamentally upon three great men, upstanding intellectually, solidly engaged in a democratic process. But this has meant that just as democracy has rested on three great personalities, institutions have not developed and therefore we have an institutionally fragile state. The time has come for us to move from a democracy supported by illuminated leaders to a democracy sustained by institutions. That is why we have assumed state reform and modernization as a basic aspect of our governmental program. Something similar occurs on the economic front; we have had a model sustained by development, by state intervention, client-oriented, and in some ways by a populism that has experienced many distortions. Therefore now it is necessary to go on to a different model, of economic openness, of economic liberalization; a model that accepts basically that development not be sustained by protected industrialization, but rather in an economy oriented towards export. All this means that we have to take apart a structure that has been in place for a long time, and as we go along create new institutions. (President Leonel Fernández, quoted by Castro 52)

THE DOMINICAN PEOPLE

For all the distinctions among Dominicans, based on ethnic origin or gender, their sense of Dominicanhood is very strong. Though in many ways the Dominicans' customs, habits, and mannerisms are typical of any person from any country in Latin America, there are enough differences to markedly distinguish them.

Columbus was the first to remark on the personality of the inhabitants of the island he called Hispaniola. He wrote in his diary about the gentle and friendly inhabitants of this island, whom he mistakenly referred to as Indian. The Taínos' and Caribs' eventual extermination notwithstanding, a description of today's inhabitants of the Dominican Republic would include "gentle" and "friendly." Other attributes would be generous, hard-working, loyal, vivacious, and extremely congenial. "It is a community that can be accurately described as possessing boundless energies and tremendous richness of spirit, along with genuine warmth unlike any other island society in the Caribbean" (Cambeira 18). These characteristics cut across social strata, racial differences, and topography.

Underlying the gaiety, Dominicans may harbor feelings of pessimism that reflect their reality—their sense that good things rarely happen. For this reason they continuously gamble, specifically with the lottery, hoping against hope itself for better times. Dominicans' sense of humor is piqued when the joke is caustic and biting. Their love for conversation leads them to discuss every aspect of life, a practice that may seem a bit forward in other cultures. Dominicans particularly indulge in discussions of health, and every Dominican is ready to offer medical advice, obviating the apparent need for physicians and pharmacists in large part. The only aspect of their lives that Dominicans are intensely secretive about is their business and how it is going. Hopelessly impatient and impulsive, Dominicans are notorious for not planning, but rather for living for the moment. Time is not money in this society, nor should life take the form of some paradigm of optimal success. "Dominican impatience is a luxury that both the rich and the poor enjoy" (Bonnelly, *Retablo* 137).

Dominicans, their culture, and their customs are mostly the products of a rich African, Taíno, and Spanish heritage. Of these, the Spanish has been the most influential. Over its history the Dominican Republic has seen an influx of immigrants who have made their presence known in the economic, political, or cultural arena. These include Arabs, German Jews, Cubans, Puerto Ricans, and others.

The Taíno Heritage

The Taíno legacy is very much present in language; agricultural practices, including food gathering and preparation; mythology and religion; and artistic representation. When one considers that the period of coexistence between the Indians and the Spaniards was a mere fifty years, the Taíno's far-reaching influence is all the more remarkable.

The system of preserving meat by salting and then barbecueing it, the use of the yucca plant as a basis for cassava bread, and the introduction of tobacco by the Taínos are examples of agriculturally related contributions. At the time of the Discovery cassava became a staple for the conquering Spaniards, as it was an ideal substitute for the customary wheat-based bread which was difficult to make during the first years of colonization. The Taínos, trying to rid the island of the Spaniards, thought that they might starve them out by refusing to bake cassava bread. Ironically, it is widely believed that the Taínos may have inadvertently accelerated their own annihilation through this tactic.

Anthropological digs have unearthed numerous samples of Taíno art, which was limited primarily to stone-carved figurines, baskets, and objects carved from wood. The current sense of renewed pride in the history of their country has seen Dominicans look to the Taínos for inspiration in music, literature, and the plastic arts. Reproductions of Taíno figurines, baskets, and wood carvings can be seen everywhere. In the 1980s, Dominican novelist Marcio Veloz Maggiolo wrote a novel into which he wove aspects of the Taíno belief system, namely the *luases* which represent fire, water, earth, and wind. The novel titled *La biografiá difusa de Sombra Castañeda* is an allegory of a country under a dictator's rule. In the mid-1990s, contemporary popular musician Juan Luis Guerra ressurrected the *areíto*, a Taíno ritual dance, by composing songs that closely mimic the rhythms of the indigenous music. Romanticized representations of Taíno culture in the nineteenth century include *Enriquillo*, a novel by Manuel de Jesús Galván; *Iguaniona*, a play by Javier Angulo Guridi; and the poem "Fantasías Indígenas" by José Joaquín Pérez. The turn of the century painter Luis Desangles memorialized the history of Taíno chieftain Caonabo and Columbus in two paintings titled *The Imprisonment of Caonabo* and *Columbus Visits Caonabo*. During the Trujillo regime José Vela Zanetti painted murals that incorporate Taíno themes to decorate the National Palace and Palace of Fine Arts in the capital.

The African Heritage

Most Dominicans are, at least to some degree, of African heritage. What makes Dominicans striking in their appearance is precisely the combination of African, Spanish, and other ethnic backgrounds. In the 1993 census, 82 percent of the adult population reported itself to be *indio*, or Indian, underscoring the continued resistance to being identified as mulatto.[5]

Traditionally it has been thought that the first blacks arrived as slaves in the New World a few years after the original explorers for the purpose of supplementing the work that was then done by Indian slaves. Blacks had been living in Spain since the Portuguese began to transport them for sale in Europe in 1441 and 1443.[6] Those that became Christian were, for the most part, freedmen. One of Columbus' ships, *La Niña*, was piloted by a black man named Pedro Alonso Niño. Other black men were involved in the discovery and exploration process, including those who accompanied Balboa, Ponce de León, and Coronado on their expeditions.

Most Africans, however, were brought to Hispaniola as slaves and were subjected to a deculturization process. Slaves from different parts of Africa were placed on the same sugar plantations so as to create friction amongst them and thus weaken any possibility of organized uprising. The goal of the deculturization process was to strip the slaves of their notion of who they were and where they were from, a process that entailed gradual erosion of the Africans' identity. Conversion to Christianity was not a priority for the Spanish, which allowed the Africans to retain their religious beliefs.

Deculturization is hardly ever 100 percent successful, and, in the case of the Africans in Hispaniola, two factors contributed to the retention of certain aspects of African culture. One was the large number of slaves (subsequently referred to as *cimarrones*) who escaped from the sugar mills, seeking freedom, to the surrounding hills where they established settlements they ferociously guarded. The other factor was that the Spaniards did not try to abolish the African customs that they did not perceive as detrimental to their main objective: the production of sugar.

Essentially, the Spaniards regarded the Africans as inferior and uncivilized peoples, a view which sanctioned, in their minds at least, the way they treated the slaves. This attitude marked the beginning of a prejudice based solely on skin color, and which was common to most of the colonies of the Western Hemisphere. To this day, Dominicans are very touchy when it comes to the topic of skin color and hair texture. Unlike the United States where a small amount of African-American blood identifies a person as black, in the Dominican Republic the exact opposite is true: any amount of "white" blood qualifies a person as white. Because of the hierarchical system of power established in the early colonial days based on skin color and the Spanish feudal concept of *pureza de sangre* (which translates roughly to "purity of blood"), the ruling class was white in all the Spanish colonies.[7] Several centuries later, the notion that being white gave one additional authority led the rising dictator Rafael Leonidas Trujillo, who was mulatto, to declare his race as white on a medical examination form as part of an application for the Dominican National Guard in 1918. Trujillo's thirty-year dictatorship was characterized by, among other things, the indoctrination it subjected Dominicans to in the name of a national identity. This indoctrination emphasized three notions that, according to Trujillo, constituted a Dominican: Spanish descent, Catholicism, and the caucasian race.

As has been written about racial status in the Dominican Republic: "despite claims of some Dominicans to the contrary, racism is present in the Dominican Republic and there is no doubt that as one moves up the social scale, race is a very important factor separating social classes and economic positions" (Wiarda, *Transition* 16–17). The late 1990s, however, witnessed a slow change toward racial acceptance and tolerance, and a gradual moving away from the obsession with "hispanicism" (Handelsman 87).

Dominicans' current gradual and ongoing acceptance and interest in their African heritage can be attributed, in part, to the experience of those Dominicans who have lived in the United States and then have returned to their country. The civil rights movement of the 1960s and 1970s in the United States imbued those Dominican immigrants with a consciousness of pride in and recognition of their African heritage.

Another feature of Dominican culture that can be traced back to an African-based social structure is the practice of polygamy that seems common in remote rural communities. Concomitant to this familial organization is the phenomenon of matrifocality, which places the mother figure in the center of the family. In many poor, rural communities, the father figure is almost insignificant when it comes to the family, whereby the grandmother and mother are in charge of raising children and running the household.

A communal conscience of mutual assistance among the members of a community is another aspect of rural life that can be traced back to Africa. The *tornapión* is the custom of helping one another out within a rural community. The help can be in the form of actual physical assistance, doing chores out on the fields, or it can relate to a system of credit referred to as the *san*. The *san* economy assigns one person, often a woman, to be in charge of collecting all the revenue of the community. No written record of the transaction is kept, rather accounts are entrusted to the memory of the person in charge. Mutual trust allows this system to be viable.

The most enduring influence of the African culture in the Dominican Republic is seen in Dominican folk music, dance, religion, some social and economic structures, and food preparation. By and large, given that the black population was for so long enslaved, predominantly in the agricultural regions, the contributions to the culture tend to be more prevalent among the rural poor.

The Spanish Heritage

"Spain gave us all it had: its language, its architecture, its religion, its customs for eating and dressing, its military science, its judicial and civic institutions, its wheat, cattle, sugar cane, and even dogs and hens" (Bosch, *Composición* 11). Although this influence began more than 500 years ago, it was enough to establish the prevalent culture which dominated from the onset of colonial times.

Those who study the evolution of Dominican cultural history emphasize the importance of recognizing the fact that the Spaniards did not arrive once, but rather continued to arrive in waves. Each group of Spanish immigrants brought traditions and customs that served to enforce those already in place. Aside from the initial wave of explorers and colonists, the first important migration was a group from the Canary Islands, who moved to Hispaniola in the seventeenth century. Their contributions were primarily economic, as they are credited with having brought sugarcane to the island. In terms of importance to Spain, Hispaniola lost favor to Puerto Rico and especially Cuba, which came to be considered more strategically located in terms of furthering exploration and conquest in the Western Hemisphere. Later, as Puerto Rico and Cuba underwent political instabilities, inhabitants of those islands took refuge in the Dominican Republic, bringing traditions and customs that were inherently Spanish in origin. Another source of Spanish immigrants were Sephardic Jews who arrived in the Dominican Republic via the Dutch Antilles (after Dominican independence in 1844). Years before, they had been persecuted in Spain, particularly during the Spanish Inquisition. Fleeing Spain they initially settled in Holland. Eventually some chose to try their fortune in Curaçao and Aruba. From there, they migrated to the Dominican Republic, bringing customs and traditions which were, once again, intrinsically Spanish. The last significant wave of Spanish immigrants occurred during the Trujillo regime. As the dictator eased all immigration restrictions so as to "whiten" Dominicans, many Spaniards fleeing the Franco regime (from the early 1940s on) took advantage of this policy. Ironically, members of this particular group of immigrants were behind Trujillo's eventual fall from power. They also have been important contributors to contemporary Dominican culture, as among them there are important musicians, painters, sculptors, and writers.

No influence is larger than that of the Spanish language. Through a process of transculturization, Dominicans have enriched Castilian Spanish with words of Taíno and African origin. But the language, essentially, is plainly recognizable as Spanish. The language has been used to weave together multiple aspects of culture, including all genres of literature and musical lyrics. Spanish is the language of the national anthem, the constitution, and the laws that govern the country. A small but telling example of the lasting quality of this influence is the very Spanish tradition of addressing married men and women as "Don" and "Doña." This custom dates back to Columbian times, and is still very much observed throughout the republic.

Roman Catholicism, brought to Hispaniola by Columbus and those who followed, is the national religion of the Dominican Republic. Dominicans have kept up with the evolutions that have taken place in the Catholic Church. For example, it is common to see a folk mass being offered in the larger cities and towns where songs are played on acoustic guitars, rather than a more traditional mass where music is typically played on a piano or an organ. Another recent development in Catholic churches are prayer groups whereby people gather to pray, read the Old and New Testaments, and discuss and interpret the readings within a contemporary context. In large urban areas of the Dominican Republic these prayer groups are referred to as *talleres* or workshops.

The influence of Spain over the Dominicans is preponderant with regard to music, dance, architecture, painting and sculpture, and in the cultural ambience of the middle and upper classes. This force has continued throughout the entire colonial period and has renewed itself with each new wave of Spanish migration. With the exception of the painters and sculptors, it is only in the last quarter century that middle- and upper-class Dominicans have emphatically turned away from Spain to seek inspiration. By contrast, Dominican popular and folk music, dance, painting, and sculpture have allowed the permeation of the African influence and, later, direct influence from Haiti for a much longer time.

The Social Class System

As in most societies, Dominicans are divided by their class status. The smallest class, but also the most powerful, is the oligarchy, which is constituted mainly by landowners. At some points in Dominican history the size and potency of the elite have been determined by politics. Trujillo's dictatorship, for example, allowed many people of other classes to become excessively wealthy while at the same time stripping power and wealth from many of the established landowners. During Trujillo's regime, many members of the upper classes made the difficult choice of pledging an allegiance, which was not heartfelt, to Trujillo, so as to protect their possessions, wealth, and class status. Today, the elite includes chief executive operators of banks and industries, such as rum and cigar manufacturers, and some landowners. This upper crust of society is further divided into the *tutumpotes* ("the all powerful") or *gente de primera* ("first-class people") and *gente de segunda* ("second-class people"). The latter includes the *nouveaux riches* who are either successful immigrants or those who married into the *gente de primera* class. It also includes an ever-growing body of professional baseball players such as Juan Marichal and Sammy Sosa, who have become immensely wealthy playing for major league teams in the U.S.

The middle and lower-middle classes consist of professionals who work both in the public and private sectors. They have no independent source of income, and the conditions for this class depend on the nation's economy. An example of the difficulties this class faces is that there is no established system of social security, so besides the daily struggle to get ahead, the household leaders must save for their retirement. Ways to get ahead include allying oneself with one of the elite families by being a loyal employee. Another way is to work for the government, a bureaucratic morass that has traditionally handsomely favored its supporters. Skin color has also been a key for upward mobility. The lighter the skin, the better chances of getting ahead. A common saying summarizes this situation: "Being white is a profession" (Franco Pichardo, *Racismo* 129).

The lower classes are divided into urban and rural dwellers. Enticed by promises of a better life, many rural inhabitants move to large urban centers where, by and large, the daily struggle is made more acute by overpopulation. The poor make their money any way they can, as there is no federally operated social welfare program for feeding, housing, or clothing the poor. Often they set up small food-vending businesses or micro-businesses, which can run the gamut from the corner store to the shoeshine boy, or the *paletero* who sells candy and cigarettes from a portable stand. It is common to see preadolescent boys washing off a windshield of a car stopped at a traffic light

To market. Courtesy of *Listín Diario.*

for a few pennies. Others work as maids, houseboys, chauffeurs, and gardeners. The urban poor suffer from conditions of high unemployment, few labor rights, and almost no unionization.

The 1980s gave rise to a manufacturing phenomenon referred to as the free-trade zone, located on the outskirts of the capital and other large cities. The fabrication of textiles and the export of garments have overtaken what used to be the main exports: sugar, bauxite, and rum (Safa 32). Owned by U.S. clothing companies such as Levi's, for example, these factories manufacture their goods at low cost as part of the Caribbean Basin initiative. The enterprises are not taxed by the Dominican or the U.S. governments. Many of the Dominican poor, especially women, have been hired by the free-trade zone companies.

The single advantage that the rural poor have over the urban poor is the relative assurance of being able to cultivate their own food for consumption. If they happen to own a small parcel of land, they can sell their crops. This land is passed down to either the eldest or youngest child in a family, one of whom is expected to stay behind and care for the parents. Most rural poor are wage-dependent and work on somebody else's land, or for a sugar mill. Tragically, over the years, Dominicans have considered themselves to be too good to cut sugarcane, so Haitians have been imported for this purpose. Haitians then constitute the lowest class and, until very recently, have been systematically discriminated against.

The frequent power and water shortages that are experienced in the large cities of the Dominican Republic are exacerbated in the countryside. Women, who often head households, have to perform chores that exceed their workload on the farm. For example, they may have to retrieve water and chop wood. The rural poor still tend to have large families, with the idea that the children can help with the farm chores, but this notion keeps the children from attending school, which in turn contributes to the rate of illiteracy and perpetuates the conditions of poverty. Most rural families are thus need-driven to provide food for the family. A relationship of interdependence is common in a small community where the landless work for food, not money, on a neighbor's lands. Giving credit is a common practice in these areas.

The Immigrant Population

In terms of cultural influence and significance with regard to the last thirty years in the Dominican Republic, the strongest has come from the United States through movies, music, consumer goods, and more recently the presence of cable television. Although American influence may not have provided access to high culture (meaning that patronized by the wealthier classes), to the intellectual branch of society, nor to formal education, it has certainly made itself ubiquitous with regard to dress style, eating habits, and changes in the language, cutting across all social classes. The youth of the Dominican Republic are the ones most easily drawn to what they perceive as a world to emulate as it is portrayed in Hollywood movies and music from the United States.

In the 1960s, the drug and hippie culture attracted mostly middle- and upper-middle-class youth. During the 1970s and 1980s Dominicans saw their youth question established values and morals, all the while testing the waters of freedom and licentiousness that was brought forth through film, radio, and, more recently, cable television and the Internet. The United States' pop culture is not entirely to blame, however. The country had undergone thirty years of a dictatorship that imposed a strict censorship that isolated the country from the world. This condition was followed by a brief, albeit bitter, civil war in 1965. Worldwide, youth felt called upon to right a series of wrongs that had been allowed to flourish, including, on a dramatic scale, the Vietnam War and, of less impact, the university student rebellions in France and Mexico in 1968. The Dominican Republic woke up from its thirty-five years of slumber to a turbulent world and to the same rapid-pace changes and globalization that are increasingly making the world smaller.

The Dominican Republic's economic dependence on the United States is another unavoidable source of U.S. influence. It assures the presence of U.S. industry in the country, along with supervisors and U.S. government agencies such as the U.S. Embassy, its consular officers, and the Agency for International Development (AID) and its personnel. The strong economic and political alliance between the United States and the Dominican Republic dates back to the late nineteenth century, for better or for worse. The United States has been the principle overseer and purveyor of technological progress to the island with such basic items as railroad and telephone services.

U.S. Immigrants

The earliest documented U.S. immigrants can be traced back to Haitian occupation under President Boyer in 1822. He established a policy for attracting U.S. freedmen to the island, offering "free passage, maintenance for four months, and thirty-six acres of land for each twelve workers" (Hoetnik 20). This migration, as well as the case of all the initiatives for enticing migration that occured during the latter half of the nineteenth century, was inspired by a desire to settle the interior farmlands with people willing to work the lands. By 1870 small groups of the descendants of these groups, who happened to be Methodists, could still be found in the capital, Santiago, Puerto Plata, and Samaná, where they had become prosperous farmers. In larger cities these immigrants became completely assimilated. In Samaná, given its isolated status, the community survived more or less in its original form, with auspices of the Methodist Church. To this day there are English-speaking black people in the Samaná peninsula area.

Sephardic Jews

Sephardic Jews, fleeing the Inquisition in Spain, wound up in the Dutch Antilles, from which they set up important commercial centers throughout the Caribbean, including the Dominican Republic. Although very few Sephardic Jews migrated to the Dominican Republic during the late nineteenth century, a notable number were extremely influential as advisors to presidents of that time. The Sephardic Jews who did migrate, quickly assimilated into Dominican society, many going so far as to join the Catholic Church. Dominicans were happy to accept this immigrant population because they were prosperous and white.

Cocolos

Cocolos is the generic and denigrating term used to describe all immigrants to the Dominican Republic from the surrounding English-speaking and Dutch-speaking Antilles. The *cocolo* men were artisans while the *cocolo* women worked as laundresses. This immigrant group thus filled a necessary void in manual labor. For the most part, the *cocolos* settled the eastern portion of the island, particularly around the city of San Pedro de Macorís. Some also dwelled in Puerto Plata and in the capital. The indiscriminate admission of these immigrants was the first to be restricted, in the late nineteenth century, by the government of Morales Languasco, for racist reasons. This policy of nonimmigration was continued by the U.S. military occupation command, and, later, by Trujillo. The *cocolos'* work ethic—physical strength, self-discipline, and overall good education (most spoke three languages and were literate)—placed them in a higher rank on the sugar plantations, where labor conditions were little better than slave labor. They were the first in the history of the country to initiate the concept of unionization and workers' rights.

In addition to the Protestant religion, which the *cocolos* practiced and propagated, they brought with them two types of folkloric dances, the *momise* and the dance of the *Guloyas*, both of which have been incorporated into the repertoire of the National Folkloric Ballet. The latter is a dance traditionally performed during carnival and represents the legendary biblical battle between David and Goliath. The dancers simulate the conflict by swinging pig bladders at each other, occasionally allowing them to fall off the float to be caught by fascinated onlookers. Stage productions that represent the same event continue to be presented by travelling troupes characterized by their imaginative and sumptuous wardrobe. The *cocolos* also introduced the pancake, or *janiqueques* ("johnnycakes"), and the dumpling to Dominican cuisine, where it has been completely incorporated. Sweets made with coconut and flour, which are very popular throughout all social classes, are also of *cocolo* origin, as is the drink guavaberry made from myrtle berries and popularized by contemporary popular composer and singer Juan Luis Guerra. Many *cocolos* have distinguished themselves in various areas including sports, literature, medical professions, politics, and as historians.

Arabs

The Arabs—mostly Lebanese, Syrians, Turks, and a few Palestinians—began to arrive in the Dominican Republic during the latter part of the nineteenth century. It is not known exactly what drove them to the island. It is speculated that seeking a better life, they headed across the Atlantic, ostensibly for the United States. The Dominican Republic was a natural first port of call on the way across. Given its natural beauty, and particularly due to the very liberal immigration policies that were still in place, many Arabs, who for the most part were in their late teens and penniless, decided to settle there. For others, there is an exact explanation of why they migrated to the republic. Originally some Arabs had settled in Cuba, which by the end of the nineteenth century saw itself saturated with immigrants. The Arabs, who were latecomers in this case, understood they were not welcome and decided to move to Cuba's close neighbor to its southeast.

This new immigrant population was quick to bring their customs to the area of commerce and marketing. They initiated the policy of sales by credit, opened stores that simulated Middle Eastern bazaars, set up open-air market places, and introduced street vendors. The Arabs' work ethic, which combined an austere life style with rigorous hours of work, took the residents of the Dominican Republic by surprise and in a short time angered other small retailers who saw these "johnny come latelies" as usurping their corner on the market. The Arab style for selling was shocking to the residents of the island, who were accustomed to a more reserved approach. They were widely accused of being dirty and of having bad manners and habits, and the government was reproached for having allowed these immigrants into the nation.

After fifty years on the island the Arabs were only second to the Spanish with regard to commercial ventures. Unlike all previous immigrants (with the exception of the freedmen in Samaná), who had been easily assimilated into the prevailing culture, the Arabs stayed very much to themselves, going so far as to return to Lebanon to marry. By the second generation, and given their ever-increasing prosperity, the Arabs gained more acceptance. They retaliated against the opposition, which they saw as aspersion against them, by obtaining citizenship and marrying Dominicans. They no longer taught their language to their children, and discontinued the practice of their own cultural customs.

Since upper-class Dominicans refused to give membership to wealthy Arabs to their private clubs like the exclusive Club de Unión, the Arabs created their own. Simplistically, Dominicans alleged that the Arabs ate raw meat and raw onions, but the real reason for refusing them as members of the upper crust was the commercial threat the Arabs presented. Over time, the Arabs gained total acceptance at all levels of society, but it is worth noting, as a postscript, that Juan Elmúdesi, a very wealthy man of Lebanese extraction, had to rely on Trujillo's influence to gain a membership into the Club Unión in 1946.[8]

Beyond the tremendous surge in commercial activity, which prior to the Arabs' arrival had been nondescript, the Arabs' influence extended to urban planning, culture, and cuisine. They were among the first to build large stores and two-story private residences throughout the country. Abraham E. Praiby published a newspaper written in Arabic, named *Al Juades*. Miguel Feris translated poems by José Deligne to Arabic. On a popular level, the Arabs provided the venue for festivals, particularly in the city of San Francisco de Macorís. The popular *quipes*, which are essentially meat fritters shaped into a ball, and *tipiles*, which is a Dominican version of the Arabic tabbouleh, are but two examples of Arabic influence in Dominican cuisine.

Other Immigrants

Other immigrants, such as the Dutch, the Germans, the Italians, and the British, exerted their influence primarily in the area of business. Most sugar plantations, which were eventually purchased by the Trujillo family, had belonged to a wide array of foreign investors. The same was true of commerce. For example, the Germans had the corner on the cigar market in the late 1800s. With regard to culture, there is some debate, as of yet unresolved, as to who introduced the accordion, an essential instrument for playing the *merengue*, the national dance. Some say it was the Germans, others, the Italians.

The wars for independence from Spain in the late nineteenth century in Cuba and Puerto Rico spurred many writers, educators, a pianist, a composer, and magicians to flee to the neighboring Dominican Republic. Many Cubans tended to settle in Santiago, where they founded schools for all levels of education (Castillo 203). Cubans also introduced the *figureo*, which is the custom of promenading along a prominent avenue of a city or town, especially on Sundays.

Puerto Ricans were imported to work under near-slave conditions on Puerto Rican–owned sugar plantations in the Dominican Republic, in the area of La Romana, during the nineteenth century. Others worked in coffee fields. The saddest case of forced migration, however, has been that of Haitians who have been brought in since the beginning of the twentieth century

Miss Dominican Republic 1994, Xiomara Gonzalez. Courtesy of *Listín Diario*.

to do physically demanding work that Dominicans have not been willing to do: manually chopping sugarcane. The Haitians have been debased and degraded by the Dominican populace, and to this day, those with very dark skin are treated differently, usually worse, because it is presumed that they are Haitian.[9] Nonetheless, the Haitian presence in the Dominican Republic has been deeply felt culturally, especially in the case of religion and art.

Women

In very general terms women are objectified by men in the Dominican Republic. Many Dominican women, regardless of social class or race, have accepted this status over the years and live their entire lives seeking male approval. Physical beauty is thus of tremendous importance and is the subject and focus of popular songs and the many beauty contests that take place throughout the country. Many women dress provocatively, usually wearing high heels and excessive make-up. There is an obsession with straight hair among Dominican women, most of whom are mulatto. It is thus not unusual to see young ladies of the lowest social stratum all decked out with large curlers in their hair, covered by a colorful scarf. So much attention is paid to physical appearance that it is often the topic of conversation. Dominican women, upon meeting acquaintances, inevitably comment either approvingly or disapprovingly on each other's appearance.

The emphasis that is placed on the physical appearance wanes at the time a woman reaches middle age, at which time she is usually accorded a great deal of respect, again, regardless of social status. The concept of motherhood is kept in very high regard among Dominicans. In fact the mother-child tie is "virtually inviolate" (Haggerty 66), meaning that the mother is expected to have a very close relationship with her children. The father, however, assumes a more distant, sterner role, the role of the strict disciplinarian. It is not considered proper for a father to show affection for his children.

Overall, Dominican men treat Dominican women abysmally. True to the Spanish Don Juan tradition the most important aspect of a relationship with a woman is the conquest. Once married, it is quite common, indeed prestigious, for the man to maintain a mistress. A wife's role at that point is to care for the children and look the other way. Men initiate their sons in the degradation of women at an early age, taking them to prostitutes to be instructed in sex. Machismo, whereby the man touts his maleness according to his conquests, and *marianismo*, whereby a woman is to be like the Virgin Mary, are alive and well in the Dominican Republic.

The double standard by which males and females are raised is introduced early on in a child's life. Boys can run around unclothed whereas girls are carefully dressed. Girls are supposed to be proper and prim, but boys can behave outrageously to the amusement and applause of family members. As they grow up, boys are actually expected to have premarital affairs and, once married, extramarital affairs, but girls must be virgins at the time of marriage. It is unconscionable for a married woman to have an affair.

The women who have broken through the rigid male stronghold are either of the lowest classes or of the highest classes. Poor women work by necessity and do not subscribe to the *marianismo* mystique, or any other middle-class constructs, but simply work to maintain their young, and possibly a mate, here and there. These women work intensely and are readily abused, sexually as well as with regard to their civil rights. In urban areas they work as maids, cooks, laundresses and pressers, as well as seamstresses in the factories of the free-trade zone.

The concept of sexual harrassment is very new to the Dominican Republic. A celebrated case of a judge in Santiago who had an affair with a plaintiff made the headlines and the talk shows in the spring of 1997 bringing light to this subject on a public level for the first time. Many Dominican males act in a way that would constitute at least a mild form of harrassment in other parts of the western world. Dominican men have a gift of rhetoric that is more notorious than that of the Cubans and Puerto Ricans. Again, regardless of age, social class, or race, they put this talent into practice by means of overtly flirting with any and all women. This flirtation or *piropo*, the history of which dates back to the Middle Ages on the Iberian peninsula, and the figure of the troubador have become art forms in and of themselves as Dominican men boldly and indiscreetly make verbal advances to women. It has been pointed out that this kind of preening underscores the male's positive self-image. He competes with other males with regard to how outrageous, if not creative, the flirtation can be. Thus, the woman becomes a pretext for the man's autoeroticism.

Discrimination against women is often enacted by omission, meaning that when it comes to making a list of successful people in whatever field, the work of applicable women is completely ignored. Women poets, short story writers, and novelists have had to fight an uphill battle to be recognized within the very tight, male-dominated bastions of literary critics and publishers, who have pretended that these literary artists do not exist, so as not to have to deal with them.

Middle- and upper-class Dominican women have been able to compete in the workplace, notably in professions such as education, medicine, and politics. It is still uncommon but not unthinkable to see a woman CEO, manager, banker, financial advisor, computer analyst, lawyer, architect, or engineer. The real reason for the scarcity of women in these positions can be better attributed to a lack of access to opportunities for education and advancement in these areas than to any sort of discrimination. It is understood, however, that women from these classes have had better opportunities with regard to schooling, and quite a few have acquired bachelor's and master's degrees abroad.

Statistics have shown that Dominican women generally have a higher educational level than men, as many more women than men complete high school. Nonetheless, women still receive lower wages than men, even when doing the same work, and even when the job in question hires primarily women, such as the free-trade zones, for example. Women are hired for positions that require less skill, while men are placed in administrative jobs. The women seem to accept this discrepancy as natural because they are "accustomed to having men in charge at the workplace" (Safa 33). Unionization does not seem to be an option because odds are good that the person on strike will simply lose her job, and, in addition, be blacklisted from other companies. A more telling reason against joining a union for women is that for the most part the women working for big corporations "feel little pride in their work, and . . . rarely identify themselves as workers in the first place" (Safa 36).

The idea that women can be engaged in nontraditional or nonconventional professions is gradually being introduced by the Center for Women's Progress (Centro de Solidaridad para el Desarrollo de la Mujer—CE-MUJER), which was cofounded and sponsored by a German foreign development agency, the GTZ. One proposed project is to train women as auto mechanics, metal workers, plumbers, blacksmiths, bricklayers, cabinetmakers, electricians, electronists, air-cooling specialists, welders, and printers to address a nationwide deficit in these technical skills. The first obstacle this organization has faced has been finding institutions willing to admit women into courses traditionally for men only. Once on the job, there are personal problems, such as losing a father's support because of holding a "man's job." One woman, a car mechanic, lost her boyfriend because he thought it improper that she worked with so many men (Martínez 164). Generally, the women who have ventured into the world previously reserved for men seem to experience the same prejudices and problems that women have experienced elsewhere.

One population of women is taken advantage of unmercifully. This is a group who is promised a better life in a foreign country, only to find themselves involved in prostitution in the Netherlands or drug trafficking in New York. The luckier ones make their way into factories or into household labor, where, since they are illegal aliens, they are more vulnerable to abuse.

National Female Figures

Several women who have been woven in the national historical fabric and are today regarded as national heroines include Anacaona, the Virgin of Altagracia, Juana Saltitopa, and the Mirabal sisters. Their deeds feed the folklore and myth that constitutes part of the Dominican national identity.

Anacaona

The Taíno Anacaona's story of courage and defiance before the ruthless forces of the genocidal Nicolás de Ovando has transcended five centuries. As Bartolomé de las Casas chronicles it, at the turn of the sixteenth century, Anacaona, Caonabo's widow, had been helpful and good to the Christians, providing assistance where needed in dealing with the Indians.[10] In 1503, when she heard that Ovando was coming to visit the land over which she ruled (having taken over for her deceased brother Bohecío), Anacaona organized a warm welcome for the dignitary. Ovando, the governor of the colony, enjoyed several days of parties and festivities, at the conclusion of which he called a meeting, asking Anacaona to gather the leaders of the area for a meeting inside the main and largest *bohío* (thatched-roof hut). Once inside the Spaniards tied the Indians' hands and then set fire to the building, killing all eighty who had been inside. In consideration of Anacaona's ruler status, she was hanged instead of incinerated. Since the beginning of the republic there have been numerous namesakes of Anacaona, as well as statues and other artistic representations of Caonabo's widow on display all over the country.

The Virgin of Altagracia

An image of the Virgin of Altagracia was brought to Hispaniola by brothers Alonso and Antonio Trejo in 1650. She became the patron saint of the island in 1692, and her shrine is in the town of Higüey. The first architect of the sanctuary is said to be named Simón Bolívar and rumored to be a direct descendant of the great Latin American liberator of the same name. The Virgin of Altagracia's most significant miracle to date is attributed to her intervention in a battle between the French and the Spanish in 1691. A battalion of 300 troops was unexpectedly able to convincingly defeat a larger battalion of better-prepared, better-armored French troops. Today, the sanctuary in Higüey, which is an architectural marvel rebuilt in the 1950s, is the site of pilgrimages and the annual celebration in honor of the Virgin of Altagracia on January 21.

Juana Saltitopa

Juana Saltitopa (Juana Trinidad) became famous for fighting along with men in the war for independence from Haiti (1843–1894). Originally from a small town in the area of La Vega, she was notorious for her masculine ways such as her passion for cock fights. When fighting the Haitians, she aligned herself with the troops, assisting in every way she could, including oiling weapons and sharpening machetes. During battles, accompanied by two other women who served as bodyguards, she ran among bullets and cannon fire, getting water for the troops who nicknamed her *La Coronela* ("The Colonel"). She died tragically in 1860, killed by an unknown assailant.

The Mirabal Sisters

Patria, Minerva, Bélgica (Dedé), and María Teresa Mirabal lived most of their lives during Trujillo's dictatorship. They became heroines when, each in her own way, they sought ways to overthrow Trujillo. Born to an upper-middle-class family, the Mirabals' social status made them unlikely candidates for political activism. Nonetheless, over time, they became Trujillo's biggest thorns and directly contributed to the eventual end of his regime. In 1957, Trujillo was quoted as saying that his two biggest problems were the Mirabal sisters and the Catholic Church. He dealt with the former by having three of the sisters (Patria, Minerva, and María Teresa) ambushed and murdered on their way back from visiting their husbands in jail. The deaths of the three sisters immediately turned into an international incident and focused world attention on Trujillo's brutality.

Today, the Mirabal sisters are highly revered and presented as role models of patriotism. Their pictures can be seen everywhere, most notably adorning the obelisk on the palm-shaded avenue that borders the Caribbean Sea in the capital, which is now painted with larger-than-life size portraits of the Mirabal sisters on each of its sides. They are depicted wearing attire typically associated with mythological Greek goddesses.

The "Dominicanyor"

At repeated times during the history of the Dominican Republic, Dominicans have left the country in mass exodus. Usually these emigrants of the middle or upper classes fled to Cuba. Those who left during Trujillo's regime went to the United States, settling in the New York area. Those who went into exile included political opponents and middle- and upper-class people who were fed up with the regime or who suffered financial losses after Trujillo's death in the early 1960s. These emigrants were from all parts of the country, with a particularly large number leaving from the Cibao area, where they had been prosperous landowners and farmers on properties taken over by Trujillo and his family. Despite the fact that it was extremely difficult to obtain a passport during the Trujillo era, as the dictator did not allow any emigration for fear that word would get out as to the extent of repression by his regime, many did manage to leave.[11]

Since the late 1970s, masses of Dominicans have left, usually illegally, in search of better living conditions. As the price and market for sugar has plummeted, and as the Dominican Republic learns to cope with globalization, which tends to benefit established economies, living conditions have become almost unbearable for the poorest Dominicans. Wages have not kept up with cost-of-living increases, and the solution for some has been simply to flee, even if it means risking one's life by sailing the treacherous shark-infested Mona passage to Puerto Rico. Few of those Dominicans stay in Puerto Rico, preferring instead to go to New York.[12]

The last thirty-five years has seen such a growth in the population of Dominicans in New York that it is now the largest immigrant group there and the state's "fastest-growing ethnic minority" (Jordan 37).[13] Many have gained political and economic clout. Guillermo Linares, for example, is a New York City councilman, and Adriano Espaillat serves in the state assembly. Approximately 20,000 New York businesses are owned by Dominicans. Nowadays, the New York Dominicans flaunt their favorite son, Leonel Fernández Reyna, who, raised in New York, became the president of the Dominican Republic in 1996.

The importance of the so-called Dominicanyor, as he or she is referred to in the Dominican Republic, and his or her relationship with the Dominican Republic is tied to a salient Dominican trait, the focus on family. This attribute, which cannot be understated or exaggerated, cuts across racial and economic lines and generations. Family members fiercely defend and protect each other against outsiders. "Family loyalty is an ingrained and unquestioned virtue; from early childhood, individuals learned that relatives were to be trusted and relied on, while those outside the family were, implicitly at least, suspect" (Haggerty 64). "At all levels of society, strong emphasis is placed upon trust, mutual aid, and familial solidarity. Individual members are socialized with a deep sense of collective responsibility for the acts of others. Members of a family share in the honor as well as the shame of the consequences of acts by one of its members" (Hendricks 32). Those who migrate from their place of origin, be it from a rural area to an urban center in the country itself, or from the Dominican Republic to some place in the United States, remain steadfastly loyal to their families and to the notion of kinship. A large portion of their income is sent back to the relatives, so much so that the money being sent back from New York City constitutes part of the national budget.

In terms of the national economy New York is the second most important city of the Dominican Republic. Businesses dedicated uniquely to sending payments back to the homeland have thrived. Depending on which of the agencies is used, once the amount is electronically wired, remittances from the United States are made in person in the Dominican Republic. It is estimated that on average, about $8 million daily is transacted through these remitting institutions, which are located throughout the United States but are most numerous in the New York area. The influx of money to the island has signified prosperity in terms of growth and commercial activity in the Dominican Republic. At times, even the parish priest might be seen fundraising in New York for a church back home.

Although many Dominicans have lived for many years in the New York area, if not all their lives, many view themselves as transient, making enough money to be able to return home. This is one of the obstacles when it comes to full political empowerment in the New York area, along with the large rate of noncitizenship among Dominicans, a perceptible lack of cohesion in political goals, and rising poverty.

In the Dominican Republic the Dominicanyor is regarded with a mixture of reverence and repugnance. On the one hand the Dominicans are impressed by the apparent wealth of those returning to the island. They usually are sporting the latest styles and have plenty of cash to spend. By the same token, this perceived wealth is snubbed by those of the upper-middle- and upper-classes who see the overt display as vulgar. The lower-class Dominicanyor has forgotten how to speak Dominican Spanish, having learned to communicate in Spanglish, a dialect whereby many words from the English language are assimilated into Spanish to the point of being almost visually and audibly unrecognizable. The Spanglish that Dominicans speak is further subdivided into "Dominicanish." The word "highways" in English becomes *jaiueyes*; "to take it easy" becomes *cogerlo isi*; "medicaid" is *mediquei*, "social security" becomes *social siguiuri*; "give me a break" is *dénme un brei*; "bosslady" translates as *bosleidi*; "Security Building" becomes *sicuri en bilde*; "to back oneself up," as in to have plenty of stock, is *baquiarse*; a quarter is a *cuora*; and so on.

Although many stories are told of the dire circumstances and harsh conditions that Dominicans suffer when they first get to New York, many learn to adapt. Upon their return to the island they are able to bring their new-found knowledge and experience back with them.[14] The harsh conditions in the United States toughen the Dominicanyor and also awaken them to the possibilities available in terms of improving conditions in general, back in their own country, especially in the areas of social welfare, health and education. This is particularly true in the case of women, whose identity and notion of self-worth are dramatically affected by their experience in New York. Much has been written about the horrendous abuses suffered by primarily Dominican and Puerto Rican women in the sweat shops of New York. They work long hours, under difficult conditions, for low wages. On the other hand, the simple fact that they have suddenly become wage earners and the idea that others are dependent on them make feminists out of women who were originally products of the Dominican machista society. These women upon returning to the Dominican Republic fight for equal rights on all fronts.

There is concern among Dominicans in New York that the United States–born generation of Dominicans may forget its traditions and be unfamiliar with its culture. This is one of the themes of the Dominican-made and produced film *Nueba Yol*. In it the second-generation daughter is accused of having acquired "American" habits of disrespect for her elders, in this case her father. Initially in the film, she does not share the notion of family that is so entrenched among Dominicans when it comes to accepting a distant relative who has moved into the family's cramped apartment in New York.

The Dominicanyor exports U.S. customs to the Dominican Republic, thus changing the standard of what is and is not acceptable. The consequential high rate of consumerism might lead to an eventual destruction of a national identity as the country aspires to be evermore like the United States. To ensure that such a nihilistic view of the country's future as an independent, unique nation with its own distinctive cultural history does not come to bear, different programs are promoted in New York for the purpose of acquainting second-generation Dominicans with their country of origin. One such initiative is called "Meet Your Brother." This program, run by the Saint George School in New York City, has a center to house, among other interests, a museum and a library called the *Centro Comunitario* or community center located in the Washington Heights area. The City University of New York sponsors the Dominican Institute, which includes a library on all things Dominican. The institute offers monthly seminars and meetings on Dominican issues ranging from education, politics, literature, economic issues, to feminism. The guest speakers include transplanted Dominicans and Dominicans who fly in to participate.

Dominicans in New York have access to local public service channels on cable television, dedicated to Dominican issues. They also keep a close watch on politics in their country, and, because of a Dominican policy that allows dual citizenship, many are able to vote in Dominican elections. Key political candidates up for election in the Dominican Republic travel to New York to campaign among the people there and thus bring the colorful and loud celebration typical of the political season in the Dominican Republic.[15]

The geography, the history, and the people of the Dominican Republic are what make it a unique and compelling place for further study. Never having posited a military or economic threat to world powers, the Dominican Republic has taken a back seat to those areas demanding more attention. Unassumingly, the Dominican people have lived out the last 150 years forging a unique identity based on traditions and an ideology that can be seen as a product of their history and the traditions and customs of the many immigrants that have settled the country since the Discovery.

NOTES

1. The design in question refers to a symmetrical layout of the city. The church or cathedral and the main governmental building are across from each other with a

square or plaza lying between. Other official buildings occupy the remaining two sides of the square. All streets are then aligned in a parallel and perpendicular fashion to the central square.

2. In the census of 1920, 1935, 1950, and 1960 the word *mestizo* was used to describe the majority of Dominicans. A *mestizo* is the product of Indian and white whereas *mulatto* is the combination of black and white. The 1993 census shows that 82.05 percent of Dominicans are mulatto, 7.55 percent are white, and 4.13 percent are black. Historian Frank Moya Pons writes: "Lately the word 'indian' has become almost universal as a descriptive of the Dominican mulatto and this is reflected in almost all official documents which ask for skin color or race for its citizens. . . . The answers of the large majority of citizens are surprising for its homogeneity: 82 of each 100 Dominicans called themselves 'indians' at the time of registering to vote" (Moya Pons, "Composición racial dominicana," 4). All quotations have been translated by the author from Spanish.

3. "Buccaneers," a word derived from the Carib Indian language that means "a place to roast beef," were neither pirates nor filibusterers. They hunted beef and pork for its skin which they traded for arms, gunpowder, shoes, wine, cloths and so on. Over time they settled in and began farming the land and making cassava bread much in the way that the Taínos had. The filibuster, in turn, was more specialized in running marine raids, piratry, and contraband. Like the pirate and the buccaneer, he did not answer to any nation's call, but was out for himself.

4. Dominican history lists Juan Pablo Duarte, Ramón Mella, and Francisco del Rosario Sánchez as *los padres de la Patria* ("the Fathers of the Country"). Actually, the insurrectional movement La Trinitaria was composed of many members, many with important roles in the struggle for independence. For more information see Ian Bell's *The Dominican Republic* or Franklin Franco Pichardo's *Historia del pueblo dominicano, Tomo I.*

5. There are many euphemisms used to designate the mulatto. These are translated as follows: light Indian, dark Indian, washed Indian, jaundiced white, and white (Albert 15).

6. There were other waves of Africans that came to the island of Hispaniola after the initial import of slaves. These came from surrounding British Antilles islands and were referred to as *cocolos*. Another group of blacks were freedmen from the United States. These tended to settle in the area of Samaná.

7. The hierarchical order during the colonial period was as follows throughout the colonized area of Latin America: those who held the highest administrative positions in government were Spaniards. Next in line were the *criollos* (creoles), whites born in the colonies. These were followed by freedmen and mulattos (mixture of black and white) or *mestizos* (mixture of Indian and white). Those on the bottom of the social ladder were the Indians and then the blacks and any racial combination thereof.

8. Even Trujillo faced great obstacles when he first tried to join the Club Unión. The members felt that his family was not worthy of this honor (Inoa 53).

9. Murray notes: "There are cultural rules regarding mutual respect and inter-personal relations which Dominicans who are strangers follow. It seems to me there are two situations for which all rules of common courtesy and mutual respect are suspended: behind the steering wheel, and interactions, when it is suspected that the other is Haitian. In the case of the corner store if the person who tries to shove him or herself before the others is Haitian, he or she would be verbally assaulted using openly racial and abusive language" (253).

10. Caonabo was the Taíno chieftain who killed the first group of Spanish settlers on the island of Hispaniola.

11. For an amusing albeit fairly realistic portrayal of the experience of well-off Dominican immigrants to New York, see Julia Alvarez's novels *How the García Girls Lost Their Accent*, and *¡Yo!* ('*Me!*'). The working class perspective is charmingly related in the 1996 movie *Nueba Yol*, directed by Angel Muñiz and performed by Luisito Martí, Raúl Carbonell, and Caridad Ravelo, by Kit Parker Films.

12. Driven by desperation, Dominicans use amazing means to illegally migrate to the United States. Some have defected from organized cultural exchange groups touring the country. Others have come disguised as priests, men dressed up as women, or women dyeing their hair and changing their appearance. Those who have managed to get visas have often provided information and the photograph of a dead person in place of their own, assuming that the deceased had better credentials. Many were found asphixiated in cargo holds of ships. Cynical observers point to the profits taken in by the funeral industry which has brought back body after body of Dominicans who succumbed to drugs and other illicit activity in the desperate effort to succeed particularly in New York.

13. Approximately 69 percent of Dominicans in the United States live in New York State, 10 percent in New Jersey, and about 7 percent in Florida, particularly in the Miami area (Jordan 37).

14. The lyrics of "Elena" by Juan Luis Guerra and the group 4.40 (*Mudanza y acarreo* 1985) tell the story of Elena who to improve her life marries an older man who smuggles her to the United States, where she is tricked into trafficking cocaine and is eventually murdered. The lyrics of another Guerra and 4.40 song, "Visa para un sueño," relate the vicissitudes of obtaining a visa from the United States embassy for a Dominican passport.

15. Although not that many Dominicans are illiterate (17% in 1996) political parties have developed a tradition of identifying themselves with a color, so as to simplify the choosing of a candidate (Pascal 239). Often, then, a campaign slogan will mandate "Vote Green" or "Vote White." Before important elections cities and towns of all sizes are fully decked out with banners representing the various candidates. Noise ordinances do not exist, so blaring megaphones play music of orchestras and singers, each of whom has allied itself with a particular candidate. Such activities last longer each day and through the night as the election day draws near.

2

Religions

The official religion of the Dominican Republic has been Roman Catholicism since the declaration of independence in 1844. Before then, Catholicism was dominant given the history of evangelization and indoctrination associated with the Spanish since colonial times. Other religions are represented in the Dominican Republic, although on a smaller scale. Officially, 90 percent of Dominicans are Catholics. The remaining population is made up of Evangelists, Adventists, Jehovah's Witnesses, Methodists, Baptists, Unitarians, Mormons, and Jews. One can find small sects of religions of Asian origin as well. The religions that capture one's imagination are those practiced in remote rural areas that are heavily influenced by the presence of Haitians. There one finds voodoo and *gagá*, both of which are products of what is referred to as synchretism, or a combination of varying degrees of belief systems, drawing from the civilizing trilogy that is the Dominican Republic: Taíno, Spanish, and African.

ROMAN CATHOLICISM

By virtue of a papal decree, Pope Alexander VI split the New World in two halves allotting territorial rights of half to Spain and the other half to Portugal in 1493. The Pope then charged the two kingdoms with the conversion of Indians to Christianity.

On his second trip to the island of Hispaniola, Columbus was accompanied by twelve priests headed by the Franciscan Brother Bernardo Boíl, who was the first to celebrate mass in the New World. The year 1502 signalled the arrival of Nicolás de Ovando along with many Franciscan monks. These monks, and others who arrived later, began setting up an educational system as well as building convents. Their primary objective was to convert the sons of the *caciques* (Indian chiefs) to Christianity, thus inculcating western European culture among the Indians. The didactic objectives of the Spaniards were reinforced by the arrival of a large contingent of monks and nuns of the Dominican order. This group initiated the defense of the Indians, whom they saw as oppressed and abused by the colonists. The most famous of the Indians' apologists, Bartolomé de las Casas, joined the order of the Dominican monks, having been an Indian slave owner himself while living in Cuba. By 1511 it became clear that the Dominicans and the Franciscans had different objectives. The former preached human rights while the latter aligned themselves with the status quo of the colonial governing board and, by extension, with the Spanish crown.

The Dominicans and the Franciscans each erected convents whose main function, aside from the religious ones of housing the monks and nuns and providing a venue for masses, was the establishment of a secular school. The Dominicans founded the School of General Studies. This academy was elevated to university status in 1538 by a papal bull of Pope Paul III, who visited the site, which was then renamed the Universidad Pontificia de Santo Tomás de Aquino, thus becoming the first university of the New World. The university later became known as the Universidad de Santo Domingo and is currently the Universidad Autónoma de Santo Domingo.

The Catholic religion is absolutely central to Dominican culture as it is throughout Latin America. The prevalence and practice of Roman Catholicism is most common in larger urban centers of the country and in New York City. In fact New York priests find that regular attendance at masses is better in New York than in the Dominican Republic. This can partially be attributed to nostalgia, or a means of connecting with the homeland through the familiar ritual and practices of the church. There is also a general perception that the rate of Catholicism is directly related to the class system as evidenced by the fact that middle- and upper-class people tend to be Catholics.

All cities and towns in the Dominican Republic have Catholic churches. If a town is small, there will be one church on the main square, in accordance to the Spanish-inspired style of city planning. If one sees the Dominican Republic in terms of north and south, splitting it along the Cordillera Central, then it can be said that the Catholic Church is more influential in the northern section, with the exception of the capital city, Santo Domingo, where it is also strong.

Side entrance to La Catedral de Las Americas (Cathedral of the Americas), the oldest cathedral in the New World. Courtesy of *Listín Diario.*

Most holidays in the Dominican Republic are based on the Catholic liturgical calendar, and most public and private functions include the presence of a church representative. *Semana Santa* ("Holy Week"), the week that culminates on Easter Sunday, is the most important religious celebration in the Dominican Republic as it is in most countries of Latin America, with Christmas and the Epiphany (Three Kings' Day) following close behind. Carnival, the time of jubilation and excessive behavior that precedes Ash Wednesday and the Lenten season, is enormously popular throughout the country. Various areas have developed their own traditions and ways to celebrate this holiday. Other important celebrations of the Catholic faith, such as Corpus Christi and the day of the country's patron saint, La Virgen de la Altagracia, involve most of the country's people. Each town has its own patron saint whose day is celebrated with parades and festivities.

It is common to read that by and large Dominicans do not take Catholicism seriously. Such a statement overlooks the daily impact of the Catholic Church on most Dominicans' lives. In fact, the Catholic Church is one of the main ways by which families reaffirm the tight bonds that bind them. For example, a child's baptism ensures two occurrences: a celebration that brings together family members, and the establishment of a new relationship for the family with the godparents of the christened child. The relationship with the godparents, the *compadrazgo,* can be formed with family members, but often involves close friends of the family that are *de confianza,* or, in other words, that can be trusted. The friends become necessarily a part of the family and enter into the circle of trust and mutual support that is pivotal to Dominicans.

Funerals, and the masses that accompany them, also bring families together. There are traditionally nine masses or *novenas* celebrated in memory of the deceased. These are announced in all daily newspapers, where invitations are extended to those who were acquainted with the deceased in any way. Such events underscore the importance that Dominicans place on mutual ties, and the origins of these celebrations can be traced back to Spanish traditions during colonial times. A very recent trend reflects the influence of Vatican II, which has encouraged lay people to directly participate in the celebration of mass and other functions. The fact that Dominicans are engaging in prayer groups and bible readings and instructions, referred to as *cursillos* or *talleres de oración,* meaning prayer workshops, can also be seen as ways to challenge and forestall the ever-increasing amount of converts to Protestant sects.

Catholicism has historically been more firmly entrenched in the Cibao region, which is generally considered to house the wealthier, better educated, and more sophisticated people of the country. The *campesinos* of this area have not been as receptive to the proselytizing of evangelicals as the eastern portion of the country, for example. Religious historians have documented the long line of clergymen and women of the church who risked their lives during the wars of independence and restoration and who were, for the most part, from the Cibao area.

The Catholic Church has not been as politicized in the Dominican Republic as in other Latin American countries. The one exception is during the latter years of the Trujillo regime, when it openly declared its opposition and was thus instrumental in mobilizing the populace against the tyrant in the late 1950s. In more recent years its role has been to mediate conflicts between the different political parties.

PROTESTANTISM

The first Methodist pastor in the Dominican Republic was Reverend Isaac Miller, who came from Philadelphia to the Samaná peninsula in the 1820s. His congregation was entirely composed of freedmen originally brought by Haitian President Boyer to the island. These American blacks faced a difficult situation in a virtual slave society, and their most lasting contribution to the

Methodist population was to teach other blacks to read and write. Gregorio Luperón, an important figure in the War of Restoration, was a notable success story of their literacy project. Although these Methodists' immediate objective was proselytical, the far-reaching notion of literacy for blacks was laudatory.

The Anglican Church, also known as the Episcopal Church, was established in San Pedro de Macorís in 1897. Today, it includes approximately fifty congregations throughout the country. The Episcopal Church is actively involved in community assistance through programs for the improvement of education and the conditions of the very poor. It has taken a defiant stance, charging the government with corruption and with negligence toward the most indigent of the population.

THE LEGACY OF THE TAÍNO BELIEF SYSTEM

The religious system of the Taíno Indians was centralized in the concept of the *cemí*. It represented divinities that were either abstract, personified, naturalist, local familial spirits, or phenomenons of nature. To explain natural elements the Taínos developed a mythology in which magic and animism were central. The Taínos saw a soul or vital spirit within all things, and believed in the immortality of the soul. They practiced various cults of fertility and of the dead. These "beings" had to be kept satisfied, otherwise the dead would terrorize the living. According to the Taíno's belief system, the dead participated in festivities and rituals and were recognizable because they lacked a belly button. The *behique*, or witch doctor, had the capacity to communicate with the *Opia* or *Hupia*, names by which the dead were designated. The *behique* could transmit the wishes of the dead to the ancestors and to the living.

The main religious ceremony of the Taínos was the *cohoba*. The *cacique* and occasionally the *behique* were charged with this ritual. To communicate with the *cemí* they would induce vomiting, so as to purify the body, and then inhale a hallucinogenic substance. Illnesses were thought to be the work of spirits, so curing methods were essentially magical animism. The *behiques* had special knowledge of medicine, botany, and related fields.

VOODOO

The very mention of voodoo incites heated debate among educated Dominicans. It is unclear what provokes the discussion: a religion shrouded in mystery, enveloped by unusual rituals and eerie beliefs, or that it originates in Haiti, which continues to signify, on a subliminal level, that which is prohibited or despised.

The Dominicans, initially for the establishment of religious hegemony, and later, in a bitter struggle for independence that lasted beyond the wars of independence, have come to associate Haiti and all things Haitian as evil. Haiti historically has been portrayed as synonymous with that which is dark and barbaric. The study of Haiti, its religious and cultural customs, and its close links with the Dominican Republic has only most recently been initiated, in an objective manner in the Dominican Republic. Numerous anthropological, sociological, and artistic studies, including music, literature, and fine arts, are being conducted in an effort to highlight the influence of what is Haitian and Afrodominican in Dominican culture and customs.

Voodoo is a belief system that today includes aspects of various myths that originated with different tribes in Africa and that incorporates aspects of Christianity. The mythology can be traced primarily to the Fon and Yoruba nations in Africa where a double deity, represented by the sun and the moon, is worshipped. There are also numerous spirits and divine beings, referred to collectively as *loas*, that mediate between humans and the spirits. Individual distinctions by name usually make reference to the place of origin of that particular *loa* in Africa. So, for example, there may be a *loa* named *yoruba*, *congas*, or *wangol*. There is always room for a new *loa* as a previously undesignated *loa* may take possession of a priest or a faithful believer and thus make its way into the pantheon of *loas* as a new *loa*. *Loas* have also been named for foreigners such as the French and Cubans. *Loas* are subdivided into the kind and gentle group known as the *rada* and the bitter, angst-ridden *petró*, who are called upon for magical purposes interpreted by many to mean witchcraft. A supreme being named *Mawu*, who is all-powerful and kind, reigns over this entire group. This particular concept made it easy for believers of voodoo to accept and assimilate the Christian god.

GAGÁ

Gagá is the Dominican version of Haitian voodoo, which assimilated the vestiges of the Taíno belief system in addition to the mythology imported from Africa. Dominican *loas* are variously referred to as beings, mysteries, and *lúa*, *sanse*, or *sane*. The *luases* (plural of *lúa*) consist of supernatural beings as well as the spirits of historical people. Just as the Haitians do, Dominicans subdivide the *luases* into subcategories, essentially breaking them down according to the following categories: earth, wind, fire, and water. The underlying mythology that explains the voodoo system is meant as both historical background and parable. It is thought that the Dominican *gagá* mythology is less complex than Haitian voodoo. The practice of *gagá* in general tends to focus more on the ritual and its mysteries than the worshipping of idols, as is the case in Haiti.

Some better known Dominican *lúases* include Anaísa, who like Aphrodite of Greek mythology is a goddess of love. Flirtatious and gay, represented by the colors of yellow or pink, she is sought out by women whose husbands have wandered and also those who have reproductive problems. The *Barón del Cementerio* ("Baron of the Cemetery"), represented by the color black, jealously guards cemeteries, serving as a mediator for the dead with regard to the purging of their sins. Since he has no anthropomorphic form he is often represented by a cross. The *Barón*, aside from being the most popular *lúa* in the Dominican Republic, is also the first one to be buried in a new cemetery. Should the deceased to be interred in a new cemetery be a woman, she is referred to as the *Baronesa Brigitte*, the *Barón's* wife. Another *lúa* is *Candelo* who is represented by the color red. He likes rum, tobacco, and dance and is the *gagá* version of the Spanish Don Juan figure since he tends to become easily infatuated. His favorite pastime, in addition to those mentioned above, is cock fights. He is turned to by those seeking luck or advice with regard to business, and he watches over the destitute. According to believers the divinities can intercede to offer solutions to problems and to hurt an enemy.

All those who practice voodoo or *gagá* in the Dominican Republic are officially Catholic. This apparent contradiction is explained by the fact that the average rural Dominican's Catholicism is circumscribed by his or her worship of Catholic saints. The loftier theories of the church, including the teachings of the New Testament and Jesus Christ, escape most people. Besides, as part of the Counterreformation movement the Catholic Church in Spain placed additional emphasis on saints, their mysteries, and other more obscure elements of the faith revived from the Middle Ages. This emphasis characterized the predominant mindset of the colonists and was the aspect of Catholicism that they favored. Catholic saints and the gifts and miraculous powers attributed to them are not that far removed, conceptually at least, from the powers and gifts of the *lúas*.

The historical explanation given for the endurance of African tribal belief systems is that the Church was comparably weak in Hispaniola during colonial times. Plantation owners were charged with the Christian indoctrination of their slaves, allowing the slaves to attend mass and so forth. In reality, the lack of churches and the time that this took away from fieldwork made it impractical for the owners. It was easy for the African slave to devote himself or herself to the cult of religious beliefs from his or her own native lands. Thus, African religion thrived as it evolved, went through a process of transculturation and arrived at the point of what today is referred to as synchretism. This synchretism conformed to two paradigms: the rural and the urban.

Synchretism began with the establishment of small churches on sugar plantations. The idea was to bring the church, particularly the worshipping of saints, closer to the slaves. The way that services were conducted was patently discriminatory, as the slaves were told to sit in the back, for example. The slaves thus turned to seeking protection from the saints who symbiotically blended with voodoo deities. Just as Saint Peter guards the gates of heaven, so does the *lúa Legba* open the doors to the spiritual world. Saint Rose watches over gardens and blooms just as *Loco* attends to herbalists. There isn't always a direct correspondence between a Catholic saint and a *lúa*, which allows for complementary assistance and a wider selection of mediation from the spiritual world. For example, the *lúa Belié Belcán* is appealed to for assistance during difficult childbirth, whereas Saint Raymond protects pregnant women.

In the larger cities and towns of sixteenth-century Hispaniola the Catholic Church established guilds that are the equivalent of today's church meeting halls. The first one in colonial Santo Domingo was the Limpia Concepción de Nuestra Señora guild, established in 1503. The guilds split along racial lines from the time of their founding; the white guild did not even allow mulattos or freed slaves to join. Such a precept promoted the creation of parallel guilds whose members were black and mulatto, and where the celebration of the feasts took on their distinct character, among other ways, by subtly, even unconsciously, focusing on African religious practices. The Church, seeing that the guilds were dedicated to a Catholic saint whose day was ostentatiously celebrated, chose to overlook the possible discrepancies with regard to how the members happened to worship.

Many Catholic celebrations and holidays are matched by *gagá* equivalents. During Holy Week, *gagá* followers cover the crosses and images of saints that adorn their altars with dark veils and cloths. In addition, *gagá* has "borrowed" the sacraments of baptism and matrimony from Catholicism. The *gagá* altar exhibits images of *luases*, as well as ritual drums, maracas, and medicinal herbs mixed in with Christian crosses, bibles, rosaries, and images of saints.

Beyond synchretism are the points that markedly differentiate *gagá* from Catholicism: the witchcraft, black magic, and possessions. *Gagá* followers believe that they can be possessed, at times without warning, by *luases* or by the evil *petró*. A witch doctor, who can be either a man or a woman, serves as an intermediary to either initiate these possessive states or to cure one of them. The dead also take possession of the living for various reasons, but usually to avenge themselves of some past wrong. When a person falls mysteriously ill it is often attributed to being possessed by the dead.[1] There have been cases where a witch doctor has determined that the only way to rid the patient of an invading spirit is to kill him or her. The *lúas* can be invoked through rituals involving magical spells that only the witch doctor knows how to formulate.

In today's Dominican Republic synchretism is limited to the rural areas. The families that migrate to urban areas bring these notions with them, but their practice is socially frowned upon. The city, with its many distractions and in the throes of modernity, tends to deemphasize the powers of the *gagá*.

SYNCHRETISM IN LITERATURE

Three recent novels by Dominican authors add legitimacy to the practice of synchretism in the same sense that history can be studied through a literary perspective and sometimes be better understood. Marcio Veloz Maggiolo's *La biografía difusa de Sombra Castañeda* ("Sombra Castañeda's Diffuse Biography") cannot be understood without a basic knowledge of the *luases* and their powers and myths. In this novel a few *luases* are central to the plot and to the character who has to deal with them. Julia Alvarez's *In the Time of the Butterflies* uses the literary device of creating a character who practices *gagá* and can therefore communicate with the dead, thus bringing the Mirabal sisters back to "life." In this case it is the household maid whose altar is made up of synchretic images and idols, and it is she who mediates with the dead sisters for the benefit of the putative author. Marisela Rizik privileges the notion of a *gagá*-practicing society concomitant to the modern world. In her novel *El tiempo del olvido* ("Of Forgotten Times"), some characters rely on the oracle of the witch doctor to make their decisions and depend on the advice of the herbalist to cure their ills.

CONCLUSION

Religious practices in the Dominican Republic contribute to the uniqueness of this nation and to the foundation of its national identity. Many manifestations of Dominican culture and customs can be traced to religious beliefs, particularly those found in the visual arts and literature and in the celebration of Carnival. The ever-increasing presence of Protestant denominations on the island does not threaten the predominance of Catholicism given the latter's importance in native culture and customs.

NOTE

1. This idea is not unique to African-based religious beliefs. The same notion has been confirmed among Australian aborigines and Chilean arauco Indians (Deive 251).

3

Social Customs

This chapter examines the daily habits of average Dominicans, including the foods they eat. Included are descriptions of a multitude of customs that date back to colonial times, with explanations of the evolution of these practices as they are carried out today. The customs of the rural and urban poor are studied in the light of the superstitions that feed them. The manner in which the national and religious holidays are celebrated along with some observations on peculiarities of Dominican language usage conclude this chapter.

From the casual greeting to the celebration of a major religious holiday, specific practices are followed judiciously in the Dominican Republic, and these customs are passed down generationally. In general terms many Dominican customs are similar and reminiscent of those in other Latin American countries and Spain and Portugal. What distinguishes Dominican customs from those of other Latin American societies is the preparation of food and the traditions that stem directly from the uniqueness of its history and the complexity of its religion: Catholicism combined with voodoo.

Dominican customs originate from the Cibao area, radiating throughout the nation from its capital, Santiago de los Treinta Caballeros. The Cibao was the area settled by ranchers and farmers, an area of stability by comparison to the capital, which is a port city and more easily susceptible to outside influences and changes. Dominicans carry on traditions and world views that date back to colonial times, meaning that many practices are Spanish in origin.

Many Dominicans subscribe, at least subconsciously, to a mentality and official discourse that is dictated by persistent Negrophobia, conservatism, misogyny, homophobia, Eurocentrism, and upper-class bias as reflected in the pronouncements of Catholic Church leaders, mainstream politicians, and state-funded intellectuals (Torres-Saillant 131). Conventional customs and their practice reflect this mindset. An alternative array of customs are reflected by those who are influenced by voodoo religious practices and African myths and legends. The customs of these marginalized Dominicans are less widely known, and to the conventional mind, their customs, steeped in superstition and fear of the unknown, seem bizarre and are dismissed as primitive.

MEALS

The Dominican workday typically runs from 8:00 A.M. through 5:00 P.M. This schedule, a reflection of globalization, responds to the current need of maintaining continuous communication with worldwide business. As recently as ten years ago, though, the workday began at 8:00 A.M. and ended at 1:00 P.M. After a prolonged lunch and sufficient time for a nap, businesses would reopen at about 4:00 P.M. and stay open through 8:00 P.M. Notorious for their lack of punctuality when it comes to social affairs, Dominicans are painstakingly punctual when it comes to business, particularly with regard to being there at the time the business opens. Meetings usually begin with a small delay, for which an excuse is always offered, even though those in attendance fully expected the delay from the onset.

Weekday breakfasts vary according to household, but most have several aspects in common. Dominican coffee is prepared by pouring hot water into a cloth sack filled with ground coffee. This filtering method is referred to as *café colado*. This coffee is served by pouring steaming milk along with hot coffee. Hot cocoa is also a popular breakfast drink. Commonly, ham and cheese or simply cheese sandwiches made with a water-based bread called *pan de agua* are eaten for breakfast. Fruit eaten for breakfast may include sliced papaya, cantaloupe, watermelon, or pineapple, which are available all year long. Weekend breakfasts may consist of fried eggs served on top of *mangú* (mashed boiled green plantains) and *queso frito* (fried cheese). Fried cheese is a dish prepared by frying a lightly spiced mild soft cheese in peanut oil, the oil of choice for all Dominican cuisine.

The time-honored tradition and ritual of the *cafecito* ("little coffee") is a demitasse of coffee served at any time a break is desired. The filtered coffee is thick and aromatic, similar, in this regard, to Turkish coffee. It is offered to guests, whether in a business situation or in a private home, on a small silver tray on which there is also a bowl of sugar. For those Dominicans who have the time to indulge in the practice, after drinking the coffee, the cup is turned over allowing for the dregs to form patterns along the insides of the cup, which are then "interpreted," similarly to Arabic practices. The resulting prophecy becomes an amusing topic of conversation.

In rural areas coffee is served presweetened and in large carafes which are shaken in circular motions to adequately distribute the heat throughout the vessel. No matter whether the visitor in question is in an urban setting or rural, it is considered impolite to refuse the offer of the *cafecito*. Dominicans are impervious to what may appear illogical to outsiders: drinking hot coffee, given the tropical climate of the country.

Served at about 1:00 P.M., lunch is the most uniformly observed meal throughout the republic when one considers the ubiquitousness of red beans, rice, stewed meat, fried plantains, and tomato and lettuce salad with a vinegar and oil dressing. This menu is fondly referred to as the "Dominican flag." The very poor may only be able to afford red beans and rice and plantains, but it can be safely said that most Dominicans eat the same lunch, give or take a few individual idiosyncrasies. The meat can be goat (considered a delicacy by Dominicans), beef, or chicken. Fish, usually served fried, substitutes for the meat dish at times. Most Dominican fish and shellfish are harvested for export, so little is consumed within the country, and when it is, prices reflect export market prices. Bread does not always accompany meals, but if it does it is usually cassava, which is made from the yucca plant. This is the same bread that the Taínos taught the Spanish to make, since flour was scarce at the beginning of the Spanish conquest of the island. Dominicans drink iced water with their meals.

Lunch concludes with a dessert that consists of any number of sweetened fruit compotes that are made of indigenous fruit such as guava, pineapple, and mango. At times these compotes are served with a cheese that resembles cream cheese. The sweetened fruit compotes, referred to as *dulces*, originated during colonial times as the Spaniards experimented with sugar and indigenous fruits and nuts such as the pineapple, the coconut (which originated in Pacific regions), and the peanut. Another favorite dessert is the *flan de queso*, a cross between a cheesecake and a custard. Dessert is followed by a demitasse of coffee.

For special occasions, the most popular dish is the *sancocho*, which is a soupy stew that includes many local varieties of root vegetables. Its preparation is complex and time consuming, mainly due to the many ingredients that make up the stew. Some of these include pork, beef, goat, sausage, cured meats, bacon, chicken, plantains, *auyamas* and *yautías* (types of indigenous squashes), yams, yucca, sweet potatoes, corn, oregano, whole garlic, salt, sour orange, vinegar, a *bouquet garni*, and *malagueta*, an indigenous spice. Ultimately the success of the *sancocho* is determined by the delicate balance of certain factors. It need be "neither too clear, nor too thick, not too greasy, nor too grease-free" (Bonnelly, *Retablo* 41). Desserts are more elaborate for these occasions, although a generous choice of the fruit compotes and cheese is always available. A red kidney bean sweetened concoction (*habichuelas dulces*) is very popular, as are cakes iced with a flavored meringue.

Family gatherings begin with a cocktail hour during which adults drink cocktails made of Dominican rum, imported spirits, or Dominican beer. Children and young adults drink soft drinks or blended fresh juices that are either milk- or water-based. The most popular Dominican blended fruit drink is the *morir soñando*, which loosely translates as "something to die for." This drink combines orange juice, milk, sugar, and ice. On very hot days blended juice may take the place of the afternoon coffee. Appetizers include *pastelitos*, which are small fried turnovers filled with cheese, yucca, or guava, and *chicharrones*, fried pork rinds. Locally grown pickled heart of palm is another favorite.

Lunch takes a long time to consume, as Dominicans enjoy talking, debating, and joking during meals, most of them refining their talent at rhetoric. Children are included and involved in every aspect of family life. At big family gatherings, siblings and cousins may share a separate table, eat less and faster, and then wander off to play, watch television, or play video games.

As is common in many Latin American countries, dinner is a light fare eaten at about 8:00 P.M. on weeknights and later on weekends. Menus run the gamut from omelets, soups, salads, pizzas, and sandwiches to breakfast-type foods such as cereals, pancakes, and waffles, accompanied by a glass of blended fresh fruit juice. Dessert typically consists of a plate of fresh fruit.

FAST FOOD

The fast food industry has grown rapidly in recent years. Most major, well-known fast food chains from the United States can be found in Santo Domingo, Santiago, and Puerto Plata. They are wildly popular, and the meals they serve tend to take the place of the evening supper, more than the traditional lunch. A few businesses have recreated the traditional lunch which they sell in styrofoam containers. These have been very successful and have assisted in the transition for those workers accustomed to a long lunch break.

VEGETABLES

The fairly recent presence of Japanese immigrants has introduced the custom of eating nontraditional vegetables, such as broccoli, asparagus, spinach, or brussel sprouts. During the second half of the twentieth century, Japanese immigrants settled mostly in Constanza, the fertile lands inland where the climate is cooler than that on the rest of the island. They brought their talent for cultivating strawberries, apples, and vegetables, in general. These crops, which are mainly grown from export, are enjoyed locally by the middle and upper classes and by foreigners. The average Dominican, however, resists eating these vegetables, preferring root vegetables, squashes, string beans, and cabbage.

A vegetable which has become a staple of Dominican cuisine, the plantain came to the Dominican Republic by way of the African slaves. A bean known as the *guandul* (a cross between a navy and a lima bean), the yam, watermelon, and the guinea hen were also brought to the Western Hemisphere by African slaves. The *tostón*, or plantain fritter, that is eaten daily for lunch is a culinary creation of the black slaves, as is the practice of steaming a mixture of meat, boiled plantain, and spices, wrapped up in banana leaves; a dish referred to as *pasteles en hoja*.

BEVERAGES

Dominican children drink powdered milk, and adolescents drink sodas, fruit juices, and shakes made from an assortment of fruit. Men prefer rum, beer, and water, as the Spanish custom of drinking wine was quickly supplanted in colonial days by the availability of rum. Women tend to drink fruit juices, and although they do consume alcoholic beverages, they drink less than men. It is believed that in the Dominican Republic for every bottle of milk that is drunk, four bottles of rum are consumed (Murray 217).

There are unspoken customs regarding drinking alcoholic beverages that span the class system. One is not to drink directly from a bottle while standing, whether on the street or in an establishment such as a bar or a store. Other dictums are that one shouldn't drink an entire bottle of rum and that one doesn't drink without loud music playing, preferably a Dominican *merengue*. There are no laws governing alcohol per se, but it is understood that men and women of all ages can drink socially. Generally, there have been few problems with regard to drinking, and there is no obsessive interest in alcohol consumption. In fact, open drunkenness is looked down upon and considered the activity of derelicts. Nowadays, perhaps as a result of encroaching modernity, children of wealthier classes have discovered alcohol and drugs as means of escape, and the disastrous consequences that accompany this kind of experimentation.

PREGNANCY AND CHILDBIRTH

Superstitions and folk remedies abound when it comes to pregnancy and childbirth in the Dominican Republic. A pregnant woman was regarded, up to the past quarter century, as a fragile object whose capricious whims had to be indulged, lest she give birth to an unhappy creature referred to as a "fish hook." According to local folklore, birthmarks occur when a craving has not been satisfied. Expectant women are kept from viewing disfigured people or hideous objects for fear that the child may look like that when he or she is born. Fortune tellers claim that the presence of a pregnant woman near their establishment signifies bad luck for their business. The consumption of certain foods is thought to have either positive or negative effects on the fetus. Eating *concón*, rice that sticks to the pot, is a good idea as it ensures the security of the placenta. It has even been documented that some women have consumed large quantities of milk of magnesia with the hope that the child will be born white.

In rural areas it is common to use midwives at the time of childbirth. The new mother and the baby are kept indoors for nine days, during which time great pains are taken to keep both away from any danger of cross-ventilation and from too much exposure to sunlight. The umbilical cord is not thrown away but rather several different practices are observed according to the traditions of the family. In some cases it is buried in the garden of the home where the baby was born. It is common, in fact, for a man to claim a particular town as his home because that is where his umbilical cord is buried. In other cases the cord is handed to the mother who tears it when the child turns seven, thus "releasing" him or her to their own fate. Others place the cord between the pages of a book with the hope that the placement of the cord will influence the outcome of the child's future. For example, the cord may be placed within the pages of an encyclopedia of music, the parents' hope being that the child will grow up to be a musician.

BAPTISMS AND GODPARENTS

The tradition of baptism is a legacy of the Catholic Church. In rural areas the practice is still referred to as the conversion of the child from Moor to Christian, and in general it is more common to talk about "pouring water on the baby" than to use the Spanish equivalent of the word baptism. Ideally the baby is baptized within the first three months of life. The baby wears a white gown trimmed in lace, if possible, one that has been passed down over generations. The satin, lace-trimmed cap that the baby wears is referred to as the *galacha*. In rural areas babies wear a gold chain with a pendant made of jet, a hard black mineral, to ward off the "evil eye." After the religious ceremony, performed in a church, the baby's parents host a party for closest family members and friends. Appetizers are served along with cocktails. Music is played and there might be dancing.

Choosing the baby's godparents is a serious endeavor. Usually the godparents are siblings of the baby's parents, or close relatives. Typically, one woman and one man are chosen. In rural as well as poorer urban areas, parents of a young baby seek out godparents who are better off than they. Ties that bind godparents with the parents of the baby are strong and unique. Godparents follow their godchild's stages as he or she grows up, often assisting financially along the way. The baby's parents and the godparents make up a new union that is considered to be as close as a familial one. Father and godfather address each other as *compadre*—a word that signifies the baptismal tie—and mother and godmother address one another as *comadre*. A formal manner of address is used among the *compadres* and *comadres*: the *usted* form, which is a respectful way of saying "you" in Spanish. Common sense rules that any one person should not have more than five godchildren. This precept was soundly undermined by dictator Rafael Leonidas Trujillo who became godfather to hundreds upon thousands of children, as yet another way to exert control over all his new *compadres*.

NAMES

Dominicans have been accused of being too individualistic for their own good, as is evidenced by people's given names. Several traditions are followed when naming a child. In remote rural areas no one really knows anyone else's full name because it is common to designate people by a nickname from a very young age. An anecdote tells of the death of a Clemente Columbano Abad Rosario Pérez. No one in the village knew where he was from or who he was until finally somebody remembered the name: Songo el de Pedro. Songo is a nickname meaning sly and the rest of this name means that he is Pedro's son, or, more literally that he belongs to Pedro. In the not so distant past one could identify oneself as the son or daughter of so and so, and indicate geographic origin as part of the name. For example, a hypothetical introduction would be, "I am Federico, son of José Pérez, from Baitoa."

Babies are named after relatives, preferably deceased, so as to better preserve their memory. Up until the middle of the twentieth century a child was given the name of a saint, usually the saint celebrated on the calendar day of the child's birth. This custom has given way to giving the baby any name in the bible, even such names as Evangelist, Bishop, or Confessor. Additional names reflect contemporary fads, international flair, musical preference, and political loyalty such as the name Grace Indhira de Mónaco, for a girl, or Pentágrama Díaz, for a boy.[1]

BIRTHDAYS

Among the middle and upper classes, birthdays are celebrated with parties, cakes, candles, games for children, dancing for adults, and presents for the feted. People of poorer classes might remember a person's birthday by extending a wish of happiness and longevity, but rarely is a birthday actually celebrated.

FIRST COMMUNION

First Communion, one of the seven sacraments of the Catholic Church, is commemorated when a child is between seven and nine years old. For Dominican Catholics, this is an important ceremony, and much attention and detail are given to how the child is dressed, particularly a young girl. Often the first-time communicants will have their picture in the social pages of the newspapers with a description of the attire they are wearing on the given day. The young girl's dress is almost as elaborate as a wedding dress, whereas a young boy typically wears a white shirt and black pants. First Communion is usually a group ceremony, meaning that a whole class of catechists go through the ceremony in unison. The individual families celebrate afterwards with close friends and extended relatives. If it is a morning ceremony the celebration will entail breakfast consisting of *churros*, which are similar to funnel cakes, and hot chocolate. A full buffet lunch or appetizer-type food (*picadera*) and drinks are served if the ceremony takes place in the early afternoon. There is always a large white cake to commemorate the occasion.

LOS QUINCEAÑOS (THE COMING-OUT PARTY)

In many middle- and upper-middle-class families, a girl's fifteenth birthday is lavishly celebrated. The occasion is announced in the social pages of the newspapers, with an accompanying photograph of the girl.

The coming-out party can resemble a miniature wedding reception. Family, friends, and relatives are invited to the party which begins around 9:00 P.M. and continues through the early hours of the morning. Dress can range from formal to semi-formal, but the birthday girl almost always is dressed in a lavish long dress. The families who pride themselves as strict traditionalists ensure that the first dance, which is reserved for the father, is a waltz. The rest of the night the music ranges from rock to *merengue, salsa, bachata,* and *bolero.* The same families that most value tradition play out a scene from Cinderella, whereupon the birthday girl is given a new "slipper," and decorated slippers make up part of the decor of the party.

DATING

Courting customs and rigorous traditions have been modernized. The current generation is the first to enjoy a fair amount of freedom when it comes to dating. Rules and stipulations are established by individual families and are typical of families everywhere. Since familial ties are close in the Dominican Republic, it is virtually impossible to carry on a courtship without involving the extended family.

Until the current generation, one-on-one dating was almost impossible. Youth went out in groups, or a chaperone, usually an unmarried aunt, *la jamona,* was called upon to accompany the couple. Men serenaded their love interests, and through the nineteenth century, paraded on horseback before the intended's home, making the horse buck and prance.

The age at which dating begins is comparable to that of any other country. There are gender-based differences with regard to the amount of freedom that is allowed. A young man is allowed to go out and stay out at an earlier age than a young woman. A young woman of the ages of twelve to fifteen is expected to be accompanied by somebody, a friend or sibling, especially if she is to stay out after ten in the evening.

From lovesick and adoring gazes in the love seat to midnight serenades, Dominicans like to think of themselves as quite romantic when it comes to courting. Not that long ago, in the Cibao area and in the south, a man in love would toss little pebbles at his intended upon running into her. If the young lady picked the pebbles up, it was an indication of reciprocity of feelings. In Moca the enamored man would hammer a small stake before his love interest's home. If she moved the stake closer to her house, it was an acknowledgment of her interest in him. Indifference was signified by not moving the stake at all.

Nowadays, few people, particularly women, want to assume the roles that society ideally expects them to play out. The age-old concepts of machismo and its necessary opposite *marianismo* have collided with modernity and women's liberation; all of which has made it necessary to redefine the roles of both the male and the female in courtship. The strong sense of masculinity, entailing aggressiveness, excessive virility, and the domination of women, as machismo is defined, is the backbone of male self-awareness as it is indoctrinated, with few exceptions, in the Dominican Republic as well as in many other Latin American countries.[2] In courtship this image remits to fantasies that predate the Middle Ages and that populate fairy tales: the image of the beautiful damsel in distress that must be saved, rescued, or won by the man, who is therefore the hero and must "conquer" the object of his affection. The term conquest or *conquista* is commonly used to designate the woman whose "heart" a man has won. The woman or young lady, for her part, has to be pure, innocent, and faithful beyond measure to her newfound love. Essentially, she should be able to fulfill the fantasy of the fair maiden. The concept of *marianismo* holds that a young woman is to be like the Virgin Mary: pure, submissive, and self-sacrificing. Of the two constructs and with the rise of feminism, *marianismo* is the one that is quickly becoming obsolete.

MARRIAGE

The *marianismo* paradigm has adjusted to modernity, in many cases, to allow for more equality within a relationship and in marriage. A deep-seated fear that has been harder to eradicate is that of becoming a spinster, or *jamona*, as this status is referred to disparagingly in the Dominican Republic. Singleness for women in their late twenties and beyond is becoming more common given rising divorce rates, but continues to be viewed negatively; the women are considered to be failures and are treated as social outcasts.

Certain rituals are carried out in hopes of "capturing" the attention of a marriageable man. These rituals reflect the symbiosis of Catholicism, voodooism, Spanish traditions, African beliefs, and other ethnic folklore inherent to the Dominican Republic. One method that ensures engagement is to place a statue or image of Saint Anthony upside down because traditionally Saint Anthony is credited with finding lost objects. At times an offering of water is made to the saint with the caveat that should he not intercede favorably in the petition, he will be "drowned" in the water. Coffee dregs are read to determine the prospects, and witch doctors are consulted for guidance. Witch doctors commonly assign different kinds of baths: some redolent, some fetid, as ways to capture a man's attention. At weddings, a guest who fears remaining single might steal the figurines that decorate the top of the wedding cake. Another furtive act is to somehow corner the groom during the wedding reception, enticing him to kiss you. Helping with wedding preparations is yet another way to ensure a future engagement, as is the use of the same soap that the bride bathed with prior to marrying. Finally, some superstitions reflect those of any part of the western world, such as catching the bouquet and garter.

Bridal showers and bachelor's parties are similar to those held in most of the western world. Engagement pictures, or pictures from the bridal showers appear in the local newspapers. The concept of a wedding rehearsal or rehearsal dinner does not exist in the Dominican Republic. Both the bride and the groom pick sponsors for the wedding. Their function and relation to the wedding couple are similar to those of the baptismal godparents. The sponsors assist substantially in covering the costs of the wedding.

After the wedding, in some areas of the Dominican Republic, the bride is still expected to prove that she was a virgin at the time of marriage. While the bride may not leave her house for nine days, her friends can visit her at which time she can discreetly reveal proof of her virginity at the time of the marriage. The friends are in charge of making sure that curiosity to that end is satisfied. This custom is losing its prevalence.

For centuries the idea that a married man could maintain a mistress was tolerated by Dominican society and even by the man's wife. Nowadays, men are increasingly feeling the pressure of societal disapproval of such practices, and the women who agree to be mistresses are increasingly the subject of unmitigated societal scorn, whereas in the past they might even have been quietly envied. Divorce is increasingly more common and more accepted, along with the accompanying rulings on alimony and child support. This is particularly significant with regard to divorced women who are no longer viewed as failures or social outcasts.

DEATH

No life passage in the Dominican Republic is as enveloped in mystery, folklore, tradition, and superstition as death. The dogma of the Catholic Church and voodoo beliefs hold that death is an alternate form of life in which the deceased embodies a different physical state. The presence of the deceased is felt by the survivors, and there are many ways of venerating them or warding off one's own death.

In the little town of Gaspar Hernández, located in the northern part of the Dominican Republic, people spray water before their houses as a funeral cortège passes. In other areas a passing funeral means that mirrors should be turned inward so as not to reflect the soul or ghost of the deceased. It is believed that a person who sees such a reflection will become insane. In

Vicente Noble, a town in the southeast of the country, mothers ensure that none of their children are lying down during an interment. Similarly, in other areas of the countryside, anyone who is ailing is propped up in bed for the duration of the funeral. Water is emptied from all inside and outside containers soon after the death of an individual because it is believed that the deceased's soul bathes in these waters. Another popular maxim holds that sleeping with one's feet pointed toward the street invites death. In many areas of the country it is considered improper to hold a wake any place other than in the deceased's home. Funeral homes' functions are strictly limited to selling coffins and renting chairs and tables.

In addition to a published obituary, through the latter half of the twentieth century, a person's death was broadcast over the radio. Nowadays, it is more common to run announcements in the newspapers that invite friends, relatives, and even acquaintances to the nine masses that follow a person's burial.

The body of the deceased is laid out in the main room of the home. Family members cry loudly and recall the deceased's many virtues. A coterie of women wailers or criers is a common sight in these rooms. These women are either acquainted with the deceased or are hired. At times the immediate family of the deceased prefers to grieve privately, in which case the hired criers function as substitutes in the public arena, all the while proclaiming the grandness of the deceased. After wailing the criers retire to a corner of the room where they silently talk among themselves. The loudest cries take place at the moment that the coffin is moved out of the house on its way to the cemetery.

A wake can last up to twenty-four hours. Bodies are embalmed only in the event that the family waits to be joined by members who live abroad. Otherwise the body is buried within twenty-four hours, or shortly thereafter. The burial is followed by nine masses offered on consecutive days. The ninth, a memorial mass, is followed by a gathering during which a sumptuous meal is offered. At this time all those who participated in remembering the deceased evaluate the procedures of the previous nine days. It is hoped that a consensus will be reached establishing that in all the observance was a "good" one.

The novenas are followed by monthly masses and ultimately the deceased is remembered in an annual mass. The custom, particularly for women, of mourning the deceased by wearing black or other subdued colors is rapidly vanishing. The nontraditionalists defend their actions by affirming that sadness and mourning are felt in the heart and not expressed by the color of the clothes that one wears. Nonetheless, the tradition of wearing black for as long as five years after the death of a spouse, child, or parent is sometimes observed.

The flowers and flower arrangements that are sent to the home of the deceased prior to interment are gathered and taken to the cemetery where they are left at the tomb site. People who visit the bereaved are not expected to bring anything other than words of comfort.

The death of a child, while commemorated similarly in urban situations as the death of an adult, is considered different in rural settings. These wakes are referred to as *baquiní.* It is popularly held that a child's death is to be celebrated in a happy way. The child is viewed as an angel whose death brings him or her that much closer to heaven where he or she can intercede on his or her family's behalf. Songs to that effect are chanted around the body of the child during the wake, and there is no crying. In the patio or in the garden, children play games in order to ensure that the deceased's parting is "fun." The deceased child's godparents pay for all the funeral arrangements.

The most superstitious in rural areas, particularly, believe that the dead leave their tombs to roam. Mashed garlic is rubbed on children so that the dead won't bother them. Accordingly *campesinos* are prepared to blurt out an exorcizing prayer should they run up against a *baká,* that appears to be dead. The first thing to do in such a case, advise the elders members of a community, is to step on the big toe of your left foot with the heel of your right foot. Others recommend crossing one's sandals at the foot of the bed to ward off evil spirits. A few seek out recently deceased spirits by taking flowers to the cemetery and asking that the deceased reveal the numbers of that particular week's lottery drawing. Some rural people have convinced themselves that the only way one can become the owner of vast territories is by striking a pact with the devil, exchanging the life of a loved one for the privilege of being a rich proprietor. Because of this many country people claim not to want any part of being wealthy.

MOTHER'S DAY

Although this holiday is an imported commercial one, it has become one of the most venerated days of the year. In the Dominican Republic Mother's Day is on the last Sunday in May. On this day, and those that immediately precede it, mothers are recognized publicly through school functions and masses, and privately with small gifts, ideally hand-crafted rather than purchased. Mothers who have died are also remembered at this time, with orphans playing big parts in school functions. The importance of Mother's

Day in the Dominican Republic underscores the high prestige that mothers hold. The mother-child bond is arguably the tightest of all human associations among Dominicans.

THE *FIGUREO*

Dominicans love to see and to be seen, a practice that is referred to as the *figureo*, and the day that is reserved for this is Sunday afternoon. From the biggest cities to the smallest towns, Sunday afternoons are dedicated to strolling along the main street, dressed up and "powdered" to appear whiter. Modernization has altered this time-honored custom by including automobiles and motorcycles as part of the spectacle. In Santo Domingo the *figureo* takes places along the *malecón*, the palm tree–lined avenue that lies along the Caribbean Sea, or along the Mirador del Sur and the Mirador del Norte parks. In Santiago the townspeople stroll up and down the hill and park that lead up to the imposing monument dedicated to the Restoration.

RELIGIOUS HOLIDAYS

The most grandly celebrated religious holidays in the Dominican Republic are Christmas and Holy Week, which begins on Palm Sunday and culminates with Easter Sunday. Of the two, Christmas and its accompanying holidays of New Year's Day and Three Kings' Day, or Epiphany, have changed the least over the past decades, with the exception of becoming increasingly commercialized. Holy Week, in contrast, once considered to be the holiest of holidays, has become little more than a spring break. Observance is limited to special religious services on Palm Sunday and Easter Sunday. As recently as a quarter of a decade ago during the entire length of Holy Week, radio stations broadcast only classical music. On Easter Sunday loud vivacious *merengues* burst forth, breaking through the solemnity of the previous week. The celebration of the day of the Virgin of Altagracia, the patron saint of the republic, and Carnival are the other two widely enjoyed religious holidays. Other religious commemorations are dedicated to local patron saints.

Christmas

Christmas is celebrated quite uniformly among Christian families in the Dominican Republic. Towns and cities are decorated for the occasion with lights, tinsel garlands, and multi-colored Christmas trees. Christmas trees are grown inland, in the fertile valleys of Constanza and La Vega, but many

Washington Monument decorated for
Christmas on the Malecón. Courtesy of
Listín Diario.

people prefer to purchase artificial trees that resemble real Christmas trees.
Others import live firs and spruces from the United States. Many use white
spray paint on the branches of a small leafless tree that is in the approximate
shape of a pear tree and then hang ornaments. Homes are not decorated on
the outside, but on the inside, by the tree, a nativity scene is set up along
with a creative exhibit of Christmas cards.

Some families choose to attend midnight mass, which is called *misa del
gallo* or the rooster's mass, throughout the Hispanic world. It is believed that
while the family is at mass baby Jesus leaves gifts. After the gifts are opened
a sumptuous dinner is served. It includes a roasted turkey or a roasted suckling pig, or both. A common menu may include, in addition to the pig whose
entire body is laid out with an apple stuffed in its mouth, festive rice, yucca   Meal.
or cheese turnovers, potato salad, stuffed banana leaves, brown sugar cake,
lerenes, and coffee. Festive rice is a rice dish with raisins and almonds, spiced
with curry. It is decorated with green peas and red pimentos, representing

traditional Christmas colors. Stuffed banana leaves are made of a dough of plantains blended with a ground beef mixture. All of this is packed into banana leaves which are then tied with raffia and steamed. The brown sugar cake, frosted with meringue, is made only with brown sugar, as its name indicates. *Lerenes*, a fruit indigenous to the island, were first introduced to the Spaniards by the Taínos. Perfectly round, these small, tart soft fruit encased in a thick rind ripen in December. Dates and other preserved fruits, apples, and nuts complete the menu, and wine and eggnog are served with the meal. Preserved and dried fruit, such as dates, figs, and apricots, used to be imported only during the Christmas season, and apples were considered a delicacy.

New Year's Eve

Throughout the Dominican Republic, the last day of the year is commemorated by attending parties at night clubs and country clubs. Dress is formal, and the color red is said to bring good luck. Some people prefer to celebrate New Year's Eve with a dinner buffet and party at their own home. At midnight, while awaiting the blast from a cannon in the original fort of Santo Domingo and the ringing of twelve bells from the old churches in the oldest part of Santo Domingo, celebrants, no matter where they may be, eat twelve grapes for good luck, one for each month of the coming year.

Three Kings' Day

Three Kings' Day, or Epiphany, is celebrated on January 6, twelve days after Christmas. Both the Wise Men and the *Vieja Belén*, a benevolent old woman, distribute gifts to children beginning on January 5 and continuing for three days thereafter. The reception of gifts is contingent upon good behavior on the part of the child. The *Vieja Belén* sends a message through the parents or godparents to the child, encouraging better behavior, should it be necessary. The word *vieja* means old woman, and *Belén* can be translated as either Bethlehem, the child Jesus, or even the nativity crib. Legend describes the *Vieja Belén* as wearing a turban and tunic. Children leave bits of hay and water next to their beds for the Wise Men's camels, and a cigar is left for the *Vieja Belén*.

Holy Week

It has been observed that "Christian writings teach that Holy Week is a time for reflection. But here in our country it is the time for huge meals for many, and a time for drunkenness at the beach and in private homes for others" (Labourt 176). Up to the last twenty-five years of the twentieth century Holy Week was dedicated in its entirety to the observation of the events that led up to Christ's crucifixion and resurrection. Beginning on Palm Sunday, which falls one week before Easter, Holy Week culminates on Easter Sunday. This is a time when *gagá* dovetails with Christianity, as important celebrations of the voodoo calendar coincide with Holy Friday observations in particular.

Houses were meticulously cleaned prior to Holy Week, so that daily chores would not interrupt Holy Week ceremonies. Special menus that did not include meat were planned for the week. The favorite food of this time was sweetened red beans (*habichuelas dulces*). On Palm Sunday little crosses were fashioned from palm leaves to be hung at home to bless it throughout the year. Holy Monday and Tuesday were dedicated to the preparation of the ceremonies to come later in the week. These preparations involved dressing the statues of saints and other holy figures to be carried in processionals on Holy Wednesday. Holy Thursday was reserved for quiet penitence in the churches whose statues were draped in purple cloth. Holy Friday saw the celebration of a lengthy mass during which Christ's agony on the cross was reenacted. Archbishops and bishops read their best sermons, which were interrupted only by Gregorian chanting. An oratorio to Christ's death was presented by the best musicians and choir members in the main churches of the larger cities. Saturday morning concluded the week of mourning with festive *merengue* music bursting forth on the radio waves. Church bells rang, sirens were turned on, and people would run out into the streets in celebration, banging pots and making noise. That evening there would be a social in the local club. Easter Sunday was marked by a mass and the changing of the vestments in the church from purple to white and gold.

Nowadays Palm Sunday and Easter Sunday are the two days that receive most attention from practicing Catholics, and if the work week is reduced at all, only Thursday and Friday are observed as holidays. Easter Sunday is a popular day to go to the beach, and is otherwise seen as any other Sunday. However, people do abstain from meat the last days of the week, particularly on Holy Friday.

Many superstitions of voodoo origin surround Holy Week in the countryside. On Holy Friday it is thought that bathing in the river at dawn will bring good luck but only if the bather is fasting at the time and he or she does not speak to anybody during the ritual. Another custom, to ward off evil is to drink a concoction of mashed garlic, some green pepper, and Holy Water on Holy Friday. It is believed that water that is left out overnight on Holy Friday becomes holy water, and a pine tree's needles will ooze blood if the pine tree was planted on Holy Friday. All these beliefs are contingent upon attending church on Holy Friday. To that end Holy Friday is one of the few days that field workers are off, besides Sundays.

The Day of the Virgin of Altagracia and Other Patron Saints' Days

On January 21 pilgrims set out to the basilica at Higüey to honor the patron saint of the Dominican Republic. Before there were good roads and centralized transportation, people walked for miles to pay homage. Nowadays buses, taxis, and private cars take the faithful to Higüey to pray before the image of the Virgin of Altagracia.

The feast of Saint Michael used to be a day of great celebration in Santiago. The belief was that the archangel descended in search of the devil who roamed free on September 29. Everybody took care of chores, made essential purchases, and so forth on the 28, so as not to have to leave the house at all on the next day.

Several customs associated with saints and their reverence were traditionally commemorated through the 1960s: the statue visitation, the *rosario*, and Saint John's Day. Gesso statues of saints were carried to private homes on religious holidays. A modest donation was made to the lay nun who brought the statue. The services of a specific saint could be requested—some saints being more popular than others. The *rosario* was an evening procession of the very devout, among them young women, children, and older adults. They walked slowly along the path symbolizing the Calvary at Golgotha, with thirteen stopping points along the way. As this group walked, lighting their way with candles, they would sing prayers and psalms. The *rosario* would conclude around midnight.

Saint John's Day, celebrated on June 24, was also accompanied by peculiar customs associated with rebirth and vigor. One began with placing the white of a raw egg in a glass of water. As the albuminoid liquid took shape in the glass of water one was supposed to be able to divine the image of a marriageable man. It is also believed that a hair cut on Saint John's Day would be stronger and shinier.

Almost every town of a significant size has its own patron saint whose day is celebrated popularly with a big party. Loudspeakers play festive music, and people dance, drink, and eat in the streets. Some customs that have disappeared include games and contests such as sack races and greasy pole climbing. One of the more challenging customs was composing and reciting couplets. The customs that have survived include the election of a queen for a day, who presides over the festivities. The parish pastor organizes the contest.

Carnival

The days leading up to Ash Wednesday, which for Catholics signifies the beginning of Lent, are filled with wild merriment and jubilation. This ancient Catholic ritual is best known internationally for its manifestation in Brazil. In the Dominican Republic, as in other Caribbean countries, this popular holiday means a week of parades and public festivities. It allows for social order to be subverted, because for those few days of Carnival everyone is king, and a form of social equality can be imagined. The celebration takes place in early spring, signifying rebirth and new life. It is a pagan festival, subsumed by Catholicism in its zeal to appease indigenous and native customs by making others' ancient celebrations its own.

In Santo Domingo, Carnival takes place the week that ends on February 27, Independence Day. That day marks the biggest celebration of all. In Santiago de los Treinta Caballeros, Carnival is celebrated the week that ends on Ash Wednesday Eve.

Parades are the most salient manifestation of Carnival. In Santo Domingo parades take place every afternoon along the *malecón*, the palm-shaded avenue that hugs the coastline. The parades are made up of dance troupes in multicolored dress, beauty queens on floats, military contingents in uniform, and people dressed up in costumes of famous people (the Pope, Fidel Castro) or well-known symbols of other countries (the American cowboy, the Dutch girl, or the Apache Indian). Big corporations have floats in the parade as well. The riders on these floats, wearing company colors, boast eye-catching decorations such as a giant beer glass on the local beer company float. The floats used to be pulled by donkeys whose heads were decorated with a crown of flowers and colorful ribbons. Nowadays it is more common to see an army jeep pulling a float.

The most intriguing paraders are interchangeably referred to as the *diablos cojuelos* ("horned devils") or *lechones* ("suckling pig"). These bizarre-looking dancers wear satin body suits, of one color or two, split lengthwise. The outfits are decorated with bells, ribbons, pennants, and small round mirrors. At times the body suit includes a cape that hangs down the back. A tight-fitting hood is worn on the head, and the face is covered with a mask made of wire and papier-maché. The masks are so festooned that over the years they have become a prized art form, decorating the homes of the wealthy and treasured in museums as folk art. Typically the masks represent either a

Ready to join the Carnival parade. Courtesy
of *Listín Diario*.

hog's snout or that of a bull. They flaunt long horns, up to two feet long,
that point upward and forward. Some of the horns are decorated with small
spikes; others are smooth. Each mask is individualized by its particular detail:
the horns on some are painted gold or silver, and the style used to paint the
facial characteristics of the mask is unique to each mask. The entire outfit is
put together by men, with minor assistance from women. The *lechones* and
diablos cojuelos are members of the lowest social class. Part of their dance or
skit during a Carnival parade is to simulate a fight (which sometimes is a
barely veiled disguise of real animosity between street gangs), with "opposing"
or "rival" masqueraders.

   The Carnival parades also include groups of people representing the different areas of the country, dressed in regional dress. Traditional dress in the
Dominican Republic is a white shirt and black pants for the man. Occasionally he may wear a straw hat to complete the outfit, or appear bare-chested.
Women wear blousy tops and full skirts that fall slightly below the knee and
are tightly cinched at the waist, allowing for freedom of movement while
dancing. Usually both men and women, dressed in traditional clothes, dance

Diablos Cojuelos in Santiago. Courtesy of *Listín Diario*.

barefoot. What distinguishes one region from another are color combinations in the women's dresses. Some dresses are all white, with a light blue ribbon at the waist, whereas others are multicolored.

Higher classes celebrate Carnival with costume balls at private clubs. As long as they are wearing masks and their identity is concealed, women are allowed to disregard social conventions, flirt, tell jokes, and in general be scandalous. Although costumes are not required, it is the custom that women who are not in costume may not dance.

NATIONAL HOLIDAYS

The two most important national political holidays are Independence Day, February 27, and Restoration Day, August 16. Independence Day dovetails with the conclusion of Carnival. The biggest celebration of Independence Day takes place in the capital city, and more modest versions are carried out in bigger towns throughout the republic. The parades of that day incorporate school children wearing school uniforms, groups of soldiers, navy officers, army officers, and police officers. The president, his cabinet, and members of the House of Representatives, the judges of the Supreme Court, and high-ranking military officers review the troops and paraders. An airplane acrobatic

Carnival reveler on motorcycle in Santiago.
Courtesy of *Listín Diario*.

show regales the crowds. The president usually addresses the nation in a nationally televised and radio broadcast speech. Among other official acts, this is the day when promotions within the military and police ranks are announced. The flag is displayed prominently along streets and in front of private homes. Some people bearing flowers visit the national pantheon, the burial place of the three heroes of the independence movement: Juan Pablo Duarte, the writer; Francisco del Rosario Sánchez, the lawyer; and Matías Ramón Mella, the soldier.

Restoration Day is almost as important as Independence Day. In a sense, it is a second independence day since it celebrates the beginning of the war for the recuperation of Dominican independence after the country had been annexed to Spain on March 18, 1861. The holiday is commemorated with military and school parades. The national anthem is played along the parade route and there is a review of the troops by top government officials.

Although the Dominican Republic is one of the few countries in the world that recognizes three founders, Juan Pablo Duarte's birthday is the one that has become a national holiday. It is commemorated on January 26 with ceremonies that take place at the national pantheon where this national hero is buried. The national altar, as the pantheon is referred to, is decorated with flowers brought by well-wishers.

May 1 is Labor Day in the Dominican Republic. Some companies treat their employees to a party. Otherwise the day is merely a holiday for workers.

THE *MERENGUE* FESTIVAL

The *merengue* festival takes place in July in both Santo Domingo and Puerto Plata. This week-long bacchanal raises the *merengue* and the costumes worn by dancers to an art form. The dancers dance in the street and on open stages and compete for an array of honors that recognize originality, fluidity, and beauty of the choreography. Posters that are designed to advertise the festival compete for originality and beauty. The crowds who come to watch the dancing and the parades that take place in the evenings also dance.

NATIONAL SYMBOLS

The Dominican flag, created by the founder and "father" of the nation, Juan Pablo Duarte, was raised for the first time to celebrate the country's independence from Haiti on February 27, 1844. The banner's design is comprised of four squares divided by a white cross. The left side is royal blue over bright red, the right side is bright red over royal blue. The country's coat of arms is at the center of the cross. The blue color represents the peace desired by Dominicans "to dedicate themselves to work and study" (Dalurzo 44), the red symbolizes the blood shed by Dominican patriots in the battlefield, and the cross represents the country's Christian faith.

The country's coat of arms bears a royal blue ribbon over it with the inscription that reads *Dios, Patria, y Libertad* ("God, Fatherland, and Liberty"). Like the flag, it is divided into four red and blue sections. In the very center is a bible open to the Gospel according to Saint John 8:32: "And you shall know the truth and the truth will make you free." There is also a small white cross above the book with two lances and four flags diagonally spread across the center background of the emblem. The emblem is further adorned by a bay leaf branch on the one side and a palm frond on the other. The bay leaves stand for immortality and the palm frond for liberty. Together they signify Glory and Triumph.

The lyrics of the national anthem were written by Emilio Prud'Homme to music by José Reyes in 1883. The hymn is played daily at all flag raisings and at the beginning of every school day, where students meet around the flagpole.

LANGUAGE

Dominicans speak slightly differently from their other Spanish-Caribbean neighbors in Cuba and Puerto Rico. Some of the words they use and proverbs that distill the common philosophical outlook on life distinguish them from other Latin American countries.

For most of their history Santo Domingo and Santiago de los Treinta Caballeros evolved independently from each other so communication between the two metropolises was scarce and difficult. Because of this, several distinctions in speech distinguished the two cities, but nowadays the distinctions are barely perceptible. The Cibao is traditionally regarded as the part of the country where the Spanish that is spoken is closest to that of the sixteenth and seventeenth centuries, particularly in the substitution of the letter *l* for *r*—instead of por, the *cibaeño* might say *pol*—and the frequent substitution of the vowel *i* for *r* (*comei* instead of *comer*, the verb meaning to eat) and for *l* (such as the definite article *el*, which is often pronounced *ei*). *Cibaeños*, as the people from the Cibao are called, would also begin the phrase, "Look here" with the Spanish equivalent *vea usté*. The *v* is pronounced as a *b*, and the final *d* in the Spanish word *usted* is dropped. City dwellers pronounce words more "properly," meaning that they enunciate more consonants. The *s* is usually dropped in common speech throughout the Spanish Caribbean and in the Dominican Republic as well. The letter *l* often replaces *r*'s: *palque* for *parque*—the word for park. The sound of *x* comes across as *ps* such as in the word for exam, which sounds like *epsamen* in popular usage.

Globalization, particularly with the advent of cable television, the Internet, and overall advanced communication systems as reflected in the media, has taken its toll on many regionalisms. Some of the words that have fallen into disuse in very recent years can be traced to Spanish archaisms, particularly from the provinces of Extremadura and Andalucía, where the majority of the *conquistadores* came from. The linguistic patterns of Spanish origin were established during the first fifteen years of colonization. Some Spanish archaisms include the word for a woman's slip, which used to be *refajo* but is now *enaguas;* the word for a man's suit, *flux*, has given way to the more common *traje*. Other words that have become part of the Dominican vocabulary reflect the occupation of U.S. forces in the early part of the twentieth century. Men's underwear is referred to as *bividí*, after BVD, and the word for garbage can is *zafacón*, an exclusively Dominican word and a deformation and mispronouncement of the U.S. Army issue "safety can."

Food terminology varies throughout the Spanish Caribbean and Latin America. The red beans that are eaten every day for lunch are called *habichuelas* by Dominicans and *frijoles* by the rest of the Hispanic world. The Hispanic world refers to oranges as *naranjas*, but in the Dominican Republic they are called *chinas*.

In all there are about 140 "Dominicanisms." Dominicans have a lexicon to remedy a momentary loss of memory with regard to naming a certain object or even an idea ("thingamajig" in English, for example). These inherently Dominican neologisms include the words *vaina*, *fuñío*, and *jodienda*. Their popular usage borders on vulgar language. Dominicans are also onomatopoeic in their speech using sounds such as *chas chas* to describe someone tearing paper and *tras* to describe the tearing of cloth.

Dominicans share other traits of communication with their Hispanic Caribbean neighbors, the Cubans and the Puerto Ricans. Dominicans gesticulate and make many facial expressions as they speak. Swearing is a well-rooted custom in the Dominican Republic. Lying is acceptable as long as an oath has not been made to uphold the lie. Some Dominicans, conscious of their own ignorance on a given subject matter, will nonetheless seek out an opportunity to use a word recently added to their own repertoire, comprehension of the word or phrase notwithstanding. Giving themselves importance and thus cloaking their fundamental misunderstanding of the word or phrase in question, these *físicos*, as they are called, will add *s* to words at random, convinced that this adds proficiency and authority to their speech. By the same token, they arbitrarily remove consonants from words: *ejas* for *cejas* ("eyebrows"); *auja* for *aguja* (needles).

Some Dominican words' etymology can be traced to Africa. *Abombarse*, a word that means inflated with water and has the connotation of something putrid, comes from the African *bomba*, a verb which means to spoil or decompose. Another Dominican word is *fucú*, which means bad luck and derives from the African word *fufú* which means spell or witchcraft.[3]

Dominican customs and language are colorful and distinctive. The preponderance of modern technology such as cable television and the Internet, and the culture it propagates has a detrimental effect on the ability to preserve certain customs. However, those customs that are based on human relations in the Dominican Republic will undoubtedly survive all threats of universal homogenization.

NOTES

1. Many names verge on ludicrous but are also a reflection of ignorance. They include Meningitis Rodríguez, Expreso Valdés, and Etcétera Vásquez (Bonnelly, *Retablo* 22).

2. The roles fashioned for men were as illogical as those for women. For example, it was not considered manly for a man to go to church on a regular basis. Men attended mass only on special occasions or major religious masses. When at mass, it was thought that kneeling in prayer was emasculating.

3. For more information on Dominican vocabulary and morphology see Alan Cambeira, *Quisqueya la bella: The Dominican Republic in Historical and Cultural Perspective* (Armonk, NY: M. E. Sharpe, 1997), 239–249.

4

Media and Cinema

There are approximately 127 AM radio stations, 52 FM stations, about 10 newspapers, a few weekly magazines, and 7 television channels in the Dominican Republic. Radio is by far the most widely distributed media in the nation. The number of print media is limited by the high rate of illiteracy or bare literacy and the cost of print media. With the exception of radio, there is a marked dichotomy between rural and urban areas with regard to the media. Even the heavily populated outer limits of urban areas have little access to the print media. The majority of Dominicans, therefore, are essentially isolated, kept in ignorance with regard to news of any kind. By extension, this group is side-lined when it comes to making political decisions or decisions in matters of public interest.

This chapter gives an overview of the short history of the print and broadcast media in the Dominican Republic. The discussion on cinema reflects the newness of this industry in this country. It also points to the excitement currently surrounding movie-making in the Dominican Republic and New York City by Dominican directors.

PRINT MEDIA

The printing press arrived in Santo Domingo in 1600. The oldest surviving document, printed in colonial Santo Domingo, dates from 1800, a time when the eastern half of Hispaniola belonged to France. This first publication is a prayer, a novena to the Virgin of Altagracia.

The first two newspapers to appear in Santo Domingo, at the time under

Haitian occupation (April 5, 1821, and April 15, 1821, respectively), were *El Telégrafo Constitucional de Santo Domingo* and *El Duende*. Both were shortlived. The first newspaper was under the direction of Dr. Antonio María Pineda, a professor of medicine at the University Santo Tomás de Aquino. The government of Spain used this paper to channel self-promoting propaganda in the hopes of quelling any notions of independence on the part of the islanders. The second newspaper was published by Dr. José Núñez de Cáceres, one of the orchestrators of eventual Dominican independence. The rapid demise of these newspapers signalled a defeat for the newspaper industry and a protracted delay for the evolution of this media in the Dominican Republic.

José María Serra is the Dominican Republic's first journalist. Juan Pablo Duarte first knew of him after reading a flier he had written denouncing Haiti. Serra's fliers, which he distributed throughout Santo Domingo, were instrumental in bringing down the Haitian forces at the time of independence because they served to unite and impassion the Dominicans against Haiti. He was present on the historic night that Sánchez and Mella stood at the entrance to what used to be the walled part of Santo Domingo, on the night of February 27, 1844, and declared independence from Haiti. Shortly after independence was declared, Serra founded the newspaper *El Dominicano*.

The occupation of the Dominican Republic by U.S. Marines (1916–1924) led to a series of publications patronized by the U.S. government in defense of the American presence in the Dominican Republic. Among these was the *Libro Azul* (*Blue Book*), a serialized publication that tried to sway public opinion with regard to the occupation.

During the government of Horacio Vásquez (1924–1930) several writers boldly criticized Vásquez's government, portraying a negative outlook as a possible consequence of the Dominican president's chummy relationship with the United States. Fabio Fiallo, the romantic poet, was also the editor of *Las Noticias*. Together with Américo Lugo, another essayist, the two wrote incisive, if not mordant articles in *Las Noticias*, deriding the prevailing political situation, ultimately landing them both in jail. Fiallo, who was under a death threat, was shot for his outspoken opinions printed in the newspaper. Fiallo's words served to raise national consciousness that had, up to that moment, passively accepted the increasing presence and influence of the United States in the country. His lavish, patriotic rhetoric was even brought to the attention of newspaper publishers in various centers of the world, including Paris, New York, and Havana, who referred to Fiallo as the "Patriotic Poet."

Trujillo understood the intrinsic value of advertising and used the various mechanisms involved in public relations to his great advantage. Before he even came into power, he oversaw the establishment in 1929 of a magazine called the *Revista militar* (*Military Magazine*). This magazine circulated throughout neighborhoods far from military quarters, where it was presumably destined. Trujillo saw to it that his ideas and that knowledge of his existence were well distributed, so that he was a known element by the time he came into power in 1930. The *Listín Diario* (1889), the oldest surviving newspaper of the Dominican Republic, remained ambivalent with regard to Trujillo until 1932 when it printed an editorial supporting Trujillo's immediate and frequent meetings with the people.

By 1935 Trujillo exerted full control and power over anything that went into print, eventually forging an entire culture centered exclusively around him. He used the newspaper to promote his campaign for changing the name of the capital to Ciudad Trujillo, to ensure his reelection, and to undo the damage done to him by the American press because of the massacre of thousands of Haitians in 1937. When Trujillo launched his campaign for the title of *Generalísimo* he controlled press criticism by restricting the amount of advertising that newspapers could sell (the newspapers of the time including *La Información, La Opinión, El Diario,* and *Listín Diario*).[1]

Despite his eventual absolute control over the national press, Trujillo realized his dream with the foundation of his own newspaper in 1940: *La Nación.* Trujillo mandated that all government employees subscribe to *La Nación,* and he forced all commercial enterprises to purchase advertisement space. Subsequently all other newspapers in the nation went out of business, unable to compete. Even the venerated *Listín Diario* was shut down. A competitor to *La Nación, El Caribe* was established in 1949. At the time of its initiation, the paper functioned as a front to prove that the government allowed a free press.

Current national newspapers include the *Listín Diario, El Caribe,* and the relative newcomer *Hoy,* which was founded in 1983. This newspaper is modeled after the American *USA Today* with many attractive color photographs, eye-catching headlines, and easy-to-read summaries. *El Nacional de Ahora* and *Ultima Hora* tend to appeal to the less intellectual reader, privileging scandal and sensational news and featuring over-sized photographs and headlines. The publishing industry is owned and controlled by an elite few, which does not allow much of an opportunity for freedom of expression.

The *Listín Diario, Ultima Hora,* and *Hoy* have web sites for providing national news, sports, and the living section, which includes news about music, musicians, painters, and advice for the homemaker. The editorial essays are also printed, as are news about money and the economy.

In 1993 the news magazine *Rumbo* made its debut. This nicely styled, informative, weekly magazine covers the gamut of current events, specifically those most interesting to Dominicans. The magazine contains editorial essays on history and the economy, for example, in one issue. Another number may cover the problems of education in the Dominican Republic, corruption in government, and architecture. Although there are other news magazines on the market, none has had the impact nor has appeared as objective as *Rumbo*.

RADIO

The first radio station in the Dominican Republic was HIH, begun in 1924 by Frank Hatton during the U.S. Marine occupation, for the purpose of broadcasting sporting events that were taking place in the United States. In 1926, in La Romana, T. Garip founded *La voz de la feria* ("The Voice from the Fair"), which later became *La voz del papagayo* ("The Parrot's Voice"). Rafael Western began HILA in Santiago, while Tuto Báez founded HIJK, which gained fame for its coverage of the devastating hurricane of 1932, Saint Xenon. The first commercials broadcasted live were over HIZ in 1927, the Dominican version of the American-influenced HIH.

In 1942 a new radio station was launched in Bonao, *La Voz del Yuna* ("The Voice from Yuna"), dedicated entirely to serve Trujillo. Eventually this station's home base moved to the capital where it changed its name to *La Voz Dominicana* ("The Dominican Voice") and became the spokesradio for the regime. Because Petán Trujillo, the dictator's brother and founder of *La Voz Dominicana*, loved live music, records were rarely used. By and large, all twelve hours of daily broadcasts from *La Voz Dominicana* were live. This situation served as a venue for the introduction of large numbers of musicians and singers. At times very famous foreign singers were invited to sing at *La Voz Dominicana*, including the Trío de los Panchos, Argentine Libertad Lamarque, and Cuban Celia Cruz. Another way to fill broadcast hours was through radio dramas and comedy. In 1959 a new radio station came on the air, *Radio Caribe*, whose function was similar to that of the newspaper of the same name: to neutralize blistering and ever-louder criticism that radio was state-controlled.

In general the Dominican radio transmissions that attempt to broadcast public service messages, such as a public advisory for farmers, do not take into consideration the cognitive level of the rural inhabitant. Often the language used in the announcements is too sophisticated and the message misses its cultural mark, addressing issues and problems that are not part of the poor farmer's reality. The big exception is the work done by Radio Santa María, which is located on the main highway from the capital to La Vega

Real with transmitter and antennas on the Santo Cerro. This station's edu- *Educ.*
cational programs have proved helpful with regard to teaching the Dominican *campesino* about agrarian-related matters.

Most radio stations play music that, according to the dee jays, is requested
by the listeners, giving the impression that this is popular music. With the
exception of Radio Santa María none include an educational format. Radio
stations in the southern part of the country, such as Radio Guarocuya and
Radio Barahona, have to give way to stations such as Radio Bonaire which
broadcasts from the Dutch Antilles or to radio stations from Haiti. This
points to the enormous transculturational shift away from that which is Dominican to the areas from which a large part of the inhabitants originate.

Most radio stations provide news, commercials, public service announcements, soap operas, advice to women (fashion, beauty, and recipes), horse
race coverage, live chatting, sports news, and music of all kinds, including
romantic, *ranchera* (from Mexico), *salsa* (dancing music that originated in
Colombia), American music, and the *merengue* (Dominican dancing music).
Of the fifty-two FM stations throughout the country, only one plays classical
music and operas.

Radio Guarachita is the most popular radio station in the Dominican
Republic. Established in 1965 by long-time musical production manager and
record producer Radhamés Aracena, this radio station reaches out to the
masses in a way that no previous radio station has to date. Its unique programming holds the key to this station's success. Early in the morning the
station plays old Mexican and Colombian music that appeals to the rural
population. This is followed by guitar music, mostly the *bachata*, recorded
by local musicians. The evenings feature a request program. The requested
music frames the programming decision, reflecting the desire of the station
to please its listeners. Radio Guarachita's public service announcements—
whereby anybody has access to the airwaves to express a message ranging
from announcing births, deaths, and illnesses of family members to locating
friends and relatives when moving into the city from the country—are its
most distinctive feature (Pacini 92).

Another aspect of Radio Guarachita that makes it unique and identifies it
today as an icon of Dominican popular culture is its theater. The disc jockey's
booth is located at one end of a theater that seats 100 and is open to the
public at all times, so that anyone can watch the broadcast take place. The
theater has also served as a venue for live programs including musical programs and the *programa de saludos* ("greeting show"), whereby those attending speak into the microphone and articulate greetings to friends and
relatives.

TELEVISION

Dominican television transmission was inaugurated on August 16, 1952, on Channel 4, operating from the National Palace. Channel 4, an offshoot of its sister radio station called itself likewise, *La voz dominicana* ("The Dominican Voice"). The Dominican Republic was the fourth country in Latin America to have television broadcasting. The station broadcasted some American shows as well as Mexican films. Live productions included a variety of orchestras, tríos, operas, representations of literary plays, and popular comedy shows. The programming included a few live variety shows which included funny skits featuring local performing artists. In 1959 a second television channel was added. This was Channel 7, or Rahintel, which stands for *Radio HIN Television* (HIN being the call letters). This station has been one of the most successful in the country and has been instrumental in launching many local artists who first performed on live noon-hour shows and afternoon talk shows.

In 1969 the first color television transmission was broadcast from the new Channel 9, *Colorvisión*. This station, based in Santiago, became a favorite of late-night viewers because of its later broadcasting hours. Channel 11, inaugurated in 1976, showed mostly Mexican movies and other Mexican programming, including soap operas. The most popular, best-funded, and most modern station (before the advent of cable television in the early 1990s) was *Tele-Antillas*, which began transmitting in 1979 on Channels 2 and 13. Its success was due to the high quality of its programming, all of it prepackaged, but nonetheless considered to contain a better offering than the companion channels, including the running of such mini-series as "Roots."

Cable television was authorized and widely established beginning in 1990. The local channels continue to broadcast talk shows, local news shows, game shows, live music shows, and news magazine shows in an attempt to entice viewers away from cable offerings. A few television stars have attained a lasting popularity, which assures that Dominicans tune in regularly to their shows. One of these is Freddy Beras Goico whose "Show de Freddy" attracts faithful viewers who anticipate the unprecedented, hilariously comedic act. In 1995 the famous pop star Juan Luis Guerra helped to establish Mango TV. This television station is directed at young people and primarily features music videos, live music, and interviews with rising and established local stars.

The only UHF station in the Dominican Republic was founded in Santiago in 1992 under the name of *Teleunión*. This station's focus is on news

magazines whose coverage centers on local issues ranging from political, economical, sports, social, tourist, and cultural issues. Most programs on *Teleunión* are live and feature well-known local figures, thus ensuring an active
and interested viewership. In 1998 *Teleunión* began broadcasting in Santo
Domingo as well.

CINEMA

Dominican movie-making is in its infancy. Given economic constraints
and political instability the history of Dominican film is limited to a few
productions. The best-known Dominican films are director Angel Muñiz's
comedy *Nueba Yol* (1996) and its two sequels. *Nueba Yol* tells the story of a
poor Dominican who moves to New York City with the hope of earning
enough money to be able to return to his homeland and contribute to his
native economy. The ups and downs of the lead character Balbuena's fate
are an apt, albeit fictional and comedic, description of the diaspora experienced by thousands of Dominicans over the past thirty-five years. The movie
is the first introduction, on a popular level, of its kind to the world of poor
and middle-class Dominican immigrants in New York. The same subject
matter is featured in *En busca de un sueño* ("In Search of a Dream"), directed
by New York–based director Freddy Vargas; *Pasaje de Ida* ("Ticket to
Travel") directed by Pericles Mejía; and *Manhattan Merengue* directed by
Joseph R. Vásquez.

Movie-making in the Dominican Republic is dependent on foreign investment and interest (primarily French), and the patronization of wealthy
Dominican investors. The Dominican government has shown only a modest
interest in sponsoring movie production. The success of the movies that have
already been made and those under production—such as *Cuatro hombres y
un ataúd* ("Four Men and a Coffin"), written and directed by Pericles Mejía—in both the Dominican Republic and among Latin Americans in New
York City and the establishment of a precedent in Dominican film-making
foretell a promising future of this art form.

CONCLUSION

The study of the printed news media, radio and television broadcasting,
and the film industry in the Dominican Republic is in embryonic stages even
in the Dominican Republic. This aspect of culture, with the exception of the
newspaper, has been a relatively recent development. The second factor con-

tributing to the general lack of documentation is the speed with which changes have taken place, particularly in the area of television broadcasting and the making of movies.

The United States has influenced the media in the Dominican Republic more than any other area of culture. Although the first newspapers were started in the late nineteenth century, the United States indirectly took over the publication of many for reasons of political control and interests. The same is true for radio, which was actually started by the U.S. military during the first occupation of the Dominican Republic in 1916. Later, the success of both radio broadcasting and television depended entirely on Trujillo, who was extremely savvy when it came to molding the media in his favor. The influence of the United States in the area of radio and television has been limited to programming, particularly in the case of television.

NOTE

1. Trujillo learned this tactic from his predecessor Horacio Vásquez who persecuted his critics in the press the same way: by limiting their advertising potential. He also hounded *Listín Diario*'s owner, Arturo Pellerano Sardá. At times he used repressive methods, alternating these with economic assistance to the newspaper, then sinking the newspaper into economic troubles, arresting Pellerano Sardá, and finally sending him abroad on a diplomatic mission. Altogether there were more than forty established newspapers throughout the country in the Trujillo era.

5

Literature

Dominican literature has contributed significantly to the forging of a Dominican cultural identity. The frustrating struggle to construct this identity, with some notable exceptions, points to a largely male-dominated form of expression informed by literary tendencies imported from Europe, other countries in Latin America, and American writers, particularly Edgar Allan Poe, William Faulkner, and Ernest Hemingway.

The history of Dominican literature reflects the particularities of the pre-Columbian, colonial, and republican aspects of its evolution. An early form of theater was staged by the Taíno Indians who performed pantomimes during religious ceremonies. Colonial times featured expository essays describing the New World and defending the Indians, while modest theatrical representations engaged in proselityzing. The establishment of the nation of the Dominican Republic in 1844 was the beginning of the long process toward the formulation of a national identity. This endeavor was at times conscious, and at others, serendipitous. In the case of nineteenth-century novelist Manuel de Jesús Galván and contemporary authors and poets Pedro Mir, Manuel del Cabral, Tomás Hernández Franco, Juan Bosch, Ida Hernández Caamaño, Aída Bonnelly de Díaz, Martha Rivera, and Julia Alvarez, to name but a few, there has been a deliberate intention, albeit elaborated in distinct voices and styles, to romanticize the Dominican nation. Other contemporary authors, poets, and dramaturgs, like Aída Cartagena Portalatín, Virgilio Díaz Grullón, Chiqui Vicioso, Marcio Veloz Maggiolo, Pedro Vergés, Viriato Censión, and José Alcántara Almánzara, realize the same objective implicitly. Over the years this romanticization has been manifested in a wide variety of ways. Variously, authors and poets have mythologized people of Dominican history, idealized the landscape and the common person, or focused on the language and folklore associated with the Dominican Republic.

Another way to see the creation of a national identity through literature is in the literature that seeks to undermine the prevailing voice of authority.[1] The Trujillo dictatorship and, to a lesser degree, Balaguer's long presidency were and continue to be sources of inspiration for many writers.[2] Therein lies an inherent and continuous struggle for the establishment of a distinguishing voice.

NARRATIVE THROUGH THE NINETEENTH CENTURY

The first narrative exposé associated with the Dominican Republic is the "Carta anunciando el descrubrimiento de América," or Christopher Columbus' first letter to King Ferdinand and Queen Isabel of Spain announcing his discovery of the New World, specifically, the island he named La Española.[3] Columbus chronicled his experiences informed both by his own cognition of literary expression and by ulterior motives. It is hypothesized that Columbus would have been familiar with the rhetoric of the epoch, and with regard to imagery, he would have been familiar with the teachings of the Catholic Church and with stories, ballads, and an oral tradition of knights and the crusades, famous for their hyperbole. Columbus' reasons for depicting in a positive light the land he had discovered, with its implicit promises of riches, was to convince the King and Queen of Spain to continue to subsidize his voyages.

Another author whose writings are associated with the Dominican Republic (then La Española) is Fray Bartolomé de Las Casas (1484–1566). The *Historia general de las Indias* (*General History of the Indies*), a lengthy description of the Spanish conquest of the New World, was never completed (Las Casas did not work on it after 1561). It nonetheless serves as a valuable resource for understanding the beginning of colonization in the Western Hemisphere. The *Brevísima relación de la destrucción de las Indias* (*A Brief Account of the Destruction of the Indies*) (1552) was written to denounce the exploitation of the Indians by the Spaniards. It is the first work in Europe to caution against the complete annihilation of a native culture and the first to postulate the consequences of colonization from the point of view of the Indians.

Many authors in colonial times were monks and nuns in convents or members of the ruling class. Their styles and themes adhered to the literary paradigms of the times, which came mainly from Spain. Their works have an intrinsic importance to the study of the period and a perspective that may prove to be unique. With a few rare exceptions they have not been critically researched and for this reason only a few are singled out here.

Several Dominican writers of the late nineteenth century and early twentieth century gained prominence, some even worldwide recognition, for their works. These include Manuel de Jesús Galván (1834–1910), brothers Max Henríquez Ureña (1885–1968) and Pedro Henríquez Ureña (1884–1946), Virginia Elena Ortea (1866–1903), and Federico García Godoy (1857–1924).

Manuel de Jesús Galván wrote the romantic-historical novel *Enriquillo* (1882). It seeks to recover the colonial past of Santo Domingo for the purpose of establishing a feeling of nation in the new republic. The eponymous protagonist, a Taíno Indian named Enriquillo had been mentioned in Las Casas' nonfictional account *Historia general de las Indias*. The young heroic Indian, baptised and raised by the Spaniards, negotiated a truce with the Spaniards as they fought renegade Indian tribes. Galván used this story as a premise for his novel that is rich in allegory and whose message is conflictive, as Galván himself was torn between believing in white supremacy on the one hand and the defense of the Indians on the other. His personal struggle notwithstanding, the artfulness of the writing and the popularity of the theme of the novel since its writing have given it its own place in history: it is the only Dominican literary text that is required reading in Dominican schools. The fictional characterization of the noble Enriquillo has transformed the Taíno Indian into a national hero and symbol.

The Henríquez Ureña brothers are a rare occurrence in the literary world as siblings contributing significantly to the art of literary criticism, philosophy, and cultural studies. Max and Pedro Henríquez Ureña were born of distinguished parents. Their mother, Salomé Ureña, was the first woman poet of renown in the Dominican Republic. She was also a teacher and in this role understood the importance of educating women. Francisco Henríquez y Carvajal, their father, was briefly president of the Republic. Forced into exile due to his opposition to the dictatorship of Ulíses Heureux (Lilís), along with the boys' sister Camila, the Henríquez family moved first to New York, and then to Cuba. As adults, the brothers lived variously in Mexico, Puerto Rico, and Argentina. Max Henríquez Ureña is remembered for his essays on art, music, and literature, specifically a history of the Latin American literary movement of the late nineteenth century and early part of the twentieth century called modernism. He also wrote for the Dominican newspaper *Listín Diario* (1889) under the pseudonym of Hatuey. Pedro Henríquez Ureña gained the distinction of being one of the primary thinkers of

Latin America along with Mexicans Alfonso Reyes and José Vasconcelos with whom he founded the *Ateneo de la juventud*, a cultural think tank based in Mexico.

Pedro Henríquez Ureña's writings promote the value of secular education, advocate freedom and justice for all citizens of Latin America, and warn against American imperialism. He searches to define that which is common throughout Latin America given the common language, religion, and legal system that are the result of Spanish colonialism. Henríquez Ureña strikes a balance in the long-running debate that pitted tradition against innovation in cultural expression, tackling the critics who lament what they see as a blatant imitation of all that is European or American and those who oppose originality, which they see as a denial of the shared Spanish experience. The Dominican social philosopher is one of the first to espouse the vision of a universalization of culture (Alcántara Almánzar, *Escritores* 129).

Pedro Henríquez Ureña was principally an essayist and philologist. His studies of Latin American culture are highly esteemed for their far-reaching analysis of the problems facing the search for an authentic Latin American voice. Among his many works, encompassing topics from history, music, art, poetry, drama, architecture, and painting to the study of linguistics, perhaps his most prominent is the book of essays titled *Seis ensayos en busca de nuestra expresión* (*Six Essays in Search of Our Voice*) (1928). Pedro Henríquez Ureña is viewed first as a Latin American writer and then as a Dominican writer. In the latter capacity he wrote *El español en Santo Domingo* (*Spanish in Santo Domingo*) (1940) and *La cultura y las letras coloniales en Santo Domingo* (*Colonial Culture and Writings in Santo Domingo*) (1936).

Virginia Elena Ortea (1866–1903) has only recently been rediscovered. She is characterized as the first Dominican woman novelist, short story writer, and playwright as well as being a poet. From her marginalized position as a woman, Ortea gingerly delved into social criticism, tackling public subjects such as the politics of her time at the turn of the century, from a private space. Her style is one of realism, and her approach is one of equilibrium. For example, she juxtaposes the good in one story, "Recuerdos y sonrisas" ("Smiles and Memories"), against the bad in another, "La mala madrastra" ("The Bad Stepmother"), ultimately arriving at a balance.[4]

NARRATIVE IN THE TWENTIETH CENTURY

The novels written between the time of Lilís' assassination and the U.S. occupation are, like *Enriquillo*, historically based. The depiction of the prevailing reality is either idealized or presented in an unequivocally direct manner. The works of Federico García Godoy (1857–1924) and Tulio M. Cestero (1877–1955) are notable for their historiographic contribution, the refined articulation of the language, and particularly the detailed portrayal of customs and landscape.

García Godoy was a journalist, literary critic, and novelist. He founded several papers in La Vega where he lived, including *Patria* ("Fatherland") (1910) and *El Día* ("The Day") (1914–1916). The literary criticism he wrote revealed a humanistic preparation and was published in national as well as international journals. García Godoy wrote historical novels that focused on the effort of restoration of independence for the young republic after the country had annexed itself to Spain: *Rufinito* (1908), *Alma dominicana* (*Dominican Soul*) (1911), and *Guanuma* (1914). His works are commended for the descriptions of the customs and settings in his native province of La Vega.

In *La Sangre* (*Blood*) (1914), Cestero narrates the collapse of the Heureux regime. The gripping realism of this novel brings forth those historical happenings of the years shortly preceding U.S. occupation. Its language is authentic of the era, and the characters are well-executed fictionalizations of real people.

Juan Bosch (1909–) is a writer, essayist and politician who has distinguished himself internationally like his predecessors the Henríquez Ureña brothers and Manuel de Jesús Galván. He is best known for his short stories because of the simplicity of the language, the realistic portrayal of the downtrodden peasant, and the immediacy of the characters. The story lines are absorbing and swiftly resolved. In addition, Bosch has written an essay proposing the poetics of short-story writing. Here he emphasizes the importance of clearness and unity when writing a short story: the fewer characters and the fewer plot contrivances, the better.[5] Bosch proposes new points of view whereby the narrator is not necessarily an omniscient voice. He also anticipates later trends in the art of narrative that involve the reader's participation by not explaining everything and by leaving room for the reader to explore and fill in.

Aside from his many stories, most of which he wrote while in exile from the Trujillo regime, Bosch wrote several novels.[6] The best-known and the most influential of these, from a literary point of view, is *La mañosa* (1930). The protagonist of the novel is the anarchy that prevailed in the years leading up to the occupation by the United States. It is written from the perspective of a sick child. This technique doubly marginalizes the point of view: childhood and illness.

A novel, compeling as much for its genesis as its topic, is *Over* (1940) by

Ramón Marrero Aristy. Written from the point of view of a minor clerk that runs a small store stocked with basic provisions and staples on a sugar plantation it describes the horrors and inequities that took place at the plantation with regard to the treatment of the slaves. The novel also describes the eventual corruption and moral decline of the clerk. *Over*, written at dictator Rafael Leonidas Trujillo's insistence, is the first Dominican novel of denunciation. The dictator wanted to have a monopoly over the sugar mills by nationalizing those owned by foreigners. The title in English refers to the amount that the clerk is supposed to cheat the slaves who buy from him. The fact that the title is in English emphasizes the foreign nature of the enterprise.

Pedro Peix, a literary critic and writer, believes that Dominican narrative was "strangled" for approximately a quarter of a century, from 1940 to 1965 (32). After Trujillo's assassination and the civil war of 1965, there was a sudden eruption on the scene of exemplary writing that reversed the long silence. These writers can be divided into two groups by age, themes, and aesthetics. The first generation, which includes writers Marcio Veloz Maggiolo, Pedro Vergés, Aída Cartagena Portalatín, Pedro Mir, José Alcántara Almánzar, Aída Bonnelly de Díaz, and Viriato Sención, was highly influenced by the novelists of the Latin American boom. For the most part their works respond to a search for a national identity. The second group includes among many others the works of Julia Alvarez, Angela Hernández, Marisela Rizik, and Martha Rivera. Their writing is permeated with feminism along with studies of diaspora, revisionist history, and postmodern expression of the personal.

Marcio Veloz Maggiolo's (1936–) many areas of expertise include anthropology, history, sociology, religion, and folklore. He is a literary critic, an essayist, a historian, a poet, a short story writer, and a novelist.[7] As a novelist and short story writer he is vastly experimental. Some of the characteristics typical of the boom novels, and those that preceded and followed them, are also evident in Veloz Maggiolo's work. Notably, the absence of an implicit narrative voice, the lack of chronology in the story line, the focus on history, and the suggestion of an alternative interpretation of it are all characteristics of the boom novel and Veloz Maggiolo's texts.[8] Veloz Maggiolo examines the Trujillo era and explores Taíno and *gagá* mythology, intricately weaving them into his works. In this way, he has raised Dominican conscience over the importance of these aspects of Dominican history as part of the foundation of its culture. His most important novels include *Los ángeles de hueso* (*Angels of Bone*) (1967), *De abril en adelante* (*From April On*) (1975), and *La biografía difusa de Sombra Castañeda* (*Sombra Castañeda's Diffuse*

Biography) (1980). *La biografía difusa de Sombra Castañeda* won the National Prize for the Novel in the Dominican Republic for that year.

Pedro Vergés (1945–) has written essays on culture and language. His one novel *Sólo cenizas hallarás* (*bolero*) (*You Will Find Only Ashes* [*Bolero*]) (1980) was the winner of the prestigious Blasco Ibáñez award in Spain and received the first prize in the Crítica Española award. Vergés has pointed to the need of representing the Dominican Republic in a realistic manner through the novel. His novel achieves this within the scope of its projection. *Sólo cenizas hallarás* (*bolero*) takes place during the transitional period between Trujillo's assassination and the election of Juan Bosch in 1962. Vergés pits characters that are nostalgic for the Trujillo era and its false sense of order and security against those who are anxious to modernize, most typically, by imitating all that is American. The novel's many characters are richly developed reflecting a faithful reproduction of the language and sentiment of the time; the author's ironic criticism of Dominican society constitutes the framework of the novel.

Most Dominican writers are prolific in more than one genre. Aída Cartagena Portalatín (1918–1997) is no exception. Her work as a poet, which will be examined later, is of paramount importance to the study of the "Poesía Sorprendida" ("Surprised Poetry") movement. Cartagena Portalatín wrote several novels, but the most interesting, if not the most complex and highly experimental, is *La escalera para Electra* (*A Stairway for Electra*) (1970), which essentially affirms the struggle of a twice marginalized writer—a woman, in a third-world country—to write a novel. The fictional author in *La escalera para Electra* proposes that the story narrated in the Greek myth of Electra could just as easily have taken place within the confines of the Dominican countryside. The novel interweaves many levels of discourse as language and folk song of a Dominican peasant are mixed in with the fictional author's self-reflexive musings regarding her position *vis-à-vis* contemporary French writers of the *nouveau roman*. *La escalera para Electra* was a finalist in the prestigious Seix Barral competition in the year that the award was won by Chilean writer José Donoso.

Pedro Mir (1913–) is the poet laureate of the Dominican Republic. His novel *Cuando amaban las tierras comuneras* (*When Common Lands Were Loved*) (1978) did not achieve popular distribution within the Dominican Republic presumably due to its experimental nature: the novel lacks punctuation. Its importance lies in its subject matter and in the experimentation. The novel allegorically deals with American occupation and its devastating consequences on the Dominican collective sense of identity. This theme underlines an ongoing dichotomy between modernity and nationalism—a subtext for most Dominican creative output. Modernity is seen as slavish imitation of the artistic production of industrial nations. Nationalism, the objective of idealizing all that is one's own while rejecting outside influence, is the opposite force.

The prolific writer, critic, and sociologist José Alcántara Almánzar (1946–) is best known within the Dominican Republic as a student of literature, both national and international. Beyond the Dominican Republic he is recognized foremost as a short-story writer. In fact he is one of the few Dominican authors whose works are anthologized in collections of representative works from Latin American writers.

Alcántara Almánzar's writing is polished, refined and indicative of his humanistic preparation. A Fulbright scholar, Alcántara Almánzar has placed the Dominican Republic on the map of world literature, along with compatriots Manuel de Jesús Galván, Pedro Henríquez Ureña, Manuel del Cabral, Juan Bosch, and Julia Alvarez. His critical writings are held in high regard, winning the prestigious national award for journalism in 1997 for his critical essays on literature and culture. Besides his many works of literary criticism and literary histories, Alcántara Almánzar is a short story writer who admits an admiration for the works of Argentine writer Julio Cortázar. Other influences include Franz Kafka, Ernest Hemingway, Jorge Luis Borges, and Mario Benedetti. Alcántara Almánzar experiments with the fantastic, toying with reality and with the reader in his early collections of short stories *Viaje al otro mundo* (*A Trip to the Other World*) (1973) and *Callejón sin salida* (*Dead End Street*) (1975). In his later works the use of the fantastic becomes more serious as his characters struggle with inner voices, repressed feelings, obsessions, irrational fears, and erotic dreams that are then opposed to the cruelty and violence of the political reality of his country: *Testimonios y profanaciones* (*Testimonies and Profanations*) (1978) and *La carne estremecida* (*Quivering Flesh*) (1991).

Los que falsificaron la firma de Dios (1992) was written in the South Bronx of New York City by Viriato Sención, who had been living in the United States since the late 1970s. It has been translated to English by Asa Zatz as *They Forged the Signature of God* (1995). This surreal portrayal of the first twelve years of the Balaguer presidency is a denunciation of the corruption and violence that permeated all levels of society and government. This novel has been a best-seller in its Spanish version since its publication in the Dominican Republic because the sordid tale it weaves features numerous characters who are unmistakably familiar to Dominican readers. Another theme of the novel that has become increasingly familiar to Dominicans is that of diaspora. One of the characters in the novel writes about his experiences in the New York winter, a metaphor for the difficulty of the immigrant experience.

Aída Bonnelly de Díaz is the Dominican writer of manners par excellence. Whether writing fictional short stories or essays on manners, Bonnelly de Díaz focuses exclusively on Dominican customs from the perspective of a woman of upper-middle-class privilege. Her writing on manners is almost always foregrounded by a kind sense of humor, poking fun at national customs, thus acknowledging how different they must seem to a foreign observer, such as seen in her collection of essays titled *Retablo de costumbres dominicanas* (*A Retable of Dominican Customs*) (1991). A musician by training, Bonnelly de Díaz has written a significant book on the history of music and song in the Dominican Republic.

Bonnelly de Díaz began writing as a hobby, submitting editorial articles to the *Listín Diario*, the oldest Dominican newspaper. They have been collected in *Por los trillos del arte* (*Along Art's Many Paths*) (1996). These submissions include articles of literary criticism, literary portraits of national and international artists, and impressions of the Dominican landscape. Bonnelly de Díaz has also written a book of short stories, *Variaciones* (*Variations*) (1984) and stories for children, *Los niños, Las artes; Cuentos para niños* (*Children and the Arts; Children's Stories*) (1994).

The newer generation of short story writers and novelists is composed primarily of women, the most notable exception being Junot Díaz. Women writers had privileged poetry over prose because of the sheer impossibility of being accepted in a male-dominated field that continues to be extremely competitive for critical acceptance within itself. Aída Cartagena Portalatín was the first to break through this wall of resistance. Women writers tell of having to have tremendous courage to resist public opinion that at times is hostile to the mere concept of a woman writer. There is also the practical matter of time, given woman's traditional role involving children and domestic duties that impedes the concentration and dedication needed to write longer works.

As most women writers of the Dominican Republic, Julia Alvarez (1950) first became known as a poet. She distinguished herself by writing in English and by being the first Dominican to have internationally best-selling novels. Her novels *How the García Girls Lost Their Accents* (1991), *In the Time of the Butterflies* (1994), and *¡Yo!* (*Me!*) (1997) have all received national and international awards. *How the García Girls Lost Their Accents* and *¡Yo!* deal with the experience of diaspora from a personal angle. Alvarez's use of English displaces traditional syntax, lending her prose a sense of otherness, of foreignness. She uses Spanish liberally throughout her works in a way that, for the most part, is understood contextually by the English-speaking reader. Her second novel *In the Time of the Butterflies* is important for its focus on the lives of four sisters, three of whom were martyred by Trujillo's henchmen in 1959. The Mirabal sisters were well-known opponents to the regime while at the same time being unlikely revolutionaries. In her novel Alvarez invents a youth for all four sisters to underscore their conventionality, making the tragedy of their brutal assassination all the more appalling. The publication of *In the Time of the Butterflies* had a tremendous impact on the Dominican Republic. It began a flurry of interest and activity regarding the Mirabal sisters, their home town, and their actual impact on Dominican history. It is widely thought that their assassinations, which occurred at about the same time that the Church withdrew its support from Trujillo, were two of several actions committed by Trujillo that ensured his own assassination in 1961.[9]

Like Julia Alvarez, Junot Díaz (1969–) writes in English. Díaz is a short-story writer (*Drown* [1996] and *Los Boys* [1996]). He has won almost instant acclaim as an American writer. Born in the Dominican Republic, Díaz moved to New York when he was seven. In 1996 he was singled out by the January 15 issue of *Newsweek* as one of the ten most promising young "new faces" of the United States. His stories have been included in the 1996 Houghton Mifflin edition of *The Best American Short Stories* and in the 1997 edition of *The Best American Short Stories.* Díaz writes about destitute Dominicans in New York. In his tales he juxtaposes the experiences of the child against that of the despair of the adult as he or she faces daily survival in a hostile environment. The importance of national identity through customs and the community is brought to the fore in his stories.

Angela Hernández (1956–) is a poet, essayist, and a prolific short-story writer. Her involvement in the feminist movement of the Dominican Republic has lasting influence on the thematics of her narrative and vice-versa. She is the author of various essays on women's issues including the ones in *Machismo y aborto* (*Machismo and Abortion*) (1983), *10 prejuicios sobre el feminismo* (*10 Prejudices About Feminism*) (1985), and *Emergencia del silencio. La mujer dominicana en la educación* (*Emergence from Silence. The Dominican Woman in Education*) (1986). Hernández's collections of short stories *Las mariposas no temen a los cactus* (*Butterflies Are Not Afraid of Cacti*) (1985), *Alótropos* (*Allotropies*) (1989), and *Masticar una rosa* (*To Chew on a Rose*) (1993) are critically acclaimed. She consistently writes thought-provoking, stimulating stories dealing with female victimization, female-to-female relationships, female identity, and assertion. Hernández's stories are part of the required reading for sociology courses at the Universidad Autónoma de Santo Domingo.

Marisela Rizik's personal story is an example of how jealously protective the literary world of the Dominican Republic can be. This Dominican author has lived outside the Dominican Republic, and not in New York, since 1981. Shunned by Dominican critics who seem to consider her an outsider, Rizik, nonetheless, is receiving due recognition for her narrative work by literary critics of Hispanic literature in the United States. She has published short stories and essays that have appeared in scholarly publications that include creative work such as *Letras Femeninas.* Her meditative interpretation of Dominican history as it appears in *El tiempo del olvido* (*Of Forgotten Times*) (1996) is innovative and alluring. The language of this novel is direct and unadorned, and the chapters are brief. Rizik tells the story of four generations of women who are descendants of slaves. The last of the four generations is the daughter of a cold-blooded dictator of an unnamed Caribbean country. The personal odyssey of these women is a tribute to women's solidarity. The novel itself, with its magical realism that weaves in voodoo practices, proposes an alternative reading of Dominican history.

Martha Rivera's novel *He olvidado tu nombre* (*I Have Forgotten Your Name*) (1997) won the Casa de Teatro prize for best novel for 1996. The entries for fictional writing for that year included those of more established authors from Puerto Rico (Ana Lydia Vega) and Cuba. The virtually unknown Rivera's psychological feminist thriller won the coveted award. Rivera's at once assertive and lyrical narrative takes the contemporary Dominican novel to a new height. She distances herself from the themes that had consumed novelists of the recent past, notably the historical novels, to deal on a very intimate level with the identity crisis that the protagonist suffers through the late years of adolescence on into full womanhood. Although it is clear from the text that the novel takes place primarily in Santo Domingo in the 1980s because of oblique references to the political situation and specific locations, the novel takes on universal proportions that are not limited by time or space.

Other Dominican novelists who have distinguished themselves in the latter quarter of the twentieth century include Hilma Contreras (1913–) and her personal short-story anthology *Entre Dos Silencios* (*Between Two Silences*) (1987); Virgilio Díaz Grullón (1924–), who wrote short stories of merit for their polished style and engaging plots, among them *De niños, hombres y fantasmas* (*Of Children, Men and Ghosts*) and *Los Algarrobos También Sueñan* (*The Carob Trees Also Dream*) (1977); Carlos Esteban Deive (1935–) and his historical novel important for its study of the destruction of the northern coast that took place in colonial times in the early seventeenth century; *Las Devastaciones* (*Devastation*) (1979); and Efraim Castillo (1940–), author of the novel *Curriculum: El síndrome de la visa* (*Curriculum or the Visa Syndrome*), which denounces Balaguer's years in the presidency in a story about a Dominican family desperate to flee the country.

LITERARY CRITICISM

Literary criticism in the Dominican Republic tackles works by native writers as well as internationally known authors. The critics most frequently publish their essays in the literary supplements that are attached to weekend newspaper editions. The most important Dominican literary critics of the twentieth century, in addition to the comprehensive work of José Alcántara Almánzar, include Soledad Alvarez, Joaquín Balaguer, Diógenes Céspedes, Daisy Cocco de Fillipis, Carlos Fernández-Rocha, Hector Incháustegui Cabral, Bruno Rosario Candelier, Manuel Rueda, Diógenes Valdez, Marcio Veloz Maggiolo, and Chiqui Vicioso.

POETRY

The Dominican Republic is a land of poets. Due to its usual brevity, this genre lends itself to quicker execution and, more important, easier and more economically feasible distribution. The first poetic works of distinction in the history of Dominican poetry are related to the movement of independence and are patriotic by definition. Works take on a romantic vein as they idealize the beauty of the country and its people, particularly speaking of the past. The Indian that once inhabited the land is brought back to life; the black presence is overlooked. The early part of the twentieth century saw poets firmly in line with the many derivatives of vanguard poetry. Later, while Trujillo sanctioned unremarkable poetry, an underground movement called *La poesía sorprendida* experimented with new styles, featured talented poets, and undermined the status quo. During the years that followed Trujillo, poetic movements dovetailed with the experience of poetry worldwide, meaning that Dominican poets experimented, as did their international contemporary counterparts, with style, language, symbolism, image, and rhythm.

Nineteenth Century

The lyrics to the national anthem of the Dominican Republic were written by Emilio Prud'homme (1856–1932). The martial words to the national anthem befit the spirit of patriotism being conveyed. This prolific poet wrote romantic poetry that was deeply meditative, much of it religious or metaphysical.

José Joaquín Pérez (1845–1900) and Salomé Ureña (1850–1897) were the most representative poets of the young country. Their patriotic poems affirm the need for the establishment of an identity unique to the young republic. Pérez's most lasting work is his collection of poems titled *Fantasías Indígenas* (*Indian Fantasies*) (1877). These descriptive romantic poems dramatize episodes between Taíno chiefs and their wives and amorous encounters with Spanish *conquistadores*. The Indians are depicted as magnificent warriors, handsome men, and beautiful women who eventually are remorseful for their actions against the Spaniards. Perez's patriotic poems are inspired by his feelings against the annexation of the Dominican Republic to Spain and by the contemporary movements for independence in Cuba and Puerto Rico.

Salomé Ureña, a highly respected poet during her time and a muse for all future Dominican poets, particularly women poets, wrote patriotic verse and poems about her private world. Her poetic style, for the most part, is neoclassical with regard to rhythm, rhyme, and verse, and the themes of her work are characteristic of romantic poetry. She does experiment with modernism occasionally, but only with regard to meter. The poems that are most often anthologized include *"Ruinas"* ("Ruins") (1876), *"Sombras"* ("Shadows") (1880), and *"Mi ofrenda a la patria"* ("My Offering to the Fatherland") (1887).

Modernism, which apexed in 1910 in most of Latin America, was a late arrival to the Dominican Republic. This poetic movement, which exalted rhyme, musicality, color, and sensuality and focused on the portrayal of exotic and exquisite objects, was most memorably represented in the Dominican Republic by Fabio Fiallo (1856–1942). Fiallo was popular even in his lifetime, known for his erotic, brief, and captivating love poems, and in an unrelated vein for his anti-U.S. journalism. Another modernist of note was Enrique Henríquez (1859–1940). The style of his nocturnes, which is the form he preferred, is quiet, intimate, and elegiac.

Twentieth Century

Unlike its counterpart in the area of prose, poetry of the twentieth century in the Dominican Republic has kept abreast of contemporary movements in poetry abroad. One such movement called *vedrinismo*, named after French pilot acrobat Vedrin, was invented by Dominican poet Vigil Díaz (1880–1961). This style is the first example of free verse in Dominican poetry. The refusal to adhere to the formality of classic poetry and the bold experimentation with images are known as the vanguard movement. Although Chilean poet Vicente Huidobro is credited with the invention of vanguard poetry, Díaz's experimental work predates that of the more celebrated Huidobro.

There was a confluence of poetic styles during the first half of the twentieth century as varied manifestations of the vanguard were being written. Concomitant to these experimental styles was folk poetry and poetry of négritude. The vanguard in the Dominican Republic included the following movements: *Postumismo, los Nuevos, Independientes del 40, Poesía Sorprendida, Grupo del 48,* and *los Independentistas del 48.* Of these, *Postumismo* and *Poesía Sorprendida* have had the most lasting effects.

Postumismo is the first movement in the history of Dominican poetry that is characterized as authentically Dominican and not, with noted exceptions, a slavish imitation of the rhymes, rhythms, and themes in the poetry of other countries. It is the first movement to blatantly and realistically address issues inherent to the Dominican Republic, including racism. Domingo Moreno Jimenes (1894–1986), a member of the *Poesía Sorprendida* group, was the founder of this movement that dared to suggest a new way of looking at reality including the most autochthonous elements such as the language of the peasant farmers, their appearance, and their lifestyle. Poetry, up to that moment, had not been inspired by these features of the country. The expression of the *Postumismo* movement is experimental for its time, as rhyme and rhythm are completely free and the object that is written about is pedestrian in nature. Ultimately Moreno Jimenes was searching for an authentic national voice, the voice of the average Dominican. This made him vulnerable to detractors who suggested that his poetry was too simplistic, that it lacked the sophistication normally associated with poetry. Moreno Jimenes' vision allowed for a change in the attitude toward poetry in general, bringing it down from the high towers of elitism. Some of his most noted collections include *Promesa* (*Promise*) (1916), *Días sin lumbre* (*Dark Days*) (1931), and *Moderno apocalipsis* (*Modern Apocalypse*) (1934).

Whereas Moreno Jimenes focused closely on Dominican themes and approached poetry from a perspective that has been deemed, among other evaluations, anarchistic, other poets of the *Poesía Sorprendida* movement took their cue from surrealism and identified with the universal man. The formation of the movement was in reaction to a step taken by the Trujillo regime to oversee artistic creation. The Trujillo regime courted certain poets with the intention of allying them to its cause. The poets of the *Sorprendida* movement did not wish to be connected to and, even less, sanctioned by the regime. The poets in this movement, aside from Moreno Jimenes, included

Franklin Mieses Burgos, Freddy Gatón Arce, Aída Cartagena Portalatín, Manuel Rueda, Manuel Valerio, and Antonio Fernández Spencer. They published twenty-one numbers of an eponymous poetic journal, *Poesía Sorprendida*. Their highly abstract poetry is generally characterized as seeing man as universal and represents man through suggestive surrealist imagery and dream-like settings. Another characteristic of the *Sorprendida* poets is that they freely borrow from all previous and contemporary movements of Hispanic poetry.

Poesía Sorprendida was also the title given to the collection of poetry that appeared from 1943 to 1948. The poets involved developed prestigious literary careers after the publication of the last issue. As a rule, the political ideology of the movement displayed ambivalence to the Trujillo regime. Its main objective was to integrate Dominican poetry into universal poetry standards as opposed to insularism, limitation, restriction, or nationalistic overtones. The group proclaimed allegiance to the working person and to freedom fighters.

Franklin Mieses Burgos (1907–1976) is seen as the leader of the *Poesía Sorprendida* group. In perfectly structured poems he writes about solitude, man's place in the universe, and death. His poetic language is refined, punctuated by symbolic images.

The surrealist movement had its greatest influence on Freddy Gatón Arce, whose automatic writing was a recognition of this art form. Gatón Arce privileges the aesthetic over meaning. The pursuit of beauty in form and sound is Gatón Arce's principal achievement.

Aída Cartagena Portalatín (1918–1994) began her prolific and award-winning literary career with the *Poesía Sorprendida*. The general literary environment was hostile to the presence of a woman poet, and Cartagena Portalatín's poetry reveals her quest to establish an identity in her own right as woman and poet. As her poetic voice matured, beyond the days with *Poesía Sorprendida*, Cartagena Portalatín offered a new perspective to such topics as woman and race. In her work she proceeded to demythify the subject of woman as it had been portrayed generally in Dominican poetry up to this time. Words and phrases such as "submissive," "cute little blond head," and "virginal" were erased from poetic discourse by Cartagena Portalatín. She took the woman out of the private recesses of the home and had her travel, showing up variously in Athens, Paris, and London. Cartagena Portalatín is the first to deal with another difficult topic, that up to this time had been anathema: race. As a poet seeking social justice, her later poetry condemns the treatment of blacks in the United States.

Contemporary to the *Poesía Sorprendida* movement was the group referred to as the *Independentistas del 40* ("the Independent Ones of the '40s"). Four of the Dominican Republic's most renowned poets came from this movement: Manuel del Cabral, Tomás Hernández Franco, Héctor Incháustegui Cabral, and Pedro Mir. This group was more directly associated with explicit and overt opposition to the Trujillo regime and included members of *Poesía Sorprendida*. Due to the suppression, censure, and persecution imposed by the ruling government, the poets resorted to allegory, metaphor, obscure language, and symbol to represent reality. Many members of the *Independentistas* preferred exile over enduring the prevailing conditions. The condition of exile paradoxically brought the *Independentista* poets closer to their country as they celebrated national causes recalling the suffering, pain, struggle, and hopes endured by their fellow countrymen and women. Their poems of denunciation emphasize the need for political change in the Dominican Republic. The language of these poems is simple, direct, and passionate.

Manuel del Cabral (1907–) is one of the Dominican Republic's most important poets with regard to world recognition, as he is the one to be most often anthologized. In the vein of Nicolás Guillén (Cuba), Aimé Césaire (Martinique), and Luis Palés Matos (Puerto Rico), he is the first one to bitterly protest the condition of the black and mulatto in his native land. Unlike his contemporary poets Cabral is a pessimist on the subject of blacks. He refers to blacks with denigrating words, implying that blacks will not overcome their position in society. Other themes that he explores include love and metaphysics, and his poems accentuate human qualities. Cabral has also written prose-poems and a novel *El presidente negro* (*The Black President*) (1973).

Tomás Rafael Hernández Franco's short life (1904–1952) did not allow him to fully develop his potential as a short-story writer, poet, and essayist. For Dominicans he is best remembered as the author of the epic poem "Yélida" (1942). This poem tells the tragic story of a Norwegian named Erick and his love for a Haitian woman named Suquiete. Hernández Franco juxtaposes the two races, eventually allowing for the supremacy of the mulatto to come forth—the mulatto being the quintessential Dominican.

Héctor Incháustegui Cabral's (1912–1979) early poetry betrays a strong influence by Walt Whitman and Carl Sandburg. He elaborates themes such as nature, work, and justice and defense for the lowest echelons of society, and his later poetry experiments with surrealism to address these themes. Incháustegui Cabral was the first poet to overtly criticize the Trujillo regime. His stand on behalf of the downtrodden was seen as a direct challenge to those in power. Over time Incháustegui lost his rebellious spirit and his will to fight when he realized that ultimately his powerful poetry, which he had hoped would be a weapon, had no impact. Regrettably he found himself collaborating with Trujillo. In addition to the struggle that his poetry documents, Inchaústegui's work is important for its polished quality and refined expression.

Pedro Mir's poem *"Hay un país en el mundo"* ("There Is a Country in the World") (1949) is a loud, plaintive cry in defense of the sugarcane cutter and the railroad track layer. It is an attack on the internationally and nationally owned enterprises that exploit the peasant. His poetic acumen, facile use of language and image, and musicality of verse elevate this poet to the stature of national poet, a title he was awarded in 1982. Another poem, the *"Amén de las mariposas"* ("Butterflies' Amen") (1969), is a tribute to the Mirabal sisters ambushed by Trujillo's henchmen in 1959 for their opposition to the regime. In addition to the evocative depiction of the martyred sisters that Mir portrays, this poem is important for being one of the first recognitions of the sisters' heroism and the first denunciation of the regime in verse after the fall of the dictator. Mir assumes the voice of the collective unconscious of the Dominican lower classes in a language that is simple and direct.

Coexistent to the *Sorprendida* movement, and often seen as the continuation of it, is the work of the poets that make up the so-called *Grupo del '48* ("Generation '48"), including, among others, poets Máximo Aviles Blonda, Ramón Cifré Navarro, Abel Fernández Mejía, Lupo Hernández Rueda, Juan Carlos Jiménez, Alberto Peña Lebrón, Luis Alfredo Torres, Rafael Valera Benítez, and Víctor Villegas, and those who do not wish to be included in this movement but that are likewise contemporary to it, the *Independientes del '48* ("Independents of '48") The focus of these poets is mankind viewed from various perspectives—from introspective to universal. Given their future fame in other genres, the most notable of this group include Máximo Aviles Blonda (1931–1988), a well-known playwright, short-story writer, and essayist, and literary critic Lupo Hernández Rueda (1930). In their description of the general characteristics of their movement, the Generation '48 poets again proclaimed man and his universe, as well as his Dominican experience, central to the thematic. The *Independientes* were even independent among themselves, making it more difficult to categorize them in general terms. Among the participants, there are those who felt the need to laud the Trujillo regime in hyperbolic terms. In time the poems of this group addressed the fate of the common man, which at this point still focused on the rural figure.

The *Generación del 60* ("Generation '60") dealt with issues immediately relating to their changed reality. Their poems dealt with politics and the new urban poor. This group was also priviliged to a plethora of new material for inspiration. During Trujillo's government very little of what was written abroad was made available in the Dominican Republic. Upon the dictator's assassination, not only were works by other poets of the past third of a century read in the Dominican Republic, but also those of critics and schools of literary criticism. The Generation '60 poets were inspired by this new material and applied it to their own and new political and social reality.

This era saw the confluence of all the past generations of poets, most of whom continued writing past the genesis of their respective movements. The focus and style of these generations had adapted to the latest movements in poetic expression. The comparison between the works of young new poets and those established during Trujillo's era underscores the obscurantism evident in the former's poetry in its effort to camouflage its message.

The new poets, whose movement is divided into two periods—1961–1965 and 1965–1978—were influenced by current trends in literary criticism and responded accordingly. Highly experimental, their poetry focused thematically on the city and on the tastes of the lower middle class, including aspects of modernity such as the ever-increasing presence of cinema, nightclubs, advertisement, and cafeterias. The political instability of the four years between 1961 and 1965 led the poets to search for their own identity, to analyze their social reality, and to vituperate it, as well. The most representative of this edgy group are Miguel Alfonseca (1942–1994), René del Risco Bermúdez (1937–1972), and Jeannette Miller (1944–).

The poets of this era had access to new and faster means for diffusing their works. Aída Cartagena Portalatín founded the journal *Brigadas Dominicanas* (*Dominican Brigades*) (1961); Freddy Gatón Arce started a cultural magazine that was included as a supplement in the newspaper *El Nacional de Ahora*, while Marianne de Tolentino edited a literary supplement for the *Listín Diario*. Most poetry submitted to these journals and supplements was published accompanied by eye-catching artwork and critical commentary. The much easier access to poetry increased Dominicans' participation, interest, and demand for quality. This also allowed for a proliferation of poets and would-be poets to come on the scene throughout the nation. The poets then formed groups, each privileging a specific ideology and mode of expression.

These groups included *El Puño* ("The Fist") (1966), which included poets Iván García (also known as a playwright), Miguel Alfonseca, Enriquillo Sánchez, René del Risco Bermúdez, Ramón Francisco, and Marcio Veloz Maggiolo; *La isla* ("The Island") (1967), which included Antonio Lockward Artiles, Wilfredo Lozano, Norberto James Rawlings, Andrés L. Mateo, and Fernando Sánchez Martínez; *La antorcha* ("The Torch") (1967), which grouped Mateo Morrison, Soledad Alvarez, Alexis Gómez Rosa, Enrique

Eusebio, and Rafael Abréu Mejía; and *La máscara* ("The Mask") (1968), which included Aquiles Azar, Héctor Díaz Polanco, and Lourdes Billini. Ironically, with the birth of the alternative venue provided by the many supplements, the publication of collections of poetry substantially decreased. An influential supplement *Aquí* (*Here*), which appeared in the Saturday issue of *La Noticia* (*The News*), privileged some poets over others, leading to the group of those that were included and those that were excluded. Among the excluded was a poet that became a leading spokesperson for women's rights and whose poetry is singularly feminist and universal: Sherezada (Chiqui) Vicioso (1948–).

Chiqui Vicioso's nonconformist and defiant posture with regard to the Dominican literary establishment has earned her many detractors, which in turn has made her struggle all the more poignant. Vicioso's poetic voice is at once lyrical, intimate, and self-assured. Her themes reflect her life experiences as a member of the human race and as a woman: New York, racism, solidarity with the oppressed, and nostalgic impressions of her island homeland from which she feels doubly estranged—as a person in self-exile and as a woman who dares to speak her mind. In addition to poetry, Vicioso has written essays on the social, political, and economic conditions of women in the Dominican Republic.

Dominican poetry written between 1961 and 1978 has been variously evaluated. Some condemn its general lack of recognition for the work of national predecessors and its excess of political rhetoric. Others celebrate the quality of this plural work, which betrays strong influences of renowned Latin American poets Pablo Neruda, Nicanor Parra, and Ernesto Cardenal, the diversity of their poetic aesthetic notwithstanding.

Musician, poet, playwright, literary critic, and essayist Manuel Rueda (1921–) broke what had been considered an absolute impasse with regard to poetic expression in 1974. Political denunciation had reached the point of drowning out (with blood, as some would claim) any hope of lyrical expression. Rueda announced the foundation of the poetic movement called *Pluralismo* ("Pluralism") whose intention was to reexamine poetic expression. It proposed a vanguard approach to poetic creation including the use of technical resources—such as the musical staff, colors, and caligrammes (representation of a poem's theme, using the words themselves to configure an image)—simultaneously with writing, allowing for a multidimensional approach to the text.

In essence Rueda did not endorse the hermitism of poetic movements such as *Concretismo* ("Concretism"), which had evolved initially in Brazil in the 1950s. This poetry reduced poetic expression to the graphically visual.

Despite some similarities between the two movements, Dominican Pluralism offers the reader choices of interpretation in the images that are drawn by the words, chosen for their visual effect. Critics of this movement accused it of evasiveness for ignoring the political and historical reality of the times. The apparently random (to the casual eye) arrangement of words escaped the average reader. This poetry is replete with complex visual images, carrying the line of verse to the ultimate limits of its possible expression. Language and its multivalent, polysemous qualities is central to this poetry as is musicality and suggestiveness. Poems may represent, for example, the fleeting images captured by a car in motion (Jeannette Miller, *"Los poemas del domingo"* ["Sunday Poems"]. The most accomplished *Pluralistas* include José Enrique García (1948–) and Cayo Claudio Espinal (1955–). An important contribution of this movement is in the influence it had on the young poets of the 1980s, the *Generación de los 80.*

The *Generación de los 80* included many poets of high caliber. These poets grew up in times when moral questions, strife, and change were common everyday occurrences. The poets dealt with desperate issues such as nihilism, the absurd, the end of mankind, death, and a hope for a new order. Their style drew heavily from the free association typical of surrealism. This group was better predisposed to writing because of the opportunities they had to study, read, and surpass previous texts. It was an era of workshops, where poets gathered to discuss, read, and write poetry. The most outstanding male representative of this movement was José Mármol (1960–). His poetry is metaphysical and in many ways reminiscent of the brilliant works of the *Sorprendida* and *Independentista* movements. His poetic voice deals with the poetics of poetry, defending its ability to organize and explain reality and propose a new reality. Mármol also explores mankind's relationship with God, all the while avoiding the creation of religious poetry, as such. In this sense he projects himself and his work into the universal question of the ideal and of God, giving his poetry a timeless quality. Mármol has drawn inspiration from as varied sources as Spanish mysticism, German romanticism, the Argentine writer and poet Jorge Luis Borges, and the German philosopher Arthur Schopenhauer. Mármol's most important works include *El ojo del arúspice* (*The Eye of the Haruspex*) (1984), *Encuentro con las mismas otredades I, II* (*Meeting the Same Others I, II*) (1985, 1989), and *Deus ex machina* (1994).

Dominican poetic writing has, in a sense, come full circle. Through much experimentation and a search for a voice that would free the image but at the same time express Dominican social, political, and historical reality, poets have ultimately resorted to a highly individual form of expression. The many poetic movements have been stepping stones toward the fulfillment that is being seen nowadays. Dominican poets have transcended the impulse to interpret their surrounding reality and to convey authenticism. Rather, they emphasize the many attributes of a given word, allowing it to signify freely to the reader, endowing the reader with the power to create a poem within a poem.

The mid-1980s saw the emergence of many women poets including Soledad Alvarez (1950–), Mayra Alemán (1957–), Aurora Arias (1962–), Ida Hernádez Caamaño (1949–), Carmen Imbert Brugal (1954–), Marianela Medrano (1964–), Ylonka Nacidit Perdomo (1957–), Martha Rivera (1960–), Sabrina Román (1956–), Carmen Sánchez (1960–), and Miriam Ventura Alvarez (1957–). These women have defied the centuries-old, unspoken opinion of Dominican men that women have nothing of importance to say. Described figuratively as being parenthetical to the prevailing poetic voice, these women poets have been free to evoke their private spaces, their public presence, apparently uninhibited by established movements, standards, or expectations. The result has been the unleashing of a significant contribution to Dominican poetry in the use of image, language, and symbol.

Hernández Caamaño has written pointedly about the vulnerability sensed by a writer at the time of launching a poetic text, arguably the most personal and intimate of artistic expressions, in the small-world environment that is the Dominican Republic. The literary class in the Dominican Republic is competitive, protective, and even cruel to the newcomer. Much has been done to ease and dissipate the tension and focus that a new author brings upon himself or herself at the time of publication. The many Saturday newspaper supplements, particularly Manuel Rueda's *Isla Abierta* (1983), have facilitated the initiation of young writers in a relatively inconspicuous manner.

The current situation of literature in the Dominican Republic in all its manifestations is one of great expectation. A literary tradition is being established as names of authors and respective works are becoming known. From a slavish dependence on Spanish models to works that searched for the establishment of a national identity, Dominican authors are increasingly free to pursue their creative veins without the worry of either censure or rejection. The topics of history, culture, interpersonal relations, and transnationalism (given the success of U.S. based Dominican authors) are being explored and transformed into works that promise to enrich the national literary heritage.

NOTES

1. This politically engaged literature is characteristic of most Latin American literature. It has been extremely effective because by creating a countervoice and by

proposing an alternative and revisionist approach to the understanding of a country's political, social, and cultural history, the authors have indeed made it possible to question official dogma. After independence from Spain, most Latin American countries found themselves, at one time or another and for different lengths of time, under a repressive regime that dictated an official discourse regarding the political, social, and cultural history of its country. Such discourses tended to privilege those in power and the landed aristocracy while completely ignoring the presence of Indians and or blacks throughout the history of the country, not to mention women, and their contributions to culture. In the case of the Dominican Republic, this literature has brought to the forefront the vital presence of the mulatto and the black while at the same time rescuing the Taíno legacy from oblivion. It also has contributed to the exploration of voodoo influences upon the culture.

2. The most recent trend has been to exorcise the pernicious effects on the collective psyche of the Dominican people of the Trujillo regime and the years of the Balaguer presidency, seen by some to be a subtle continuation of the Trujillo regime. Much research is being done on the era, and those who survived the regime are being indirectly held accountable for their passivity during the dictatorship.

3. Published in Barcelona in 1493, it was translated into Latin and read throughout Europe.

4. Amalia Francasci (1850–1941) was the first woman novelist of the Dominican Republic. The style and themes of her works privileged Spain and are considered typical of the times and unremarkable.

5. Gabriel García Márquez, the renowned Nobel Prize winner from Colombia and author of *Cien años de soledad* (*One Hundred Years of Solitude*) (1967) anecdotally attributes his success as a writer in part to Juan Bosch, whom he met at a seminar where Bosch was the lecturer. It was there that Bosch presented his rules for short story writing that can be found as part of the preface of *Cuentos escritos en el exilio y apuntes sobre el arte de escribir cuentos* (*Stories Written in Exile and Notes on the Art of Story-Writing*).

6. In fact Dominican readers did not become acquainted with Bosch's writings until the late 1960s given the censure to which Trujillo subjected his country. Bosch also wrote several sociopolitical interpretations of his country's history. The most quoted is his *Composición social dominicana* (*Social Dominican Demography*) (1970).

7. In 1963 Veloz Maggiolo was the winner of the William Faulkner Foundation prize for the novel.

8. The boom and the existence of such a literary phenomenon are being revisited in today's literary studies of the Latin American novel. The term refers to the apparently sudden appearance in the mid- to late 1960s on the world market of many outstanding novels written by authors from across Latin America.

9. Two additional events that led to decreased support from the United States included Trujillo's attempt on Venezuelan President Rómulo Betancourt's life in 1956 and the mysterious assassination of Jesús de Galíndez, a student at Columbia University in New York City who was completing a dissertation on the Trujillo regime.

6

Performing Arts

Unlike literature or plastic arts, performing arts in the Dominican Republic have been informed primarily by popular tastes and trends. The roots for musical compositions and dance are firmly grounded in folkloric terrain. Broadcast media, in its history and evolution in the Dominican Republic, have also reflected this trend. Programming in television and radio has kept the interest of the lower and middle classes in mind. The only exception is the place of theater within cultural boundaries in the Republic. By its very nature, theater, even when dealing with popular material, is patronized primarily by the elite and educated people who tend to subscribe to high culture. The survival of classical performances in either theater, ballet, music, or opera depends highly on this group and government assistance. In fact formal expression of music and dance in the Dominican Republic has been largely limited to a close imitation of classical European music and ballet. Difficulties notwithstanding, many Dominicans have been successful in classical repertoire.

Music and dance, especially on the popular level, are free from the constraints and limitations of a dominating influence. Rather, given their spontaneity and ubiquity, composition and choreography are in constant development. Like their artistic counterparts (visual arts, theater, literature), they have not enjoyed universal appeal, with a few important exceptions.

This chapter deals with the evolution of music, dance, and theater in the Dominican Republic. The performing arts have not been immune to the fluxes of Dominican history from Taíno times through independence, the American occupation, the Trujillo dictatorship, the civil war of 1965, to current times. The most prominent difference with regard to the development of the performing arts in the Dominican Republic focuses on popular music and dance, which Trujillo and his family avidly supported.

FOLK MUSIC

The instruments used to play folkloric music in the Dominican Republic reflect the country's ethnic and racial history. The musical instruments of Taíno times have been researched and gradually unearthed, allowing for an increasingly holistic understanding of the music played by the first inhabitants of the land. Contemporary composers, most specifically Juan Luis Guerra, have explored the range, sound, quality, and composition possibilities of these instruments with hopes of recuperating the past. This is most notably the case with Guerra in his 1992 compact disc titled after the Taíno ceremonial dance, *Areíto.*

Influence from both Africa and Europe is also evident in Dominican music. African influence in instrumentation in Dominican folk and popular music has also been lasting. Drums and other percussion instruments have layed the foundation for the rhythms that characterize Dominican folk and popular music and dance. The Spanish influence resides primarily in the area of song, specifically Medieval romances passed down over the centuries. Also, the Spanish acoustic guitar is central to the *bachata,* a song-and-dance form that, until Guerra popularized it in 1991, was restricted to the enjoyment of the lower classes. The advent of wind and brass instruments and the accordion from Europe contributed to the completion of what was eventually going to make up the *merengue* orchestra. The *merengue,* in brisk 2/4 time, is the national dance of the Dominican Republic, and since Trujillo's time, it has been elevated to ballroom status.

The Taíno Contribution to Folk Music

The chronicles written by the Spanish *conquistadores,* settlers and explorers, in what was then called Hispaniola, specifically those by Bartolomé de las Casas and López de Gómara, describe several kinds of percussion instruments and a few wind instruments used by the Taínos for dancing and singing—both activities associated with religious rituals. Although archaelogists continue to unearth various samples of the Taíno culture (a fraction of which has been found), musicologists still have to rely mostly on the Spanish chronicles for indications of what instruments actually were used by the Taínos. Many of these instruments were originally crafted of wood, which naturally decayed over time, but those of bone, clay, stone, shell, or gold have survived.

Las Casas described a wooden instrument that, according to his description, today would be called *maracas.* This instrument had a double function in Taíno ceremonies. On the one hand, its long tongue-like extension served as a vomit inducer, used to stimulate the gag reflex. Vomiting was a way of indicating that one's insides were pure. The handle of this device, which contained little pebbles, rattled, much the way *maracas* do. The hollow handle at times was made of bone (manatee ribs) and would be ornamentally carved. Some *maracas* were made from gourds.

References are made in the chronicles to the existence of small metallic cymbals and stone castanets with metallic tips. These have not been located, and it is surmised that because the only metal that the Taínos knew was gold, the instruments fell victim to Spanish avarice. Repeated mention is made of the use of drums; large barrel-like trunks that were hollowed out and struck rhythmically with sticks; however, thus far no such instrument has been unearthed. Jingle bells were made of bones and shells strung together. The Taíno men and women would adorn their calves with rows of bells of bone and shell, emitting a sound with each dance step. Another rhythm-producing device was a clay bowl containing pebbles. The pebbles within jangled when this instrument was shaken.

The Taínos used large conch shells as horns (*fotuto*), made whistles from bone, and it is speculated, from clay as well. The carved conch shells had one end altered to form a mouthpiece. The whistles (*ocarina*) were of different sizes and shapes and produced a variety of rather shrill sounds.

African Instruments

As in the case of the Taínos, the biggest African contribution to Dominican music was in the area of percussion. But, in contrast to the Indians, the African instruments have had a lasting and profoundly influential effect on the evolution of folk and popular music in the Dominican Republic. Many instruments tend to be more regionalized, specialized, and seen only in the folkloric practices of very remote areas. Some examples include the *adenco*, the *palitos de los bailes de cinta*, spoon-playing, the metal *maraca*, the *botijuela*, and the *yon*.

The *adenco* essentially consists of two sugarcanes, each differently hollowed out and topped off, played by tapping the ground. Usually, only women play this instrument to accompany chants composed for any celebration. The *adenco* is only known in two parts of the republic: El Cañafistol and San Juan de la Maguana. Some sticks (*palitos de los bailes de cinta*) are decorated with paint and are used as part of a dance choreography and not as instrumentation, per se. The dancers lightly hit each other's sticks as they dance. Spoon-playing reaches an art form among women in remote areas of the countryside. The spoons are used as an accompaniment to children's songs, work songs, and songs for a child's funeral. The only origin that can be attributed to this rhythmic form is the use of spoons by travelling troupes of Turkish folkloric dancers. The metal *maraca*, cylindrical in shape and filled with pebbles, is most popular with *cocolos*, the African slaves that migrated from nearby British and Dutch islands to cut sugarcane. The *botijuela* is a large clay pot whose opening is covered with goat skin. This instrument, with its deep, hollow sound, is hand-played and is common at folk religious ceremonies. The *yon* is a double maraca, meaning that there is an oval-shaped gourd filled with seeds at each end of a baton-like stick, which is turned and tossed in the same manner a baton would be. The *yon* is most often used in voodoo ceremonies, in the dances of the *gagá*.

More common instruments associated with both folk and popular Dominican music include the triangle, the sticks (*palitos*), all sorts of *maracas*, the *güiro*, the *guayo*, and different styles of drums. The origins of these instruments in the Dominican Republic vary from being imported by *cocolos* to coming directly from Africa, to the unknown.

The triangle is associated with the *cocolos*. It is played by hitting a dangling piece of metal, shaped in a triangle, with a metal rod. A pair of wooden sticks (*palitos*) hit against each other constitute a percussion instrument that is common throughout the island. The sticks are not identical, as one is thicker in diameter than the other. Like the triangle, this instrument plays in the background of most folk and popular bands. Maracas can be made of a single gourd with a handle or two gourds with one handle. Another version of the maraca is a hollow piece of wood filled with beans, corked off at both ends. An instrument called the *arel* is made like this. The *güiro* is an empty gourd along whose side parallel grooves have been carved. A "scratcher," which can be either a small piece of wood with barbs, or a thick piece of frayed wire, is used to play over the surface of the indentations on the gourd, creating a scraping sound. Also essential to folk and popular music is the *guayo*. The *guayo* is a sheet of galvanized steel that is perforated, very much as a kitchen grater is. Then, it is bent to form a cylindrical vase topped off with a cone shape. A little handle is added to the middle part of the cylinder. The cylinder is played similarly to the *güiro*, by scraping it with either a thick piece of frayed wire or a barbed piece of wood. The sound of the *guayo* is more metallic in contrast to the *güiro* whose sound is muted.[1]

Drums of all types and sizes, including the conga, bongo, and *palos*, are popular instruments of Dominican folk and popular bands, and the most prevalent African instruments used in many bands and orchestras throughout the Caribbean. The main difference between drums lies in the shape of the body, which can be long and cylindrical or short and stout. Another varying factor is whether they are played with hands or with sticks. Some drums are free-standing, while others are tucked under the arm when played. Some drum heads on one end are covered with a billy goat's skin, whereas the other side is covered with a nanny goat's skin, ideally a nanny goat that has not yet been impregnated.

A common type of drum is the double-headed *timbaleta.* It consists of one stand from which extend two small identical leather-covered drum heads played with sticks. The *balsié* is short, covered with goat skin. It is usually played with both hands, the drum held in place by the drummer's knees. Most drums are referred to as *palos* and are made by hollowing out a large trunk by burning it; goat skin is strapped over the opening. Rope cords secured to the edges of the drum are used to tune the drums. These drums are free-standing or are tied ingeniously to the drummer's body with the use of fancy and decorative leather strips. The *palos* are by far the most prevalent instruments as they are used for any and all occasions. They are played in an inclined position so that the sound emerges from the back of the drum. There are three different lengths and diameters of *palos*: the *palo mayor* or *palo grande;* the *palo mediano* or the *adulón,* the medium-sized one; and the smallest, called the *alcahuete.*

Bongo drums are called *el mongo* in the Dominican Republic. Unlike the *palos,* bongo drums are two connected drums, one slightly larger than the other. The shape of the small, rather stout drum is cylindrical. A seated drummer places these drums between his or her thighs. The *tambora,* like most of these drums, is made out of a hollowed out tree trunk. Both ends are covered with stretched goat skin, and both ends are beaten as the player cradles the instrument sideways over his or her knees.

A typical folk band that is representative of the whole country would include an accordion, a *balsié,* a *pandero* (or tambourine), and a *guayo.* Depending on where one travels within the republic, or what the occasion is, different types of instruments are used.

FOLK SONGS

The Dominican Republic boasts a rich tradition of folk poets who have created ballads and chants that have been passed down over generations. The recording and documentation of this tradition is only now taking place. The folk songs have diverse themes and purposes. There are religious songs, songs of social protest, songs for entertainment, work songs, and children's songs and nursery rhymes. The legacy of folk songs is uniquely Medieval Spanish.

Music during colonial times was both religious and secular, inspired by the styles popular in Spain since Medieval times. It was used for the celebration of High Mass and for theatrical presentations, which included comedies, religious mystery plays, and farces. Music also accompanied dances that took place either in the courtyard, by the cathedral, or by the Dominican convent. The African population, separated by unions that were sanctioned by the colonial governing body, had the opportunity to create their own forms of celebration and musical expression. These unions, or brotherhoods, formed the tradition of recognizing the day of a patron saint, especially that of St. John the Baptist, with eight days of festivities, masses, and sermons. For the purpose of public prayer they organized other forms for celebrating rituals.

Popular religion—such as that practiced in rural areas, semiurban areas, and in the slums surrounding large metropolitan areas—with its mix of Catholicism and magical-religious manifestations, usually is practiced without the presence of a priest because the praying rituals and corresponding ceremonies are led by women and men charged with the task of praying. One of the most common rituals is that of the *vela*. This is usually a day of devotion dedicated to the Virgin or to a patron saint. The day begins early with a mass. This is followed by chants accompanied by the *pandereta* (small tambourine), the *güiro*, and hand-clapping. Some *velas* can last all day and night and include a parade during which the participants sing psalms and other prayers like the rosary, the Lord's Prayer, and songs of praise and adoration. The polyphonous chants blend male baritones with female mezzo sopranos and sopranos.

The lyrics of these religious songs are derived from Medieval Spain. The stanzas comprise six- or eight-syllable couplets with a consistent rhyme. This simple form is preferred for its musicality. There are songs written in free verse whose rhyme is not quite as structured. The different parts of a prayer are alternatively sung by a soloist to a choral response, but there are cases when one choral group responds to another. Generally speaking, there is no exact and uniform representation of these songs, as there are new variations with each performance.

Tonadas are folk songs, accompanied by kettle drums, *maracas*, and *güiros*. These songs are used in *velas* but also during magical-religious festivities and during burial rites. Their lyrics combine secular language with religious, and the invocations are as much Catholic as they are *gagá*. These songs are peppered with exclamations such as *ay!* and vocalized sections. The spectator public is expected to interject words into the song as well as join in the chorus. The lyrics of the *tonadas* are often improvised. The composition of the *tonadas*, the accompanying instruments, and the lyrics themselves vary depending on the geographic area.

Songs for entertainment traditionally are sung at the conclusion of the *velas.* The overall structure of these songs, which tend to consist of stanzas of ten octosyllabic verses, is similar to that of Spanish Medieval songs. The most common of these folk songs is the *mediatuna.* The refrain tends to identify the particular song as it functions as a response to the theme presented in the main body of the song. The themes include love, social protest, disdain, and disillusionment, and there are some that are humorous or satirical.

Christmas carols (*villancicos*) in the Dominican Republic tend to be of European origin and are the same ones that are sung in the neighboring islands of Cuba and Puerto Rico. These simple tunes consist of choruses and familiar melodies. One custom, which is not unique to the Dominican Republic, is to go from house to house singing these carols with the hope of either being invited in or of receiving a small token of appreciation. The custom is referred to as the *asalto* ("assault").

Work songs are a collective effort whereby workers set a pace for their manual labor through the rhythm of the songs. The singing alleviates the arduousness of the task on hand. The workers are either rural workers who pick coffee, harvest crops, or chop trees or urban workers doing road construction, selling flowers, or constructing buildings. The lyrics of the songs are arranged in octosyllabic verses, alternating refrains between soloist and chorus. Street vendors advertise their wares or services with sonorous, melodic chanting.

Children's songs and nursery rhymes sung in the Dominican Republic are common to all of Latin America. They are taught in elementary school and in catechism classes, which are often held on Saturdays. The songs are often part of a game with opposing sides singing different verses or in games that involve dance-like movements, holding hands in a circle around one child in a guessing game.

FOLK AND POPULAR DANCES

Dancing, whether by those of the upper class or by those of the rural communities, is the favorite mode of entertainment for Dominicans. It is a means of sociability by which they can express their innermost feelings, and almost all festive occasions are celebrated with dance.

Dominican folk dancers. Courtesy of *Listín Diario*.

The *sarandunga* is a folkloric dance that is accompanied by three small drums and a *güiro*. Its choreography and rhythm evoke a Spanish peasant dance from which it is undoubtedly inspired. It can be danced by many at a time, or take on the role of a spectacle with one woman dancer coyly rejecting the advances of her partner by pushing him away gently with her shoulder. The woman defines a circle and never looks up as she dances. The man stands tall, holding a handkerchief that he waves at her. Besides her feet, the woman's body barely moves. At times the partners' shoulders touch. The dance comes across as a game. Although the *sarandunga* is a folk dance, classical musicians like Julio Alberto Hernández have composed music based on its rhythms for violin and piano.

The *guarapo* and the *sarambo* are both tap dances whose origins can also be traced to Spain. Other than the fact that the *sarambo* is faster paced than the *guarapo*, the dances are similar. Each is danced in different parts of the country. Only one couple dances this dance on the dance floor with a basic choreography of the partners approaching each other only to step away. The male keeps his hands to his side while the female lifts her skirt to her knees.

The *yuca* is danced in groups of four pairs. While a soloist sings and a

Traditional folk dancers. Courtesy of *Listín Diario*.

chorus responds, the dancing pairs alternate an approach and retreat chore-ography while tap-dancing. The *güiro* imitates the sound of the shuffling or sweeping feet, one of the moves that is made as dancers change partners.

Although named after a Spanish slow dance, the Dominican *bolero* is markedly different, particularly with regard to the lyrics of the song. The Dominican *bolero* is inspired by intimately personal feelings ranging from happiness to sadness to hopefulness. The *bolero* is the most sentimental and romantic of songs, similar in this sense, to the Mexican *ranchera*.

The *carabiné* is a dance that originally came from the Spanish, but under Haitian occupation the dance evolved somewhat and adopted the name that characterizes it today. It is a popular folk dance with as many as five variations throughout the country. The dance is accompanied by an accordion, a *balsié*, a *güiro*, and a tambourine. The *carabiné* is a complex dance involving chang-ing partners, whose raised arms meet, draw apart, embrace, form circles of all females surrounding a circle of all males, then reverse that pattern. Much as in square dancing, there is an announcer, the *bastonero*, who directs the dance steps.

The *merengue* has become the national dance of the Dominican Republic. For most of its history it was snubbed by the upper classes, considered to be a dance limited to the rural and urban poor. While the lower classes danced the *merengue*, the upper classes danced waltzes, mazurkas, foxtrots, and pol-kas. The early, crude form of the *merengue* was played by guitar, violin, saxophone, and common percussion instruments. The accordion was added to the *merengue* band between 1874 and 1880. The saxophone was added at the beginning of the twentieth century. In the typical band, the accordion player sits in the center and then, in the form of a triangle, the *bambotero*, or drummer, sits on the right and the *güira* player on the left. The characteristic rhythm of the *merengue* is established by the drum played with the palm of the left hand while the right hand beats a rhythm with a small drumstick.

Some of the first *merengues* were composed by Dominican musician and composer Juan Bautista Alfonseca in the mid-1880s. Bautista Alfonseca was a classical musician with a keen and close understanding of popular tastes. He wrote the wildly popular *"La Juana Aquilina,"* which was based on an actual police case. Bautista Alfonseca's approach set the standard for the composition of *merengue* lyrics since then. Every aspect of life is recorded in the lyrics of the *merengue*, which usually tells a story. There are *merengues* about politics, love, lust, money, history, voodoo, modern technological advances, fads, and sociological problems. Often the lyrics are humorous, mordant, and satirical and very often replete with double entendres.

The *merengue* as it is known today began to take shape in 1915. The first report of it in print was in 1854, in an article in which upper-class detractors thought of the *merengue* as indecent, presumably because of the fact that dancing partners were united by a close embrace, dancing chest to chest, with hips swaying. The dance was accepted into high society in the beginning of the 1920s when musician Emilio Arté added the walking stroll to the dance. This movement is similar to what takes place in the jitterbug whereby the partners separate, the male dancer twirls the female around, she spins him around, and so forth. What ultimately brought recognition to the *merengue* by the upper classes of society was when classical musical composers played *merengue* music during classical musical performances.

Trujillo loved *merengue* and did much to popularize it, institutionalize it, and provide financial support to the bands he favored. Thus, the Trujillo era was also known as the big band era in the Dominican Republic. Some of the band leaders who gained prominence at this time include Luis Alberti, who is credited with being the first to modernize the *merengue*. Among his most famous *merengue* compositions is the one titled *"Compadre Pedro Juan,"* which gained international status for this dance and its music. Alberti added new instrumentation to the basic *merengue* orchestra including the saxophone, the clarinet or trumpet, and a piano. The diatonic accordion was replaced by the *bandoneon*, which is the same type of accordion used to play the Argentine tango.[2] Alberti made the *merengue* more sophisticated, distancing it from its folkloric roots, as he lowered the singing pitch; high-pitched singers were typically heard accompanying the more rustic, smaller *merengue* bands. Alberti's modifications to the *merengue* band changed its essential constitution to the point that the music of the "big band" *merengue*, with as many as twenty members at times, began to be seen as middle- and upper-class. The smaller, simpler groups with a high-pitched soloist were deemed primitive but kept alive with groups such as the Reynoso Trío and the Isidoro Flores Band.

Other composers that became famous during the Trujillo era and who directed bands include Papa Molina, Rafael Solano, and Antonio Morel. These, along with Alberti, went on to become internationally renowned. Joseíto Mateo was a popular vocalist for the Super Orchestra San José and the Voz Dominicana Radio Station. With the advent of television in 1952, Mateo went on to become the choreographer for live orchestral shows. With Mateo and the flourishing steps he added, the *merengue* acquired ballroom status.

The big band era ended after Trujillo's death. It became more practical, especially with regard to television studios, to feature smaller bands consisting of eight to ten members, a so-called combo. The advent of rock and roll music and the new dances that accompanied it in the United States influenced the essential constitution of the *merengue* band. The band itself became smaller, the music was played faster, the band members began to dance to their own music in a synchronized fashion, and many bands added a few dancers. Johnny Ventura was the vocalist and musician who spearheaded these new changes. Ventura is a wildly popular, charismatic singer whose fame is as established in the Dominican Republic as it is in New York City and Miami, where he has his own clubs.

Felix del Rosario and his *Magos del Ritmo* ("Rhythm Magicians") added new instruments to the *merengue* band including a baritone and a tenor saxophone, as well as a xylophone and a flute in 1964. Wilfrido Vargas' orchestra added the electronic piano and bass in the 1970s. These instruments and the increased acceleration in the rhythm made it possible for the *merengue* to compete on an international level and to capitalize on the gradually increasing interest in Latin American music worldwide.[3]

Another important step in the evolution of the *merengue* and its establishment as the national dance of the Dominican Republic was the compositions of the brilliant Juan Luis Guerra. Guerra and his band the 4.40 burst onto the scene in the 1980s, taking the Dominican musical scene by surprise. Guerra's creative and at times provocative lyrics, catchy melodies, and remarkable vocal arrangements have assured him an international reputation that no Dominican had ever achieved before in the entertainment industry. Trained in the United States at Berklee College in Boston, Massachusetts, Guerra was initially a student of jazz. His first record with 4.40, a group that over its history has shifted from five to four members, is reminiscent of the music of the American jazz quartet the Manhattan Transfer. Guerra's second and subsequent records experimented with Dominican music including the *merengue*, the *bachata*, and the simple folk ballad. Guerra's later records were as significant for the excellence of the music as for the lyrics that confronted Dominicans' sense of identity, which according to Guerra is based on a false assumption of an Indian heritage, a rejection of their black ascendance, and a slavish imitation of all things European and American. Other songs have explored Taíno rhythms, resurrecting the Taíno *areíto* while experimenting with Taíno instruments and chants. After an absence of about five years, during which time Guerra conducted the National Symphony of the Dominican Republic and helped other artists launch their careers, Guerra released his latest album, *Ni es lo mismo ni es igual* ("It's Not the Same Nor Can It Be Compared"), in December 1998. It explores, among other themes, the influence of modern technology on everyday lives.

BACHATA

Although Guerra is responsible for making the *bachata* acceptable beyond its lower-class roots with the release of his *Bachata Rosa* album in 1991, this ballad-type song and slow dance can be identified with the Dominican Republic almost as much as the *merengue*. Although the *bachata*'s emergence occurred at the beginning of the 1960s, the word *bachata* has traditionally signified a dance or a party involving food and drink. Since the 1960s and up to the time that Guerra modernized it, the *bachata* was an acoustic guitar–centered ensemble, with bongo drums and *maracas* for percussion. Initially, the *bachata* was not danced to, but over time, a slow dance similar to the *bolero* was associated with the music. *Bachata* lyrics deal primarily with love and are sung in an overdramatized, melancholic, even sobbing style. The language of the lyrics is common, replete with euphemisms that border on the vulgar (Pacini 3).

CLASSICAL DANCE

Ballet in the Dominican Republic has been limited to the work of one inspired and dedicated ballerina, Magda Corbett. As part of the immigration wave that came in from Europe during World War II, this Hungarian dancer arrived in the Dominican Republic with the idea of making this form of dance familiar to Dominicans. She founded a ballet school whose range encompassed young dancers preparing to dance the "Nutcracker" to ballet dancers who have gained respectability within the world of classical dance.

Corbett's struggle for legitimization in the Dominican Republic is compounded by the fact that her school has not received any governmental support or sanction with the exception of the shortlived presidency of Antonio Guzmán. In addition to aiding the Corbett School of Dance he founded the *Ballet Clásico Nacional* ("National Classical Ballet") in 1981. The company is directed by Carmen Heredia de Guerrero. The *Ballet Clásico Nacional* has produced several outstanding male dancers who, in turn, have founded other companies such as the *Ballet Concierto Dominicano* ("Dominican Concert Ballet"), founded by Carlos Veitía and his mother Clara Elena Ramírez, and the *Ballet Roto* ("Broken Ballet"), founded by Mercedes Morales and Victor Ramírez. It was not until the 1990s that enough ballet companies were established throughout the country that a healthy rivalry could ensue, thus strengthening individual repertoire and choreographic skills.

Alina Abréu is one of the leading ballerinas in the country, and Mónica Despradel has gained fame internationally as a ballerina, as has Juan Fidel Mieses Gautreaux who has danced with the American Ballet Company. The sense is that there is a general feeling of indifference with regard to this art, and the cultural politics of the nation have not prioritized the study of ballet as an important part of a child's general education. Mieses Gautreaux and Abréu feel that ballet is an art form that has not been given enough exposure over its history in the Dominican Republic. Mieses Gautreaux has established a school of ballet geared toward attracting students from the less-privileged classes (Cruz Hierro, "Ballet").

CLASSICAL MUSIC

The history of classical music in the Dominican Republic is closely linked to that of popular music. In fact, it is common to see crossover artists, particularly from classical to pop. Many classical composers have composed music for the *merengue*, for example. The converse is true as well, as in the case of Guerra, some of whose compositions have been transcribed as symphonic arrangements. Another contributing factor to the interrelationship between classical and popular music in the Dominican Republic is that, on balance, Dominicans of all social classes tend to favor and patronize popular music and events.

The founding fathers of the Dominican Republic were also musicians.

Juan Pablo Duarte played the flute and the guitar, and Francisco del Rosario Sánchez played the flute. Several of the first Dominican composers came from the rank and file of the young republic's Army Bands. Among these, José Reyes distinguished himself as the composer of the national anthem. The orchestration of the anthem was penned by Alfredo Máximo Soler (1859–1922), and the official band orchestration was done by José Dolores Cerón (1897–1969).

As teachers of music, composers and entertainers José María Rodríguez Arreson (1875–1947), José de Jesús Ravelo (1876–1951), and José Ovidio García (1862–1919) were among those who began the tradition of providing access of classical music to Dominicans. These musicians were band leaders who earned their living by teaching how to play various instruments. They instituted the custom of playing once or twice a week in the bandstand of the town square. Concerts were also held in theaters and in private salons, as appreciation for this type of music attracted only a small number of Dominicans when compared to popular music composed for dancing. The music they composed, designed for popular appeal within a classical vein, was modeled after music composed in Europe in the nineteenth century. Some of Rodríguez Arreson's, Ravelo's, and García's compositions can be designated as crossover music in that they often bridged the gap between classical and popular expression. Rodríguez Arreson is also noted for having founded the first musical academy in the Dominican Republic.[4]

Major advances were made during the first three decades of the twentieth century in the Dominican Republic in terms of establishing a humanistic foundation in the education system in elementary through secondary school. This foundation included orchestral and choral music. Dominican school children began the tradition of singing songs, ranging from patriotic to religious and civic, before the beginning of each school day. Musical compositions were created by the composers of the time to eventually serve as the traditional repertoire for children's school songs.

The next generation of classical musicians included Luis Rivera (1902–), Enrique de Marchena (1908–), and Ninón Lapeiretta (1907–). Rivera wrote piano rhapsodies for one and two pianos and a virtuosic violin sonata. De Marchena wrote many melodies for voice and piano and for flute and orchestra. Lapeiretta wrote orchestral pieces for a soloist and orchestra. The works of these musicians have found a place in the history of Dominican classical music.

The Trujillo dictatorship did not exert influence over classical music with the exception of the music to be played during the numerous parades he staged. Composers and lyricists were forced to write hymns, marches, and songs in honor of the autocrat. On the positive side, the Trujillo regime patronized the arts, so intrepid artists were able to forward their artistic imagination, taking care not to offend the prevailing rule of authority.

During the Spanish Civil War and the beginning of World War II, many talented Spanish and Jewish musicians immigrated to the Dominican Republic. An immediate result of their presence was the revival of all cultural activities in the country. These immigrants opened a school for the study of music in the Palacio de Bellas Artes in Santo Domingo. Schools of music had existed in the major cities and towns of the Dominican Republic prior to this historic moment, but the recent arrivals' enthusiasm for and knowledge of music far surpassed that of established school directors. The Symphonic Orchestra was reorganized under the baton of Enrique Casal Chapí who was also the director of the School for Fine Arts established in 1942.[5] A conservatory of music was also founded in 1942 and at its peak boasted an enrollment of 600 students. During the same time period there were 39 schools dedicated to the study of music throughout the country.

With the advent of peace in Europe, interest in the study of classical music in the Dominican Republic waned, with the exception of the National Symphony Orchestra. Many of the immigrants who had provided so much inspiration and had initiated programs returned to their native countries, so Dominican musicians had to seek training abroad.

The National Symphony Orchestra brought in harpists, violinists, cellists, flutists, horn players, and theoriticians from Italy and France in the 1950s. These musical experts also taught, allowing for the formation of a small group of musicians who, to this day, are major influences in the teaching of music and fostering musical appreciation. The most prominent of these teachers are Aída Bonnelly de Díaz and Manuel Rueda. Margarita Luna García and Miguel Pichardo Vicioso are the first graduates in composition in the country.

Other Dominican composers of classical music include Julio Alberto Hernández (1900–), Luis Rivera (1901–1986), Manuel Simó (1916–1988), and Bienvenido Bustamante (1921–). Dominican pianists that have distinguished themselves in the area of classical music include Manuel Rueda (1921–), Floralba Del Monte (1929–), Miriam Ariza (1940–), and María del Fátima Geraldes (1950–).

Today, as in the rest of the world, classical music is a minor art. Those who appreciate it are its most ardent supporters. The Dominican Republic enjoys frequent visits from world-renowned artists who perform concerts in the theater of the Plaza de la Cultura in Santo Domingo with the Dominican Symphonic Orchestra and its conductor, José Antonio Molina, and at the

Centro Cultural del Dominico-Americano, the Casa de Francia, the Sala Teatro de Ballet, and the auditorium in the Palacio de Bellas Artes in Santo Domingo, and the Centro de la Cultura in Santiago. By and large classical musicians cannot earn a living from teaching and playing classical music alone. Many are members of popular bands or perhaps write on the side.

SINGERS

The rise of Dominican singers of popular music is closely linked to the establishment of radio broadcasting in the Dominican Republic. The Voz del Yuna radio station was founded in 1942 by José Arismendi Trujillo Molina, one of dictator Trujillo's brothers. In 1946 the Academy of Song was created by Argentine baritone Carlos Crespo. The ascendance in popularity of a large variety of singers was meteoric. These included popular ballad singers such as Lope Balaguer, Negrito Chapuseaux, Pablo Molina, Alberto Gómez, Rosa Elena Bobadilla, and Casandra Damirón, among others. *Merengue* orchestras featured outstanding singers, in particular Johnny Ventura and Luis Alberti. Others that have reached prominence through *merengue*, *bachata, salsa,* and popular styles such as soft rock include Johnny Pacheco, Luis Díaz, Sonia Silvestre, Angelita Carrasco, and the sister vocalists Jocelyn and Milly Quezada and their musician brothers Los Vecinos, who originated in New York.[6]

Despite the preponderance of popular singers, few Dominicans have excelled in opera. Some who have are Susano Polanco (1902–1991), Eduardo Brito (1905–1946), Rafael Félix Gimbernard (1912–1976), Rafael Sánchez Cestero (1912–), Gerónimo Pellerano (1927–1991), Violeta Stephen (1929–), and Tony Curiel (1931–).

THEATER

Early theatrical representations in the Dominican Republic have been attributed to the Taíno Indians whose religious celebrations involved pantomime, dance, and song. The *areíto*, for example, was a dramatic dance performed under the influence of hallucinogenic drugs.

The purpose of theater during the colonial times was either catechistic or for entertainment. The plays that were presented included all types of theater common to Spain at the time. Among these were the *entremés* (short comedy), farces, and comedies. Cristóbal de Llerena is the first Dominican-born playwright. The only work of his that remains is a short comedy he staged in 1588 in the atrium of Santo Domingo's cathedral. The play incorporated subtle criticism of the politics of colonial administration and resulted in Llerena's eventual deportation for insubordination. The theater of the next two centuries, if any, given the dire historical circumstances including the continous change in governance, the scarce population, and pirate raids and sacking, was used as a function of the Spanish aristocracy and the entertainment that they sought.

Juan Pablo Duarte, father of Dominican independence, perceived that a way to disseminate the message of independence and revolution and to fight against oppression was by staging works that conveyed this very message written by European playwrights. These works were staged throughout the Spanish half of the island even though it was under Haitian control at the time.

Felix María del Monte and Javier Angulo Guridi were the first Dominican playwrights of the free republic. Their plays were characterized by indigenous and heroic themes framed in romanticism. Del Monte wrote a political play criticizing the assassination of Antonio Duvergé: *Antonio Duvergé, o Las víctimas del 11 de abril* (*Antonio Duvergé or The Victims of April 11*) (1856). In this work, del Monte portrays despotism, class distinctions, and alienation. Structurally, the play is based on staging approaches that were outmoded at the time of its staging. Angulo Guridi's most famous play *Iguaniona* (1867) is the romantic tale of an Indian princess and is a muffled metaphor of political protest. Angulo Guridi and his contemporaries betrayed a strong dependence on Spanish culture, all the while writing plays about Spanish-speaking Indians who, as a group in their own right, had long since ceased to exist. There is no pursuit of a national voice, and there is a complete denial of the existence of blacks in the nation.

About seventy-five plays were written between 1863 and 1916. As the new republic lacked a theater tradition, most of these plays reflected tendencies and subjects that were of interest in Spain and in other countries of Latin America. The years of 1916 to 1922 saw an increase in theatrical activity by Dominican playwrights. Still, none represented a Dominican reality with the exception of the rumored existence of plays by Rafael Damirón, *Los Yanquis en Santo Domingo* (*Yankees in Santo Domingo*); Delia M. Quezada, *Quisqueya y la ocupación americana* (*Quisqueya and American Occupation*); and Ricardo Pérez Alfonseca, *La inmolación* (*The Sacrifice*), among others. These plays were written to protest the United States occupation of the country (1916–1924).

Theater during the first years of the Trujillo era was easily dispensable. It consisted of representations or adaptations of Greek theater. This classical theater was appealing to the dictator who fancied himself to be one of its heroes. Around 1945, two historical events took place that would lay the foundation for Dominican theater and for a Dominican theater tradition. The first is that Trujillo's wife at the time had the dictator build a fine arts performing center, the Palacio de Bellas Artes. The second is that the refugees from the Spanish Civil War and World War II brought innovative perspectives on contemporary theater to the Dominican Republic. Dominican playwrights Franklin Domínguez, Manuel Rueda, and Héctor Incháustegui Cabral were the first to take advantage of this new inspiration and venue by staging translations of foreign plays, incorporating the latest in production technique.

Manuel Rueda's *La Trinitaria Blanca* (*The White Heartsease*) (1957) and Franklin Domínguez's *El último instante* (*The Very Last Moment*) (1958) are considered breakthrough plays as they incorporate Dominican idiomatic idiosyncracies and atmosphere into their plays. These were the exceptions to what was otherwise seen as a long series of psychological dramas built around themes of corruption and distraction set in such universal terms so as not to be taken as criticisms of the prevailing regime. Incháustegui Cabral's *Prometeo* (*Prometheus*) (1961) is significant for being the first play based on the Greco-Latin tradition transplanted to the Dominican Republic and for thus being the first deliberate attempt to nationalize a classical myth.

True Dominican theater emerged in 1965. From this year henceforth rose the voices that are still dominant in theater today, including those of Carlos Acevedo, Máximo Aviles Blonda, Efraín Castillo, Carlos Esteban Deive, Franklin Domínguez, Iván García, Manuel Rueda, Haffe Serulle, and Marcio Veloz Maggiolo. As these playwrights became established they attracted followers who started small theater groups that performed mainly experimental works. Some of the more established of these include the Teatro Experimental Popular (TEXPO) ("Popular Experimental Theater") in the capital and the Teatro Popular del Centro (TPC) ("Popular Theater of the Center") in Santiago.

With inspiration ranging from the works of Bertold Brecht to those of Eugene Ionesco, contemporary playwrights write plays that portray social theatrical theory and the theater of the absurd. The work of some is hybrid, furiously existential, and critical of society. Ivan García's works are typical of this trend. His works present irrational worlds where communication is an impossibility. García's characters undergo isolation and alienation as a reaction to modernization, class exploitation, economic exploitation and a sense of helplessness before a society that is seen as cold and indifferent. Two of his plays are *Un héroe más para la mitología* (*Another Hero for Mythology*) (1964) and *Los hijos del Fénix* (*Children of the Phoenix*) (1965).

Other Dominican playwrights resort to historical revisionism, particularly in the case of Serrulle's plays *Duarte* and *El Hatero de Seibo* (*The Cattle Rancher from Seibo*). Yet another trend revives the one begun by Domínguez in 1961 by representing Roman, Greek, and even Babylonian plays within a Dominican context. This nationalistic creative effort responds to the urgency among Dominican artists to be a part of universal literature. It is a recurrent theme in theater productions and in literature.

A venerated Dominican institution, the Casa de Teatro, under the direction of actor and director Freddy Ginebra, inaugurated an annual competition for theater and the short story in 1983. This incentive has attracted many entries, has underscored the importance of Dominican theater and literature, and has established the foundation for the growth of a theatrical tradition in the Dominican Republic.

Many small theater companies have sprouted throughout the Dominican Republic in the last fifteen years, usually around academic institutions such as the Universidad Autónoma de Santo Domingo, the Universidad Nacional Pedro Henríquez Ureña, and the Instituto Tecnológico, all in Santo Domingo; the Universidad Católica Madre y Maestra in Santiago; and the Universidad Nacional del Este in San Pedro de Macorís. These groups include the Jockey Club Group, the Popular Experimental Theatre (1976), INTEC Projection (1978), and *Chispa* ("Spark"). Franklin Domínguez created his own independent group, and Danilo Ginebra and others who formed the Gratey Theater can be credited for the writing and distribution of many new plays and for inaugurating the first ever national popular theater festival.

Despite the youth and condition of the development of Dominican theater, two Dominican playwrights have been honored in prestigious international competitions. Reynaldo Disla won the Casa de las Americas prize in 1985 for his play *Bolo Francisco*. In 1996 Manuel Rueda won the prestigious Blasco Ibañez award for best play of the year in Spain. His play *Juana la Loca* is based on the life of Juana, the daughter of King Ferdinand and Queen Isabel of Spain.

In the history of Dominican theater, actresses are more memorable than actors both in the Dominican Republic and in New York. In the Dominican Republic, Margarita Reid Baquero is a thespian of lasting quality who has tackled theatrical roles that run the gamut from comedic to tragic, from absurd to roles in children's plays. Dominican actresses of prominence in New York include Ilka Tanya Payán and Josefina Báez. Payán (1943–1996) acted on stages in Spain, Puerto Rico, and the Dominican Republic. She also starred in a Spanish-speaking soap opera on Telemundo, one of the Spanish-speaking cable television stations. Báez (1960–) is an actress, dancer, teacher, poet, and playwright. She founded a theater company in New York called Latinarte which serves as a thriving center for dramatic performances dealing with Hispanic issues. Some of her works are one-woman shows, whereas others are collaborative efforts with New York–based Dominican playwright Claudio Mir. Her plays, which deal primarily with the experience of being a black female immigrant in New York, include *Negritud dominicana* (*Dominican Blackness*) (1986), *Lo mío es mío* (*What's Mine Is Mine*) (1994), and *In Dominicanisch* (1996).[7]

CONCLUSION

Of all possible cultural manifestations, the area of performing arts is where the Dominican Republic has made the biggest impression in terms of world recognition. This aspect of culture has been best able to harness those salient characteristics of Dominicans when viewed as a whole: exuberance, vitality, charm, ingenuity, and the transcultural debt owed to its many immigrants. These traits have easily been channeled into music, dance, and theater, understandably the most accessible of all art forms.

NOTES

1. Musicologists and anthropologists have studied the origin of the *güiro* extensively. There are even two accepted spellings of this instrument: *güiro* and *güira*. Some historians claim that the instrument is indigenous whereas others point to its origin as Africa. Although some musicologists see the *guayo* as being a replacement of the *güiro* there are *merengue* orchestras in which both are played.

2. A diatonic instrument is limited to the eight notes of a major or minor scale and is not able to produce chromatic variations.

3. Three companies have established dance troupes to preserve and perform the *merengue*. The first of these was founded by Casandra Damirón who staged her folkloric dance shows at the Hotel Embajador. The *Cueva Colonial* ("Colonial Cave") was a dance troupe directed by René Carrasco. This dance group focused on representing all folk dances in addition to the *merengue*. Fradique Lizardo's Dominican Folkloric Ballet is the latest addition to the list of national folkloric dance ensembles.

4. Ravelo composed a string quartet, a requiem for a mass, and an oratorio dedicated to the death of Christ, which has been critically acclaimed. García wrote two string quartets and the *Quisqueyana Symphony*, which was played for the first time in 1941 and was well received by the audience. Today it constitutes part of the National Symphonic Orchestra's repertoire along with the three symphonies written by Enrique Mejía Arredondo (1901–1951), whose promising musical career was stunted by an early death.

5. The Palacio de Bellas Artes is an imposing architectural structure built in the neoclassic style. During Trujillo's time it saw the establishment of an art school, a music school, and a ballet school.

6. Milly Quezada has gone on to a solo career. The lyrics of her songs are noted for their feminist stance. Quezada is very popular among women fans and has been credited for advancing the women's movement in the Dominican Republic. She is currently the star of a theater production based on her life.

7. Chiqui Vicioso, who is better known as a poet, literary critic, and women's movement activist, has made a successful foray into playwrighting. *Whisky Sour,* a performance art play, was written and staged in New York. It deals with the difficulties of middle-aged womanhood particularly from the point of view of the Dominican-American woman.

7

Architecture, Art, Sculpture, and Photography

The visual arts in the Dominican Republic evolved from a close imitation of European-inspired works to an individualized expression that today is gaining international recognition, particularly with regard to painting and architecture. These works in architecture, painting, sculpture, and photography are testaments to the artistic potential on this island nation since its independence.

This chapter offers a survey of architecture through the study of extant buildings. Some of the buildings date from colonial times, others are products of the 1990s. Painting is studied from the time of independence, as the colonial period did not lend itself to much original artistic representation particularly in the mediums of painting and sculpture. A short overview of the evolution of photography concludes the chapter.

ARCHITECTURE

The study of architecture and interior design in the Dominican Republic is divided into four historic periods: colonial, Republic, Trujillo era, and contemporary. These periods are not inclusive, but they serve as points of departure for the study of architecture during these times and others. Although architectural creations are more numerous in the capital city, there are outstanding buildings and monuments throughout the Republic, most notably in Santiago, Puerto Plata, Montecristi, Higüey, San Pedro de Macorís, and La Romana.

Construction in the Dominican Republic has relied on natural resources and imported materials. Stone is amply available and was used until the technology for the production of reinforced concrete was introduced. There are ample supplies of marble, limestone, pine, ebony, and mahogany. It was not until the end of the nineteenth century that prefabricated materials and modular components made their way into architectural designs. Primitive homes have always been made of the ubiquitous palm tree. Its trunk is cut into thin planks which constitute the walls of the modest abode, whereas the fronds cover the roof. Some of these houses, many of which have no modern conveniences, are painted in bright, festive colors, dispelling the true nature of the poverty of its inhabitants.

The Colonial Era

One of the legacies of the Balaguer presidency is the restoration of the colonial part of the capital. Long in disrepair as the burgeoning capital grew outward and away from the port, the colonial part of the city suffered the same neglect seen in most major metropolitan areas of the world during the twentieth century. Modern commercial areas sprouted in relatively distant points throughout the wide expanse of what is today Santo Domingo, creating alternative business hubs and thus drawing people away from the downtown area.

The advent of the year 1992, however, was significant for focusing Dominicans' attention on their own country and its appearance, as it became the center of the world's attention for the celebration of the 500-year anniversary of the Discovery. The decades preceding the commemoration of the quinquecentennial saw the restoration of the downtown area of Santo Domingo, making it appear very much as it did during Columbus' lifetime.[1] Today this area is mainly a tourist attraction, brimming with restaurants, souvenir shops, and important museums. The cathedral, a convent, churches, Columbus' son's house, other homes of prominent figures of colonial times, and part of the wall that surrounded the original city have been fully restored.

Colonial architecture responded to five distinct objectives: religion, health, defense, residence, and sugarcane production. Convents and universities were built to address the first need. Hospitals, forts, and walls fulfilled the second and third needs; while palaces, homes, and factories responded to the last objective.

Frey Nicolás de Ovando can be credited with the actual layout of the city of Santo Domingo. His plans were then copied by settlers throughout the New World. The streets were parallel or perpendicular to a central square. The central square boasted a cathedral on one side, faced by governmental buildings. The buildings on the lateral sides of the square were usually governmental in nature as well, or served as apartments. Most buildings in colonial times were built of stone or of brick and rubblework. Ovando oversaw the building and design of churches, a hospital, a walled fortress, and numerous private homes. These lavish residences are typically Spanish in that the outside of the building is a plain wall, sometimes adorned with a balcony, with a massive wooden door as the main portal. On the inside, by contrast, there is a large open courtyard with a fountain in the center, framed by arched walls.

Ovando was replaced as governor by Diego Colón, son of Christopher Columbus, who built the Alcazár, a palace which was to be his home. The Alcázar, with its coral limestone facade, betrays a blend of Spanish, Italian, and Moorish styles. In its history it has suffered from neglect and destruction occasioned by earthquakes, hurricanes, and wars. It was fully restored in 1968 according to specifications of colonial times.

Other imposing structures originally built during colonial times include the Ozama Fortress, the *Casa de Bastidas* ("the Bastidas' home"), the cathedral, the *Casa de Tostados* ("the Tostados' home"), and the San Francisco monastery. Some of these were restored during Balaguer's governance. Others, like the San Francisco monastery, can only attest to their former splendor by the magnitude of what today lies in ruins.

The Ozama fortress was designed to protect the young city from coastal attacks. Today social and cultural functions are held there. The neoclassic portal that adorns the entrance to this structure is the third one, built in 1787. The Bastidas' home interior court opens into the Ozama fortress. In its time it was considered one of the more elegant homes. Today the elongated rooms that border elegant courtyards serve as a workshop where masterpieces are restored, and as an exhibit hall for colonial items that are still being found in archeological excavations.

The cathedral's most imposing feature is its western portal, which is in a late plateresque style, a hyperbole of bas-reliefs typical of the early period of Spanish Renaissance. Seven chapels line three parallel naves. These serve as mausoleums for illustrious Dominicans. Paintings by precursors of renowned seventeenth-century Spanish painter Diego Velázquez hang in the chapels. Columbus' remains were kept in a magnificent bronze and marble sarcophagus behind four baroque columns carved to resemble royal palms. The Cathedral's limestone facade ranges from Gothic Elizabethan to intricate baroque, with occasional traces of Mudéjar (combination of Moorish and Gothic) influences in some of the interior columns, doorways, and window trims.

Sarcophagus with Columbus' remains. Courtesy of
Listín Diario.

The Casa de Tostado is the only colonial house in the New World that boasts large twin Gothic windows. Today it is a museum of the evolution of furniture from colonial times through the present. It doubles, in this regard, as a chronicle of the lifestyles of prosperous Dominicans throughout their history.

The San Francisco Monastery ruins where the Franciscan order had established a permanent residence attest to the existence of three structures: a church, a convent, and what is referred to as the Third Chapel. Its original architect, Rodrigro de Liendo, was commissioned in 1554 to build a church to resemble the church of San Gerónimo in Granada, Spain. The location of the Franciscan monastery is the highest promontory of the colonial capital. Liendo never completed his work, as his initial efforts were leveled by a hurricane in 1545 and earthquakes that followed. Sir Francis Drake added to the destruction by setting fire to the church and convent and by completely destroying the Third Chapel. The Haitian invasions in 1805 ensured its complete annihilation as Dominican defenders climbed on the roofs of the church and monastery with heavy artillery to fight the attackers. With the departure of the Franciscan monks, the San Francisco church fell into ruin. The monastery became an insane asylum in the latter part of the nineteenth century and continued in this capacity well into the twentieth century. The chains used to restrain the patients are still attached to the ancient walls. The restoration of this important colonial building has been hampered by modern expansion of the capital, whereby small private homes line the streets immediately adjacent to the structure, thus impeding access for restoration work.

Rodrigo de Liendo was also responsible for building the Convent of Mercy or Iglesia de las Mercedes. Its cloister is the only one of the many that were built in colonial times that has survived the ravages of weather and war intact. The first Masonic Lodge of the Americas makes its home in part of the cloister. The lodge jealously guards the room where the celebrated seventeenth-century Spanish playwright Tirso de Molina stayed during the years he lived in Santo Domingo. He wrote his most famous play "Don Juan Tenorio" here, and it is thought that he based the character of Don Juan on Christopher Columbus' grandson, Luis Colón (Rueda, *Todo Santo Domingo* 43).[2]

An excellent example of military-style architecture can be found in Puerto Plata. The San Felipe Fortress, named posthumously for Philip V, king of Spain, was finished in 1577. It was desgined by Francisco de Ceballos but ultimately built by Pedro Rengifo y Angulo. Teódulo Blanchard was charged with its restoration in the 1960s. The fortress includes 2,000 meters of built up area, buttressed by two large fortified, crenellated towers that are 80 feet in diameter. There are three identical interior naves with communicating passages. Two watchtowers overlook the Atlantic Ocean, which is also where the chain-operated drawbridge is located.

The National Pantheon was built in 1714 as a Jesuit monastery. After the expulsion of the order, the building became a theater and was ultimately designated as a national pantheon by Trujillo in 1955. Its architectural style is described simply as eighteenth-century religious (Rueda, *Todo Santo Domingo* 19).

In 1762 twenty-nine sugar mills were registered throughout the colony. The most interesting of these, given its magnitude, is the rubblework Boca de Nigua mill located in La Romana. Besides the mill, the complex included boiler rooms, drying rooms, living quarters, slave rooms, and warehouses.

The Republic

Economic prosperity brought on by the sugar industry ensured the foundation of a solid urban middle class composed mostly of immigrants. Architectural styles of the nineteenth century are similar throughout the Caribbean and New Orleans, Louisiana. These consist of those variously described as Stick Style, Gingerbread, or Victorian. The newer residences are light, airy, open, and colorful, responsive to the prevailing climate.

Toward the end of the nineteenth century entire prefabricated buildings were imported from France, Belgium, and the United States such as would be used for train stations (Calventi 35). A few vestiges of these buildings and the ornamental accessories that were characteristic of the period can still be found in the towns of Pimentel, Hostos, Arenoso, Villa Rivas, Puerto Plata, and Montecristi. These towns varyingly feature elaborate ironwork street lamps, bandstands in parks, and clock towers, the most prominent being the one in Montecristi.

Modest urban residences continued to be built of rubblework, the most common construction material in the Dominican Republic. These distinguished themselves with varying slopes on rooflines, decorated windows, and long balconies with intricate detail.

The Trujillo Era

Trujillo's thirty-one-year dictatorship was characterized by a significant building spurt that responded, in part, to the dictator's nationalistic ideology. As the country readied itself to celebrate its centennial in 1944, many buildings of note were built allowing for the rise of and prominence of individual Dominican architects. The Casino at Güibia, the national hippodrome, the Central Fire Station, hospitals, and churches built for this commemoration flaunted a contemporary international style. The most outstanding expression of modernity was achieved by José Antonio Caro Alvarez and his design for the School of Medicine on the campus of the Universidad Autónoma de Santo Domingo. Its "subtly curved contraflexured facade created an aesthetic tension" that was new to the Dominican world of architecture (Calventi 43). Many of the constructions, such as the numerous schools that were built throughout the country, are not architecturally memorable given their highly functional, simple style.

Some buildings and monuments created during Trujillo's rule have endured. Among these are the National Palace, the Palace of Fine Arts, the basilica at Higüey, the World's Fair, and the Universidad Autónoma de Santo

The National Palace in Santo Domingo. Courtesy of *Listín Diario*.

Domingo. Trujillo also began the restoration process of downtown Santo Domingo. During his regime, the capital city, which he had renamed Ciudad Trujillo, faced its first incidence of urban sprawl. Many large avenues were built on the city's outskirts to accommodate projected growth in that area.

Italian architect Guido D'Alessandro built the National Palace in a renaissance style. This building, which is the headquarters for the government, is located midway between the colonial area and what is referred to as the Ciudad Nueva, or New City. Inaugurated in 1947 it is a three-story building with sculpted gardens. The ground floor contains archives, communications systems, a kitchen, and quarters for the servants. The second floor houses the president's and vice president's offices as well as those of other important functionaries. The third floor is the location of reception halls, salons, and sumptuous bedrooms for visiting dignitaries. Its mahogany floors are elaborately inlaid, and there are decorative accents in the rooms made of Dominican marble and alabaster. Other rooms feature French Baccarat lamps and mirrors. Ambassador Hall, which is used to welcome newly appointed ambassadors, is decorated with Persian rugs, brocade drapes, and empire-style furniture whose trim is gilded with twenty-two carat gold.

Over the years the National Palace had fallen into disrepair. For Leonel Fernández Reyna, the current president of the Dominican Republic, the seat of government needs to uphold its importance as a national symbol. He has ordered a complete restoration including painting the huge edifice, which has always been white, a tropical pink color.

The construction of the Our Lady of Altagracia Basilica at Higüey was begun in 1954. French architects André Jacques Dunoyer de Segonzac and Pierre Dupré were contracted for this project. The church, which has an ultramodern appearance and is graced with tall parabolic arches placed in ascending succession, was inaugurated in 1971. Dunoyer de Segonzac has explained that there is symbolism in the arches as they relate to the pilgrim's voyage in counterpoint to polyphonic music. All this combines with a harmonic equilibrium of the walls themselves and the lighting and polychromatic quality of the vividly colored stained glass windows (Rueda, *Todo Santo Domingo* 119). Dominican sculptor Antonio Prats Ventós is responsible for the Virgen de Altagracia's image which is carved in wood surrounded by the symbolic orange trees associated with her miraculous appearance during colonial times. The leaves and fruits on the trees are painted gold. Large murals by José Vela Zanetti, the Spanish painter who made the Dominican Republic his home for many years, grace the inner sanctuary.

There was a great boom in residential and private construction in the period following the U.S. military occupation (1916–1924) and throughout the Trujillo era. In this area architects were freer to express and experiment with new, innovative styles. The homes built at that time were in the Mediterranean domestic style. Red tile roofing replaced corrugated steel roofs, and arches were added as a decorative element to the cement block house. This style, popular in Florida, California, Havana, Cuba, and San Juan, Puerto Rico, has also been referred to as neocolonial. The concepts of Art Deco, on the one hand, and functionalism, on the other, were introduced by architects who had studied in the United States, including Humberto Ruiz Castillo, José Antonio Caro Alvarez, brothers Leo and Marcial Pou Ricart, and Guillermo González. The most interesting buildings of this period include the *casa vapor* ("vaporous house") by musician and self-taught architect Henry Gazón and the headquarters of Esso Standard Oil by José Antonio Caro Alvarez.

While these architects imposed modernistic ideas in their creations, Henry Gazón, the official architect of the regime, turned to neoclassicism with its columns and elaborate cornices as the most appropriate style, particularly for government buildings and the National Palace of Fine Arts completed in 1956.[3] Another style favored by Trujillo was one that can only be described as monumental given the physical enormity of the buildings involved. The buildings include those built for the World's Fair that took place in Ciudad Trujillo in 1958, the palaces of the Dominican Political Party, Trujillo's

The National Theater. Courtesy of *Listín Diario*.

private residence in San Cristóbal, and the monument to peace in Santiago. These buildings bear symbols of Trujillo's authority, including five stars depicted horizontally, and a royal palm. Other buildings and monuments that were built throughout the Republic attesting to Trujillo's regime included obelisks and monuments modeled after Paris' Arc de Triomphe.

Contemporary Architecture

The 1970s saw a boom in construction of public buildings in the Dominican Republic. These include, among others, the edifices of the Cultural Plaza, the national airport, and the central bank. The architectural style of all of these buildings is modern and sleek. Most are at least three-story buildings that feature full-length columns and windows, and are painted white. The entrance lobby, in most cases, is a spacious atrium featuring large plants indigenous to the area.

The Cultural Plaza complex, or Plaza Cultural, houses the National Theater, the Gallery of Modern Art, the Museum of Dominican Man (*Museo del Hombre Dominicano*), the National Library, the National Museum of History and Geography, and the Museum of Natural History. All of these modern buildings lie within a large complex shaded by trees that are centuries old. They are connected by paved walkways with outdoor sculptures, gardens, benches, decorative pavilions, and fountains completing the setting. Of all the newer structures in the Dominican Republic, this plaza is thought of as the most individual, authentic, and successful expression of a national identity through architecture.

Completed in 1973, the National Theater, designed by Teófilo Carbonell, has earned a reputation as an important venue for the performance of concerts and theater productions by national and international symphonic orchestras and theater companies. The main stage is ranked fourth in the world with regard to size. Natacha Sánchez, the current director of the theater, has visions that are at once international and intrinsically nationalistic. She actively seeks international engagements for the theater's stages while at the same time promoting the local actor, storyteller, dramaturg, musician, and dancer.

The Modern Art Gallery, designed by José Miniño (1976), exhibits collections of art by both Dominican and international artists. The Museum of Dominican Man, designed by José Antonio Caro Alvarez (1973), teaches about the evolution of Dominicans through archeology, physical and cultural anthropology, and natural and social sciences. Special areas throughout the museum are designated research areas. The museum publishes books, journals, and newsletters pertaining to Dominicans. The National Museum of Natural History was designed by Héctor Tamburini (1974). It is used to exhibit the flora, fauna, and natural land and marine habitats of the Dominican Republic. The National Library, which was also designed by José Antonio Caro Alvarez (1971), is a four-story building with a floor plan designed to provide flexibility in its use.

The Central Bank (*Banco Central*), designed by Rafael Calventi, houses a cultural center, besides being the headquarters for the main bank of the country. This complex also includes an office tower and a parking garage. The attractive and ultramodern four-story building hosts conventions, seminars, and numerous cultural and artistic activities, including exhibits and concerts. Its auditorium, which seats 900, is equipped with facilities for simultaneous translation in four languages along with other state-of-the-art multimedia services.

The Altos de Chavón is the location of an art and interior design school, affiliated with New York's Parsons School of Design. This is a small village built in the 1970s but made to resemble a sixteenth-century Mediterranean village that sits on a bluff overlooking the Chavón river in La Romana, and a vast wooded area is also a cultural arts center. Cobblestone streets are lined with lanterns and wrought-iron balconies. The village buildings, the church St. Stanislaus of Krakow (named after the patron saint of Poland in honor of Pope John Paul II's visit in 1979), and the outdoor amphitheater simulate primitive structures, all made of stone, brick, and wood.

The Columbus Lighthouse or *Faro a Colón* was first conceived during the Trujillo era. An international competition was held to select the best rendition of the lighthouse. British architect J. L. Gleave won. Work on the lighthouse came to a halt with Gleave's death in 1931. It was resumed shortly prior to the quinquecentennial and was completed in 1992. The lighthouse is faithful to Gleave's plans. Viewed from above, the complex resembles a massive cross. From ground level, what has been described as a stern fascist construction towers high, resembling a pyramid.

The Monument to the Restoration of the Republic, designed by Rafael Calventi (1986), is a tribute to the feats that restored independence to the Dominican people after annexation to Spain. It is a collection of highly symbolic abstract forms recalling various aspects of the struggle. The truncated columns at the main entrance recall the destruction of colonial power. The large blocks of concrete lie horizontally throughout the monument. On the front of one of them is a mural by sculptor Antonio Prats Ventós.

William Reid Cabral, Sr., is among the more prolific and influential architects and sculptors of the modern era in the Dominican Republic.[4] His individualized style, which emphasizes the design of buildings that best conform to the climate and intrinsic geographical characteristics, has been referred to as sensitively human. He has labeled his work as a symbiosis of romanticism and pragmatic realism with regard to nature. His works optimize functional economy with regard to use of space. He is best known for the construction of international bank buildings, such as the Chase Manhattan Bank, the Bank of America, and the Royal Bank of Canada in Santiago de los Treinta Caballeros. Reid Cabral, Sr., has also built many private residences, the National Savings and Loans offices, and apartment buildings. His son, Carlos Reid Baquero, and daughter, Patricia Reid Baquero, are young architects that contribute further to the Reid Cabral legacy, particularly in the area of private residence construction. Reid Cabral maintains that one cannot speak of Dominican architecture per se. Architectural works in the Dominican Republic are by and large adaptations of an international style of architecture (Moré Guaschino).

There are three trends in today's architecture in the Dominican Republic: (a) a modern international style that rejects colonial and national cultural influences; (b) postmodern architecture reflected in various ways: a contextual meld integral to extant nature or to nationalism, an eclectic style that blends architectural styles of the past, "incorporating formal elements of historical architecture removed from their origins, abstract and separate from the physical and cultural environment" (Calventi 15); and (c) a style rich in neocolonial influence.

PAINTING AND SCULPTURE

The development of fine arts in the Dominican Republic is closely linked to its sense of identity as a nation. Dominican painting and sculpture were highly derivative and highly influenced by movements and tendencies first appearing in Europe through the 1930s. Many Dominican artists studied in Europe at one time or another in their careers, adapting their work from paradigms learned abroad. These artists by and large focused on a Dominican theme, but applied techniques learned elsewhere. From the 1940s through the late twentieth century, Dominican painting, sculpture, and photography have earned universal recognition given the uniqueness of the subject matter and the very experimental nature of its expression. The art world has been slow to recognize Dominican talent throughout the twentieth century, preferring to privilege Cuban artists or those of other Caribbean islands for political reasons and for reasons of ignorance and lack of exposure on the part of Dominican painters, sculptors, and photographers. This wrong is being righted particularly due to the wide exposure that these artists are gaining from their active participation in the many competitions held throughout the Caribbean and elsewhere in Latin America.

The history of painting and sculpture in the Dominican Republic begins with the nation as an independent republic in the 1840s, with the works of Alejandro Bonilla (1820–1901), Leopoldo Navarro (1856–1908), Luis Desangles (1861–1940), and Abelardo Rodríguez Urdaneta (1870–1933). The work of these artists is generally characterized as romantic in conception, neoclassic in practice.

Although Bonilla was trained in Caracas in portraiture, he was the first Dominican painter to paint the sugarcane plantation and the machinery associated with the production of sugar. Desangles is credited with experimenting with impressionism, and Navarro is credited for mastering the movement that ultimately saw its epitome in the work of the first of many women Dominican painters, Celeste Woss y Gil. Desangles' works, most of which are portraits, can be found in museums in Santo Domingo and in Santiago, Cuba. His most famous works are romantic in style and depict historical events. These include the large oil of the Taíno chieftain Caonabo in chains, and *El regreso de la canoa* (*The Return of the Canoe*). Urdaneta, whose mentor was Desangles, is regarded as the most skilled of the four painters and can be regarded as the founding father of painting as an art form in the Dominican Republic. He was a sculptor, draftsman, painter, photographer, and a musician, and his works are the first to be qualified as having "national significance" (Miller 120). This claim is substantiated by the fact that his famous sculptures, such as that of the Taíno chieftain Caonabo and the piece titled *Uno de tantos* ("One of Many"), and many of his paintings are all property of the national government.

Celeste Woss y Gil (1891–1985) and Enrique García Godoy (1885–1945) are grouped as the immediate succesors to the painting and sculpting traditions established by the founders of Dominican plastic arts. García Godoy is best remembered as a teacher. His masterpieces, all of which depicted historical scenes, were either neoclassic or romantic in style. Both Woss y Gil and García Godoy founded painting academies—the former in Santo Domingo and the latter in his birthplace of La Vega. Of the two, Woss y Gil is by far the most famous, incidentally because she was a woman, but specifically because her paintings, which were highly impressionistic in style, were groundbreakers in format, statement, and impact. Woss y Gil had lived and studied in Cuba and in the United States, thereby learning about the latest in trends and techniques. Her work, nudes and portraits, bears a trademark of neutral tones. Woss y Gil's experimentation with the use of light in her paintings is considered innovative for the time.

The artists described thus far were exceptional in their craft, but their work was derivative, the style, approach, and inspiration relying heavily on western European influences. The first Dominican painters to distance themselves from the influence of European art are also considered the first Dominican artists of the modern era: Yoryi Morel (1901–1979), Jaime Colson (1901–1975), and Darío Suro (1917–). Their works depict Dominican settings and a use of light that better reflects a tropical approach.

Morel, who never travelled abroad and who was essentially self-taught, is acclaimed for his focus on Dominican topics. His impressionistic paintings feature different aspects of the Cibao including the sexual tensions of the *merengue*, the Dominican peasant smoking his pipe, and cockfights. His style has been labeled "vigorous" and his use of light "sensual" (Miller 121). Morel remains one of the most popular Dominican painters of all time and is considered to be the father of authentic Dominican painting.

Colson is credited with being the first Dominican artist to feature the mulatto. His artistic history is long and reflects the many influences he encountered including cubism, surrealism, and, at times, neoclassicism. The unique combination of artistic trends ensures a signature style for this artist from Puerto Plata. Colson is equally renowned as a teacher of art and has recently been "discovered" by museums in Europe.

Darío Suro was initially a student of his uncle García Godoy in La Vega. He then studied in Mexico with, among others, the famous Mexican muralist Diego Rivera. This contact was to have profound influence on his work, which went through a period emphasizing social conditions. He is the only Dominican painter to admit so much Mexican influence in his art. Mixing surrealism with images of pre-Columbine art, Suro confesses his debt to Frida Kahlo, the painter and Diego Rivera's wife, with regard to inspiration. As Colson's art evolved, he found his own voice in abstract expressionism, developing a style that is uniquely his. Suro depicted Dominican reality through landscapes, architecture, people, and customs.

The Trujillo regime's positive contribution to the culture of the Dominican Republic lies in the establishment and the building of proper venues from which to perform, view, or make art. The National School of Fine Arts was founded in 1942 in the Palacio de Bellas Artes. Biennial competitions began to be held through 1960. (They were resumed in 1972.) The Trujillo regime also had works of art commissioned for the purpose of decorating the halls of the presidential palace and other public areas. As happened in other areas of the arts, the self-exiled Spanish and European refugees who fled, respectively, the Spanish Civil War and World War II, arrived in the Dominican Republic invited by Trujillo.[5] These multitalented professionals were up to date with the latest artistic movements and techniques. For the most part the painters and sculptors of the group continued the work they had carried out in Europe. But their influence and mere presence in the country left a lasting impression on a large new generation of artists of the mid–twentieth century.

The four most influential Spanish painters and sculptors who immigrated to the Dominican Republic were José Gausachs (1889–1959), José Vela Zanetti (1913–), Eugenio Fernández Granell (1912–), and Manolo Pascual (1902–). Gausachs, who established the School of Fine Arts in Santo Domingo, was an indefatigable teacher of post-impressionism and art appreciation in general. Among his most outstanding students who earned national and international acclaim in their own right are Gilberto Hernández Ortega (1924–1978), Clara Ledesma (1924–), Fernando Peña Defilló (1928–), and Ada Balcácer (1930–). Vela Zanetti (1913–) was a painter and muralist who was commissioned to paint murals in many public buildings. Among others he painted the mural featured in the United Nations headquarters in New York City. In the Dominican Republic his most famous murals are those with a religious theme in the Church of la Merced in Santo Domingo and the murals in the Palace of Justice, the National Bank, and the School of Medicine and National Library of the Universidad Autónoma de Santo Domingo. His style is epic and realistic with an occasionally geometric-based perspective. In addition to being a teacher of painting in the School of Fine Arts, Fernández Granell was the founder of the National Symphony Orchestra in 1941, and its first violinist. He also was one of the founders and the editor of the *Poesía Sorprendida* poetry review, and was a writer for the *La Nación* newspaper. Manolo Pascual, a sculptor, was the first director of the School of Fine Arts. Some of his protegés include Domingo Liz (1931–), Luichy Martínez Richiez (1928–), Antonio Prats Ventós (1925–), and Antonio Toribio (1924–).

Dominicans influenced by European visitors, such as Gausachs, deserve mention here. Hernández Ortega's art evolves from neorealism through works that achieve an assimilation of man and landscape. From there he moves to expressionism where a predominance of black and deformed images depict the horrors of the 1960s in the Dominican Republic. Ledesma paints mermaids, stars, and flowers to evoke the magic of the island. In her early years she dealt with the topic of the black man and woman in schematic drawings. Peña Defilló, considered one of the premier abstractionist painters of the Caribbean, spent the decade of the 1950s in exile in Madrid and Paris realizing abstract paintings. Upon his return in 1963, he dedicated himself to works of gigantic proportions in which he explored popular religious practices through spiritual and symbolic expression. Balcácer returned from self-exile in New York in 1962. She then produced a series titled the *Bacá* after the religious deity present in Dominican synchretism. Her portrayal of this mythical character borders on caricature. She also studied the Dominican woman, fusing her with nature, and most recently has experimented with the effects of light and color. Guillo Pérez, (1926–), a disciple of Yoryi Morel rather than Gausachs, paints abstract-expressionist painting, which he defines as "tropical structuralism." Pérez has enjoyed enormous commercial success as his paintings appeal to the tastes of the upper and middle classes.

One of the art subjects that was introduced by the Europeans was that of the black person, a figure that was very popular in Europe as of the 1920s but not widely considered a source of inspiration for Dominican artists, with the possible exception of Colson. The mulatto and the black were painted as products of their society and culture including voodoo magic and poverty. The means for portraying these situations included surrealism, magical-realism, neorealism, and expressionism.

Two important visitors during the 1940s also contributed to the rapid modernization of Dominican art and the search for a new image in painting and other aspects of culture. One was Wilfredo Lam, a Cuban surrealist painter. He spent three months in the Republic in 1941 exchanging ideas and techniques. André Bréton, the father of surrealism and the author of the manifesto for the movement, spent some time in the capital on two occasions. In 1941 he arrived with celebrated ethnologist and sociologist Claude Lévi-Strauss, and the second time he visited was in 1946. On both occasions he showed great interest for the work of the *Poesía Sorprendida* movement, and was an inspiration to all the artists who met him.

The turmoil of the 1960s with the assassination of Trujillo, the short-lived presidency of Bosch, and the Civil War brought about a marriage of literature with the visual arts. Groups associated with literary trends such as *El Puño* (*The Fist*), *La Máscara* (*The Mask*), and *La Isla* (*The Island*) incorporated poets, narrators, playwrights, painters, draftsmen, muralists, and sculptors. Poetic texts appeared as part of a painting or a poster, and to this day the collaboration between the painter and the poet is immediate. A newly published book of poetry is valued as much for its content as for the images on its cover, two expressions of the same work. Another manifestation of this collaboration is in the use of poetic text as part of a collage. This approach was limited to the political art of the 1960s and 1970s. The painters who distinguished themselves during this period include Cándido Bidó (1936–), José Cestero (1937–), Silvano Lora (1931–), Elsa Núñez (1943–), Ramón Oviedo (1927–), Soucy de Pellerano (1928–), José Rincón Mora (1938–), Danilo de los Santos (1944–), Jorge Severino (1946?–) and Iván Tovar (1942–). Bidó paints peasant customs featuring highly stylized figures with classic countenances. The paintings, in primary colors, have been extremely popular, assuring Bidó the position as one of the better known painters of the country. Cestero uses neorealism and postimpressionism to depict street people and scenes. Lora has earned international fame with his performance art posters and murals. These collages, which feature large plates, funeral wreaths, or airplanes dropping bombs, are made from raw materials and rubbish and always depict his island nation in the landscape. Núñez's focus on the woman evolved from dark expressionism to decorative lyricism. For her, the body and the landscape can be mixed to represent the island. Oviedo denounces social injustice and painfully portrays the horror of the 1960s, emphasizing the color red. In more recent times his interest has focused on a representation of Taíno art. Pellerano applied geometrically conceived images to the construction of mobiles made from metal wastes. She is the pioneer for this media and for the creation of artistic installations and scenes. Rincón Mora has tackled different artistic media including painting, drawing, engraving and stained-glass work. His works feature the color gold, crosses, and thick slabs of black along with movement and color to express existential fear combined with religious mysticism. He has lived in Munich,

Germany, since 1963 where he has created stained-glass windows for German churches. Rincón Mora has also worked on the stained-glass windows of the Cathedral in Santo Domingo. Severino's salient contribution is the dignity he bestows upon the black race through his dramatic portraits with their stale color-contrasts of black and white. Danilo de los Santos and Iván Tovar are painters of surrealism. De los Santos' works betrays African influences. He is currently an art historian and curator of Dominican art. Tovar has been more influenced by European tendencies in surrealistic expression, having lived seven years in Paris, and having participated in numerous European exhibits where he is well known.

The art of engraving, previously championed by Ada Balcácer, was revived by Frank Almánzar (1946–1985) and Rosa Tavárez (1939–) in the 1970s. Almánzar worked with silkscreening, within which he depicted topics of everyday politics and alienation. Tavárez portrayed social injustice and women's submissiveness using harsh images of abuse, thus denouncing this troubling reality in the Dominican Republic.

The artists who came of age in the 1970s represent current forms of artistic expression, a symbiosis of and experimentation with all recent artistic trends, at times neorealistic, while at others abstract. Expressionism, surrealism, paintings that function as sculptures, installations, mobiles, multimedia presentations, and performance art are all at play simultaneously. Many of the artists of the 1970s lived in Paris or Madrid and returned in the 1980s. They include the first Dominican to experiment with photorealism, Alberto Bass (1949–); Dionisio Blanco (1954–); metal sculptor Joaquín Ciprián (1950–); García Cordero (1951–); Alonso Cuevas (1953–); Aurelio Grisanty (1949–); Antonio Guadalupe (1941–); José Miura (1948–); Manuel Montilla (1948–); José Perdomo (1943–); Alberto Ulloa (1950–); and Fernando Ureña Rib (1951–).

The artists of the 1990s, whose art is highly individual, participate in biennial competitions and exhibit their works in galleries throughout the world. These include Tony Capellán (1955–), José García Cordero (1951–), Martín López (1955–), Marcos Lora Read (1965–), Jorge Pineda (1961–), Belkis Ramírez (1957–), Raúl Recio (1965–), Freddy Rodríguez (1945–), Uruguayan-born Fernando Valera (1951–), and Bismarck Victoria (1952–). Capellán is a mixed-media artist combining engraving with painting and installations. García Cordero is an architect whose work is inspired by dreams and depicts auguring fragmented landscapes and figures. López works with film and video in addition to being a painter and an art critic. Lora Read sculpts in bronze, whereas Pineda is an expert lithographer whose works denounce social injustice. Ramírez combines many techniques in her works, including silk-screening, engraving, lithography, intaglios, and mixed-media installations, usually on a very large scale. Ramírez's themes also explore social conditions. Recio is a draftsman and engraver, Rodríguez is a textile designer, Varela is a graphic arts painter, and Victoria is a marble sculptor.

Dominican visual artists in New York have struggled for recognition just as their compatriots in the Republic have. In the 1980s a group including Bismarck Victoria, Freddy Rodríguez, Eligio Reynoso, Magno Laracuente, and Tito Cánepa founded an association called Dominican Visual Artists of New York whose aim was to give exposure to Dominican art by both New York–born and Dominican-born artists. Over time this group has been successful in convincing art patrons to sponsor exhibits of Dominican art in highly frequented venues.

PHOTOGRAPHY

Photography as an art form has been slow to develop in the Dominican Republic. As is the case in many countries, the technique and experimentation associated with it were explored in the latter part of the nineteenth century. The first photography club of the republic was founded in Santiago in 1968 by, among others, Domingo Batista. A colleague and fellow photographer Wilfredo García established a similar club in the capital the same year. The objective of these clubs was to underscore the legitimacy of photography as an art form and as an important component of the cultural world. In the Dominican Republic photography was recognized officially as an art form when it was sanctioned to participate in its own category in biennial competitions beginning in the late 1970s.

The father of Dominican photography was Epifanio Billini (1823–1892), who as part of La Trinitaria group was known for his portraits of leading figures in the movement for independence. Other amateur photographers, among them those who distinguished themselves as painters, sculptors, and architects, have left samples of their experimentation. It was not until the 1990s that Dominican photographers gained international recognition for their work. The most renowned Dominican photographers are Domingo Batista and Polibio Díaz. Others who have been honored for their work include Carlos Acero, Pepa Acedo, Maritza Alvarez, Clara Barletta, María Rosa Jiménez, David Martínez, Luis Nova, Martín Rodríguez, Carlos Sanlley, José Alfredo Victoria, and Vicente Yens.

Domingo Batista, who was born in Santiago, is by far the most recognized name in Dominican photography, not only because of the remarkable quality of his art but for his commercial success. His photography is considered to be beautiful, elegant, and traditional with regard to his favorite subject matter: the landscapes of his native country, captured in the light of all times of the day and night. Díaz, who was born in Barahona, is the rebel photographer. A civil engineer who studied photography at Texas A&M University, he deliberately goes against all traditional precepts with regard to photographing under specific lighting requirements. He works under the merciless light of the noonday sun. His photographs are spontaneous and have even been described as frenetic. Whereas Batista paints a paradisical country with his photographs, as revealed in such collections as *Color dominicano* ("Dominican Color") and *Tiempo de luz* ("Time for Light"), Díaz searches for Dominican identity in its people, exploring particularly the racial dilemma that plagues this nation. He also studies popular culture as is evidenced by his collections of photographs titled *Espantapájaros del sur* ("Scarecrows of the South") which are actually voodoo effigies erected in fields for the purpose of thwarting evil spirits. Another subject of study for Díaz is the celebration of Carnival and its many manifestations, collected in the book *Imágenes de carnaval* (*Images of Carnival*).

CONCLUSION

Through architecture, painting, sculpture, and photography, Dominican artists have immortalized their interpretation of the Dominican landscape, its history, its religious practices, its customs, and its people. Dominican architects strive for an individual expression as their building designs are continually more embracing of the local flora and fauna. Dominican painters and sculptors have seemed the most free of all artists with regard to governmental control and suppression perhaps because, for the most part, their work has not been politically inspired. Social conditions have been a source of inspiration for painters and photographers particularly as many have portrayed the life and conditions of the common person. The work that Dominican photographers, sculptors, painters, and architects have achieved sets the Dominican Republic apart and merits further study.

NOTES

1. One of Joaquín Balaguer's major political objectives was the promotion of the tourist industry. As a result, many parts of Santo Domingo and the surrounding areas experienced an unprecedented surge in building activity during his presidential terms. There was an explosion in hotel construction to accommodate the anticipated

arrival of tourists. The renovation of the colonial area was also a part of this endeavor. The activity therein accelerated with the quinquecentennial celebration plans.

2. Rodrigo de Liendo is the Dominican Republic's first architect of note. He proposed many projects, among them, a double arched bridge to traverse the Ozama River. The collapse of this bridge as it was being built so angered those who had financially supported the project that Liendo was forced to build something for free to benefit colonial Santo Domingo. The result was the first aqueduct of the New World. This aqueduct was unearthed while restoring colonial buildings in preparation for the quinquecentennial celebration (Báez López-Penha 79).

3. Neoclassicism with its inference to universal cultural refinement, ideal order, and the implication of authority was the quintessential expression of Trujillo's power.

4. Many architects have significantly contributed to the urban landscape including Milán Lora, Mariano Sanz, Eduardo Selman, and Plácido Piña.

5. Santo Domingo in 1939 was a small provincial city. The refugees coming from Spain were for the most part Republicans fleeing the newly established dictatorship of Francisco Franco. Other Europeans who arrived at the same time, mostly from France, were for the most part Jewish professionals willing to go anywhere to escape Nazi concentration camps. The group included sculptors, painters, draftsmen, muralists, musicians, writers, professors, and journalists. Their arrival began the process of modernizing city life and brought western-style culture to the country.

Bibliography

Abreu de Suriel, Nilda. *Los ménus de Navidad de Doña Nilda.* Santo Domingo: Taller, 1985.

Alba, Orlando. "A propósito de la identidad lingüística dominicana." *Eme eme: Estudios dominicanos* 72 (1984): 31–34.

Albert, Celsa. *Los africanos y nuestra isla.* Santo Domingo: Búho, 1987.

Alberto Hernández, Julio. *Música tradicional dominicana.* Santo Domingo: Julio D. Portigo, Editores, 1969.

Alcántara Almánzar, José. *Antología de la literatura dominicana.* Santo Domingo: Editora Cultural, 1972.

———. *La aventura interior.* Santo Domingo: Banco Central de la República Dominicana, 1997.

———. *Callejón sin salida.* Santo Domingo: Taller, 1975.

———. *Los escritores dominicanos y la cultura.* Santo Domingo: Instituto Tecnológico de Santo Domingo, 1990.

———. *Las máscaras de la seducción.* Santo Domingo: Taller, 1980.

———. *Narrativa y sociedad en Hispanoamérica.* Santo Domingo: Instituto Tecnológico de Santo Domingo, 1984.

———. *Panorama sociocultural de la República Dominicana.* Santo Domingo: Amigo del Hogar, 1997.

———. *El sabor de lo prohibo.* Río Piedras: Universidad de Puerto Rico, 1993.

———. *Testimonios y profanaciones.* Santo Domingo: Taller, 1978.

———. *Viaje al otro mundo.* Santo Domingo: Taller, 1973.

———, ed. *Imágenes de Hector Inchaústegui Cabral.* Santo Domingo: Taller, 1980.

Alegría-Pons, José Francisco. *Gagá y vudú en la República Dominicana: Ensayos antropológicos.* Santo Domingo: El Chango Prieto, 1993.

Almánzar, Ramón. "La Cadena Sur lleva el programa de Corporán a los países árabes, Asia y Europa." *Listín Digital* Online, 2, no. 712, Internet, 1998.

———. " 'La vida hoy' sustituye a los meridianos del Canal 4." *Listín Digital* Online, 2, no. 715, Internet, 1998.

Alvarez, Julia. *Homecoming.* New York: Grove Press, 1984.

———. *How the García Girls Lost Their Accent.* Chapel Hill, NC: Algonquin Books, 1991. Reprint, New York: Plum 1992.

———. *In the Time of the Butterflies.* Chapel Hill, NC: Algonquin Press, 1994.

———. *¡Yo!* Chapel Hill, NC: Algonquin Books, 1997.

Alvarez-Altman, Grace. "Literary Onomastics Typology in Manuel Rueda's Dramas." *Literary Onomastic Studies* 10(1983): 285–299.

Alvarez Vega, Bienvenido. "La República: Más allá del 2000; los medios de comunicación." *Rumbo*, May 14, 1997: 52.

Angulo Guridi, Javier. *Iguaniona.* Santo Domingo: Imprenta de J. J. Machado, 1981.

ASIEX. *Living in the D.R.: A Transcultural Handbook to Life in the Dominican Republic.* Santo Domingo: Dominican Association of Foreign Investment Companies, Inc. (ASIEX), n.d.

Baciu, Stefan. "Juan Bosch un hombre solo." *Eme eme: Estudios dominicanos* 11, no. 63 (1982): 1–71.

Báez, Clara, and Mercedes Matrillé. *Mercado laboral para las mujeres formadas en ocupaciones no tradicionales: caso los Mina Norte.* Santo Domingo: CE-MUJER, 1994.

Báez Díaz, Tomás. *La mujer dominicana.* Santo Domingo: Editora Educativa Dominicana, 1980.

Báez López-Penha, José Ramón. *Por qué Santo Domingo es así.* Santo Domingo: Amigo del Hogar, 1992.

Baeza Flores, Alberto. *La poesía dominicana el siglo XX: Historia crítica, estudio comparativo y estilístico.* Santo Domingo: Orfeo, 1986.

———. *Los poetas dominicanos del 1965: Una generación importante y distinta.* Santo Domingo: Orfeo, 1965.

Balaguer Ricardo, Joaquín. *El Cristo de la libertad: Vida de Juan Pablo Duarte.* Madrid: Talleres de Selecciones Gráficas, 1970.

———. *Historia de la Literatura Dominicana.* 5th ed. Buenos Aires: Gráfica Guadalupe, 1972.

Balcácer, Juan Daniel. *Algunas reflexiones en torno a la democracia dominicana.* Santo Domingo: Corripio, 1993.

Bandon, Alexandra. *Dominican Americans.* Parsippany, NJ: New Discovery Books, 1995.

Banham, Martin, ed. *The Cambridge Guide to Theater.* Cambridge: University Press, 1995, 299–300.

Bell, Ian. *The Dominican Republic.* Boulder, CO: Westview Press, 1981.

Benerías, Lourdes. *Reproducción, producción y división sexual del trabajo.* Santo Domingo: Ediciones Populares Feministas, 1984.

Berroa, Rei, ed. *Revista Iberoamericana: Número especial sobre la literatura dominicana en el siglo XX* 54 (1988): 142.

Betances, Emelio, and Hobart Spalding. "The Dominican Republic—After the Caudillos." *North American Congress on Latin America (NACLA)* 30, no. 5 (1997): 16–19.

Blonda Acosta, Máximo Aviles. *Las manos vacías.* Ciudad Trujillo: Arte y Cine, 1959.

———. *Teatro.* Santo Domingo: Sociedad de Autores y Compositores Dramáticos, 1968.

Bobea, Lillian. "An Experiment in Local Democracy." *NACLA* 30, no. 5 (1997): 27–30.

Bonnelly de Díaz, Aída. *Breve historia de la música dominicana.* Santo Domingo: Banco de Reservas, 1984.

———. *En torno a la música: Guía para la apreciación musical.* Santo Domingo: Taller, 1978.

———. *Los niños. Las artes: cuentos para niños.* Santo Domingo: Amigo del Hogar, 1994.

———. *Por los trillos del arte: vivencias, semblanzas e inquietudes.* Santo Domingo: Amigo del Hogar, 1996.

———. *Retablo de costumbres dominicanas.* Santo Domingo: Taller, 1991.

———. *Variaciones.* 2nd ed. Santo Domingo: Taller, 1986.

Bosch, Juan. *Composición social dominicana: Historia e interpretación.* 14th ed. Santo Domingo: Alfa y Omega, 1984.

———. *Cuentos escritos antes del exilio.* Santo Domingo: Alfa y Omega, 1980.

———. *Cuentos escritos en el exilio y apuntes sobre el arte de escribir cuentos.* Santo Domingo: Librería Dominicana, 1962.

———. *La mañosa.* 1936. Santo Domingo: Alfay y Omega, 1982.

———. *Más cuentos escritos en el exilio.* Santo Domingo: Alfa y Omega, 1980.

———. *El oro y la paz.* 1976. 3rd ed. Santo Domingo: Amigo del Hogar, 1978.

———. *Trujillo: Causas de una dictadura sin ejemplo.* Lima: Populibros Peruanos, 1959.

Brusiloff, Carmenchu, and Juan Alfredo Biaggi. *Santo Domingo.* Santo Domingo: Imprenta Vallejo Hermanos, n.d.

Cabral, Manuel del. *Obra poética completa.* Santo Domingo: Alfa y Omega, 1976.

Cabrera, José. *Crisis de la publicidad y la mercadotecnia en la República Dominicana.* Santo Domingo: Taller, 1980.

Calder, Bruce. *The Impact of Intervention.* Santo Domingo: Fundación Cultural Dominicana, 1989.

Calventi, Rafael. *Arquitectura contemporánea en República Dominicana: Contemporary Architecture in the Dominican Republic.* Santo Domingo: Banco Nacional de Resevas, 1986.

Cambeira, Alan. *Quisqueya la Bella: The Dominican Republic in Historical and Cultural Perspective.* Armonk, NY: M. E. Sharpe, 1997.

Capitan, Marien A. "Una semana conociendo a la patria." *Hoy,* March 26, 1998.

Cartagena Portalatín, Aída. *Escalera para Electra.* 2nd ed. Santo Domingo: Taller, 1980.

———. *Tablero: doce cuentos de lo popular a lo culto.* Santo Domingo: Taller, 1978.

———. *La tarde en que murió Estefanía.* Santo Domingo: Taller, 1983.

———. *Una mujer está sola.* Santo Domingo: Colección La Isla Necesaria, 1955.

———. *Vísperas del sueño.* Santo Domingo: *La poesía sorprendida,* Colección El Desvelado Solitario, 1945.

———. *Yania tierra.* 1945. Santo Domingo: Colección Montesinos, 1981.

Casas, Bartolomé de las. *Brevísima relación de la destrucción de las Indias.* 3 vols. 1552. Buenos Aires: Ediciones Mar Océano, 1953.

———. *Historia de las Indias.* 5 vols. 1520. Madrid: Impresora de M. Ginesta, 1875–76.

Casas, Fray Bartolomé lás. *Historia de las Indias.* 2 vols. Agustín Millares Carlo, ed. 2nd ed. México: Fondo de Cultura Económica, 1951.

Cassá, Roberto. *Historia social y económica de la República Dominicana.* 2 vols. 8th ed. Santo Domingo: Alfa y Omega, 1986.

———. "Negotiated Elections: The Old Boss Steps to the Side." Translated by NACLA. *NACLA* 30, no. 5 (1997): 20–23, 26.

———. *Los taínos de La Española.* Santo Domingo: Universidad Autónoma de Santo Domingo, 1993.

Castillo, José del. "Las inmigraciones y su aporte a la cultura dominicana (Finales del siglo XIX y principio del XX)." In Bernardo Vega et al., *Ensayos sobre cultura dominicana.* 5th ed. Santo Domingo: Amigo del Hogar, 1997.

Castillo, José del, and Manuel A. García Arévalo. *Antología del merengue: Anthology of the Merengue.* Translated by Jeannie Ash de Pou and Giselle Scanlon. Santo Domingo: Corripio, 1989.

Castillo, Efraím. *Curriculm (el síndrome de la visa).* Santo Domingo: Taller, 1982.

Castro, Aníbal de. "El hombre, el presidente y el compromiso de liberar al país de las miserias." *Rumbo,* December 9, 1996: 48–58.

Censión, Viriato. *Los que falsificaron la firma de Dios.* Santo Domingo: Taller, 1992.

Céspedes, Diógenes. *Lenguaje y poesía en Santo Domingo en el Siglo XX.* Santo Domingo: UASD, 1985.

Cestero, Tulio Manuel. *La sangre: una vida bajo la tiranía.* 1914. Santo Domingo: Ediciones Saber, 1974.

Chang-Rodríguez, Eugenio. *The Lingering Crisis: A Case Study of the Dominican Republic.* New York: Las Américas Publishing Company, 1969.

Chang-Rodríguez, Raquel, and Malva E. Filer. *Voces de Hispanoamérica: Antología literaria.* 2nd ed. New York: Heinle and Heinle, 1996.

"City Found by Columbus Found Again." *Mobile Register,* March 29, 1997: 2.

Cocco de Filippis, Daisy, ed. *Antología de cuentos escritos por mujeres dominicanas.* Santo Domingo: Taller, 1992.

———. *Bilingual Anthology of the Poetry of Aída Cartagena Portalatín.* Translated by Emma Jane Robinett. Santo Domingo: Taller, 1988.

————. *Estudios semióticos de poesía dominicana.* Santo Domingo: Taller, 1984.

————. *Sin otro profeta que su canto: Antología de poesía escrita por dominicanas.* Santo Domingo: Taller, 1988.

CODETEL. *Dominican Republic Tourist Guide 93/94.* Santo Domingo: Compañía Dominicana de Teléfonos (CODETEL), 1994.

Contín Aybar, Nestor. *Historia de la literatura dominicana.* 3 vols. Santo Domingo: Taller, 1982.

Contreras, Hilma. *Cuatro cuentos.* Ciudad Trujillo: Stella, 1953.

————. *Entre dos silencios.* Santo Domingo: Taller, 1987.

————. *El ojo de Dios. Cuentos de la clandestinidad.* Santo Domingo: Ediciones Dominicanas, 1962.

Cordero, Margarita. "La ciudad que no muere." *Rumbo,* December 30, 1996: 48–72.

Crassweller, Robert D. *Trujillo: The Life and Times of a Caribbean Dictator.* New York: Macmillan, 1966.

Cross Frías, Elvira Angélica. *Sarna con gusto no pica y si pica no mortifica: Proverbios e idiotismos dominicanos y quijotescos.* Caracas: Torino, 1995.

Cruz Hierro, Ynmaculada. "El ballet comienza a dejar de ser cenicienta de las artes." *Listín Digital* Online, 2, no. 730, Internet, November 1998.

————. "Tremendo bonche en la celebración del tercer año del canal de Juan Luis Guerra." *Listín Digital* Online, 2, no. 710, Internet, October 1998.

Cuello H., José Israel. *Contratación de mano de obra haitiana destinada a la industria azucarera dominicana: 1952–1986.* Santo Domingo: Taller, 1997.

Dalurzo, Beatriz F. *La República Dominicana: País símbolo.* Santo Domingo: Editora Cultural Dominicana, 1975.

Deive, Carlos Esteban. "La herencia africana en la cultura dominicana actual." In Bernardo Vega et al., *Ensayos sobre cultura dominicana.* 5th ed. Santo Domingo: Amigo del Hogar, 1997.

————. *Las devastaciones.* Santo Domingo: Alfa y Omega, 1979.

————. *Tangomangos.* Santo Domingo: Fundación de Cultura Dominicana, 1997.

Díaz, Junot. *Drown.* New York: Riverhead Books, 1996.

Díaz Grullón, Virgilio. *Antinostalgia de una era.* Santo Domingo: Fundación Cultural Dominicana, 1989.

————. *De niños, hombres, y fantasmas.* Santo Domingo: Colección Montesinos, 1981.

————. *Los algarrobos también sueñan.* Santo Domingo: Taller, 1978.

————. *Más allá del espejo: Cuentos.* Santo Domingo: Taller, 1983.

Dobal, Carlos. "Herencia española en la cultura dominicana de hoy." In Bernardo Vega et al., *Ensayos sobre cultura dominicana.* 5th ed. Santo Domingo: Amigo del Hogar, 1997.

————. *Vodú y magia en Santo Domingo.* Santo Domingo: Taller, 1996.

Domínguez, Franklin. *El último instante. La Broma del senador.* Ciudad Trujillo: Editora Arte y Cine, 1958.

————. *Teatro, Espigas maduras, Antígona-humor, Los actores, El encuentro.* Santo Domingo: Ediciones de la Sociedad de Autores y Dompositores Dramáticos, 1968.

Duarte, Isis et al. *Población y condición de la mujer en la República Dominicana.* Santo Domingo: Instituto de Estudios de Población y Desarrollo, 1990.

Ferguson, James. "The Two Caudillos." *NACLA* 30, no. 5 (1997): 24–25.

Fernández, Felix. "La estructuración gramatical del español dominicano y la identidad de los dominicanos: Una interpretación." *Eme eme: Estudios dominicanos* 72 (1984): 45–58.

Fernández Olmos, Margarita. *La cuentística de Juan Bosch: Un análisis crítico-cultural.* Santo Domingo: Alfa y Omega, 1982.

Fernández-Rocha, Carlos. "Los machos coquetos." *El Caribe,* November 2, 1996: 29.

Ferreras, Ramón Alberto. *Las Mirabal.* Santo Domingo: Media Isla, 1982.

Fiallo, Fabio. *Obras completas.* Santo Domingo: Sociedad Dominicana de Bibliófilos, 1980.

Franco Pichardo, Franklin. *Historia del pueblo dominicano.* 2 vols. Santo Domingo: Taller, 1992.

————. *Sobre racismo y antihaitianismo (y otros ensayos).* Santo Domingo: Vidal, 1997.

Galván, Manuel de Jesús. *Enriquillo: leyenda histórica dominicana (1503–1538).* 1882. Santo Domingo: Taller, 1985.

Galván, William. *Minerva Mirabal.* Santo Domingo: UASD, 1982.

García, Ivan. *Más allá de la búsqueda.* Santiago: Universidad Católica Madre y Maestra, 1967.

García Godoy, Federico. *Alma dominicana.* Santo Domingo: Imprenta La Cuna de América, 1911.

García Márquez, Gabriel. *Cien años de soledad.* 1967. 5th ed. Madrid: Cátedra, 1994.

————. *Guanuma: novela histórica.* Santo Domingo: Imprenta La Cuna de América, 1914.

————. *Rufinito.* 1908. 2nd ed. Santo Domingo: Secretaría de Estado de Educación, 1968.

Gerón, Candido. *Juan Bosch: Vida y obra narrativa.* Santo Domingo: Alfa y Omega, 1993.

Gil Fiallo, Laura. "Ada Balcácer y su Academia de Luz." *Rumbo,* January 13, 1997: 56–57.

————. "Alberto Bass en el Museo de Arte Moderno: La dirección vehemente." *Rumbo,* February 24, 1997: 56–57.

————. "Altos de Chavón: Más de una década en la senda del arte." *Rumbo,* September 23, 1996: 58.

————. "Belkys Ramírez e Inés Tolentino en la Bienal de La Habana." *Rumbo,* December 9, 1996: 72.

————. "Darío Suro: La última metamorfosis." *Rumbo,* February 3, 1997: 56–57.

———. "El dominicano Jaime Colson en la vanguardia barcelonesa." *Rumbo*, March 17, 1997: 56–57.

———. "La etapa barcelonesa de Jaime Colson." *Rumbo*, September 8, 1997: 57–58.

———. "Exposición de fotografías en beneficio de fe y alegría." *Rumbo*, October 7, 1996: 59.

———. "Exposición de instalaciones: Historia y contemporaneidad en el Museo de Arte Moderno." *Rumbo*, September 2, 1996: 46–48.

———. "Exposición fotográfica del grupo Objectivo 10." *Rumbo*, June 23, 1997: 61.

———. "Gaspar Mario Cruz y el retorno de la escultura: un libro y una retrospectiva." *Rumbo*, November 3, 1997: 58.

———. "José Alcántara Almánzar: la función del crítico es orientar." *Rumbo*, September 11, 1996: 58–59.

———. "*Lengua de paraíso* de José Mármol." *Rumbo*, June 16, 1997: 57–58.

———. "Las migraciones españolas y el arte dominicano." *Rumbo*, October 28, 1996: 57–58.

———. "Natacha Sánchez y el nuevo giro en la dirección del Teatro Nacional." *Rumbo*, February 10, 1997: 59.

———. "Oviedo & Guayasmín: Un encuentro afortunado." *Rumbo*, August 4, 1997: 57.

———. "La semiótica de los materiales en las instalaciones de Tony Capellán." *Rumbo*, June 9, 1997: 57–58.

———. "La sobrerrealidad del eros en la pintura de Iván Tovar." *Rumbo*, March 30, 1998: 55–57.

———. "Vida y muerte de la pintura dominicana y el conscurso Hoteles Barceló." *Rumbo*, November 25, 1996: 56–58.

Gleijeses, Piero. *The Dominican Crisis: The 1965 Constitutionalist Revolt and American Intervention*. Translated by Lawrence Lipson. Baltimore, MD: The Johns Hopkins University Press, 1978.

Gómez, Alfau, and Luis Emilio. *Ayer: o Santo Domingo de hace 50 años*. Ciudad Trujillo: Pol Hermanos, 1944.

González, Nancie. "El carnaval en Santiago de los Caballeros." *Eme eme: Estudios dominicanos* 9(1973): 80–95.

Guerra, Juan Luis. "Elena." *Mudanza y acarreo*. Santo Domingo: Discos Karen, 1985.

———. "Visa para un sueño." *Ojalá que llueva café*. Santo Domingo: Discos Karen, 1988.

Guerrero, Miguel. *Enero de 1962: ¡El despertar dominicano!* Santo Domingo: Mograf, 1991.

———. *El golpe de estado: Historia del derrocamiento de Juan Bosch*. 3rd ed. Santo Domingo: Corripio, 1993.

———. *Los últimos días de la Era de Trujillo*. Santo Domingo: Corripio, 1991.

Gutiérrez, Franklin, ed. *Antología de la poesía dominicana del siglo XX (1912–1995)*. New York: Ediciones Alcance, 1995.

Guzmán, Reyes. "Lope Balaguer ve incierto proceso de mejoría para los artistas dominicanos." *Hoy*, March 26, 1998: 14D.

Haggerty, Richard A., ed. *Dominican Republic and Haiti: Country Studies*. 2nd ed. Washington, DC: Federal Research Division, 1991.

Handelsman, Michael. "Balaguer, Blas Jiménez y lo afro en la República Dominicana." *Journal of the Southeastern Council on Latin American Studies* 29 (March 1997): 85–91.

Hendricks, Glenn. *The Dominican Diaspora: From the Dominican Republic to New York City—Villagers in Transition*. New York: Teachers College Press, Columbia University, 1974.

Henríquez Ureña, Max. *Breve historia del modernismo*. México: Fondo de Cultura Económica, 1954.

———. *La cultura y las letras coloniales en Santo Domingo*. Buenos Aires: Universidad de Buenos Aires, 1936.

———. *Panorama histórico de la literatura cubana*. New York: Las Américas Publishing Co., 1963.

———. *El retorno de los galeones y otros ensayos*. México: Ediciones de Andrea, 1963.

Henríquez Ureña, Pedro. *Las corrientes literarias en la América Latina*. México: Fondo de Cultura Económica, 1949.

———. *Estudios de versificación española*. Buenos Aires: Universidad de Buenos Aires, 1961.

———. *Estudios mexicanos*. México: Fondo de Cultura Económica, 1984.

———. *Historia de la cultura en la América Hispánica*. México: Fondo de Cultura Económica, 1964.

———. *Literatura dominicana*. New York: Bailly-Bailliere, 1917.

———. *Obras completas*. 10 vols. Juan Jacobo de Lara, ed. Santo Domingo: Universidad Nacional Pedro Henríquez Ureña, 1976–1980.

———. *Seis ensayos en busca de nuestra expresión*. 1928.

———. *La utopía de América*. Pról., Fafael Gutiérrez Girardot. Compilación y cronología, Angel Rama y Rafael Gutiérrez Girardot. Caracas: Biblioteca Ayacucho, 1978.

Hernández, Angela. *Alótropos*. Santo Domingo: Editora Impretur, 1989.

———. *Las mariposas no le temen a los cactus*. Santo Domingo: Editora Universitaria, 1985.

———. *Masticar una rosa*. Santo Domingo: Editora Impretur, 1993.

Hernández, Ramona. "The Construction of a New Identity for Dominican Women Workers." *The Women of Hispaniola: Moving Towards Tomorrow: Selected Proceedings of the 1993 Conference*. Daisy Cocco de Filippis, ed. New York: City University of New York, 1993, 41–51.

Hernández Caamaño, Ida. *Viajera del polvo*. Santo Domingo: Instituto Tecnológico de Santo Domingo, 1993.

Hernández Franco, Tomás. *Yélida.* 3rd ed. Santo Domingo: Taller, 1975.

Hernández Soto, Carlos. *Morir en Villa Mella: Ritos funerarios afrodominicanos.* Santo Domingo: Centro Para la Investigación y Acción Social en el Caribe (CIASCA), 1996.

Hoetnik, H. *The Dominican People 1850–1900: Notes for a Historical Sociology.* Translated by Stephen K. Ault. Baltimore, MD: Johns Hopkins University Press, 1982.

Holston, Mark. "La República Dominicana en doble exposición: En espectaculares imágenes, Domingo Batista y Polibio Díaz revelan la contrastante realidad de su país natal." *Américas* 49, no. 1 (1997): 30–39.

Inchaústegui, Arístides. *Por amor al arte: Notas sobre música, compositores e intérpretes dominicanos.* Santo Domingo: Editora Centenario, 1995.

Inchaústegui Cabral, Héctor. *De literatura dominicana siglo veinte.* 2nd ed. Santiago: Universidad Católica Madre y Maestra, 1973.

Inoa, Orlando. "Los árabes en Santo Domingo." *Estudios Sociales* 24, no. 85 (1991): 35–58.

Jiménez, Luis A. "El sujeto femenino fin-de-siglo en la cuentística de Virginia Elena Ortea." *South Eastern Latin Americanist* 42, no. 1 (1998): 13–20.

Jiménez, R. Emilio. *Al amor del bohío: Tradiciones y costumbres dominicanas.* Vol. 1. Santo Domingo: Montalvo, 1927.

Jordan, Howard. "Dominicans in New York: Getting a Slice of the Apple." *NACLA Report on the Americas* 30, no. 5 (1997): 37–42.

Jorge, Bernarda. *El canto de tradición oral de República Dominicana.* Santo Domingo: Amigos del Hogar, 1996.

Knight, Melvin M. *The Americans in Santo Domingo.* New York: Arno Press, 1970.

Kuret de Rainieri, Haydee. "La mujer y el turismo en República Dominicana." *Rumbo,* September 30, 1996: 12–13.

Labourt, José. *Sana, sana, culito de rana.* . . . Santo Domingo: Taller, 1982.

Lebrón Saviñón, Mariano. *Historia de la cultura dominicana.* Vol. 4. Santo Domingo: Universidad Nacional Pedro Henríquez Ureña, 1982.

Lemonick, Michael D. "Before Columbus: Destroyed Almost Overnight by Spanish Invaders, the Culture of the Gentle Taíno Is Finally Coming to Light." *Time,* October 19, 1998: 76–77.

Lewis, Samella. *Caribbean Visions: Contemporary Painting and Sculpture.* Alexandria, VA: Art Services International, 1995.

Lizardo, Fradique. *Danzas y bailes folklóricos dominicano.* Santo Domingo: Taller, 1974.

———. *Instrumentos musicales folklóricos dominicanos: Idiófonos y membranófonos.* Santo Domingo: Editorial Santo Domingo, 1988.

———. *Metodología de la danza.* Santo Domingo: Taller, 1975.

Lockward, Alanna. "La herencia de Georges en el ojo místico de Juan Fidel Mieses." *Listín Digital* Online, 2, no. 723, Internet, November 1998.

Mariñez, Pablo A. "El proceso democrático en República Dominicana: Algunos rasgos fundamentales." *Estudios sociales* 26, no. 93 (1993): 27–39.

Marin Lezaeta, Ximena. "José Francisco Peña Gómez: 'Me apoyarán partidarios de Balaguer.' " *Cambio*, July 1, 1996: 60–61.

Mármol, José. *Deus ex machina.* Santo Domingo: Ediciones de Casa de Teatro, 1994.

———. *Encuentros con las mismas otredades I.* Santo Domingo: Colección Egro, 1985.

———. *Encuentros con las mismas otredades II.* Santo Domingo: Amigo del Hogar, 1989.

———. *La invención del día.* Santo Domingo: Instituto Tecnológico de Santo Domingo, 1989.

———. *Lengua del paraíso.* Santo Domingo: Ediciones de la Universidad Nacional Pedro Henríquez Ureña, 1993.

———. *El ojo del arúspice.* Santo Domingo: Colección Luna Cabeza Caliente, 1984.

Marrero Aristy, Ramón. *Over.* 1939. 8th ed. Santo Domingo: Taller, 1976.

Martí Martínez, José. "Bachata: amor, sexo y género." *Hoy*, July 2, 1997: 15D.

Martínez, Lusitania. *Actitudes femeninas frente a los oficios no tradicionales.* Santo Domingo: CE-MUJER, 1994.

Mejía-Ricart, G. Tirso. *La universidad, la iglesia y el estado en la República Dominicana.* Santo Domingo: UASD, 1980.

Miller, Jeannette. *Historia de la pintura dominicana.* 3d ed. Santo Domingo: Amigo del Hogar, 1983.

Minshall, Peter. "Carnival and Its Place in Caribbean Culture and Art." In E. Nancy Eickel, ed. *Caribbean Visions: Contemporary Painting and Sculpture.* Alexandria, VA: Arts Services International, 1995.

Mir, Pedro. *Amén de mariposas.* Santo Domingo: Nuevo Mundo, 1969.

———. *Cuando amaban las tierras comuneras.* México: Siglo XXI, 1978.

Moré Guaschino, Gustavo Luis. "Entrevista con el arquitecto William Reid Cabral." *Arquivox*, 1, no. 1 (1984): 11–14.

———. "Notas sobre forma e identidad en la arquitectura de 'La era de Trujillo.' " *Arquivox*, 1, no. 1 (1984): 3–10.

Moscoso Espinosa, Lulio, ed. *Historia de la televisión.* Santo Domingo: n.p. [1994?].

Moya Pons, Frank. "Los aliados de los restauradores." *Rumbo*, November 11, 1996: 8.

———. "Alimentos coloniales." *Rumbo*, February 17, 1997: 4.

———. "Cinco terremotos." *Rumbo*, December 16, 1996: 10.

———. "Composición racial dominicana." *Rumbo*, November 4, 1996: 4.

———. "Demografía 'mestiza.' " *Rumbo*, August 19, 1996: 4.

———. "Huracanes coloniales." *Rumbo*, September 16, 1996: 8.

———. "La literatura dominicana en cifras." *Rumbo*, May 5, 1997: 6.

———. "Maderas y tabaco durante la dominación haitiana." *Rumbo*, October 28, 1996: 8.

———. *Manual de la historia dominicana.* 10th ed. Santo Domingo: Caribbean Publishers, 1995.

———. "Mao y Valverde." *Rumbo,* March 17, 1997: 4.

———. "Los muertos de la Anexión." *Rumbo,* November 18, 1996: 4.

Murray, Gerald F. *El colmado: una investigación antropológica del negocio de comidas y bebidas en la República Dominicana.* 2nd ed. Santo Domingo: Amigo del Hogar, 1997.

Olivera, Otto. *Bibliografía de la literatura dominicana (1960–1982).* Lincoln, NB: Society of Spanish and Spanish-American Studies, 1984.

Olivo Peña, Gustavo. "La Mirabal: Una familia admirable." *Rumbo,* September 9, 1996: 26.

Ordoñez, Miguel Angel. "Cine 'Made in R.D.' la fábrica de sueños avanza al pasito." *Rumbo,* November 18, 1996: 53.

———. "El Pomier: La explosiva agonía de las 'pirámides dominicanas.' " *Rumbo,* September 23, 1996: 49–53.

Ortea, Virginia Elena. *Obras.* Catharina Vallejo, ed. Santo Domingo: Búho, 1997.

———. *Risas y lágrimas.* 1901. Santo Domingo: Editora Corripio, 1981.

Ossers Cabrera, Manuel Augusto. *La expresividad en la cuentística de Juan Bosch: Análisis estilístico.* Santo Domingo: Alfa y Omega, 1989.

Pacini Hernández, Deborah. *Bachata: A Social History of Dominican Popular Music.* Philadelphia: Temple University Press, 1995.

Pascal, Nanette R., and María P. Rojas. *Relaciones comerciales.* Lexington, MA: D.C. Heath, 1996.

Peix, Pedro. *La narrativa yugulada.* Santo Domingo: Alfa y Omega, 1981.

Peña, Angela. "Consígueme un dominicano." *Hoy,* July 8, 1997.

———. "Mondongo scam: Josefina Báez Pérez." *Hoy,* August 5, 1997: 12.

Peña Battle, Manuel Arturo. *Ensayos históricos.* Juan Daniel Balcácer, ed. Santo Domingo: Taller, 1989.

Pérez, José Joaquín. *Fantasías indígenas.* 1877. Santo Domingo: Taller 19781

Pérez, Renato. "Las aves acuáticas del Lago Enriquillo." *Rumbo,* September 30, 1996: 2–5.

———. "La extraña historia del Lago Enriquillo." *Rumbo,* September 16, 1996: 2–5.

———. "Mirada fría: Cocodrilos criollos en el Lago Enriquillo." *Rumbo,* October 28, 1996: 2–5.

———. "Monstruos bonitos." *Rumbo,* October 14, 1996: 2–5.

———. "Un mar de vida: Los arrecifes de coral." *Rumbo,* November 11, 1996: 2–5.

Pérez, Sara. "Las habilidades de un juez para no encontrar justicia." *Rumbo,* August 4, 1997: 38.

———. "Santos y señas de los santiagueses." *Rumbo,* October 7, 1996: 14.

Pessar, Patricia R. "Dominican Transnational Migration: Uneven Benefits Back Home and the Contingency of Return." In Emelio Betances and Hobart A. Spalding, eds. *The Dominican Republic Today: Realities and Perspectives.* New York: Bildner Center for Western Hemisphere Studies, 1996, 151–171.

Piña Contreras, Guillermo. *Doce en la literatura dominicana*. Santiago: Universidad Católica Madre y Maestra, 1982.

Poet, J. "He'll Make Latin Lovers of Us All." *Utne Reader* 57 (May-June 1993): 28–32.

Polanco Brito, Hugo. "Aporte de la iglesia en el Cibao a la causa nacional 1844–1880." *Eme eme: Estudios Dominicanos* 8, no. 48 (1980): 21–31.

Ramírez de Carías, María. *La cocina dominicana*. 2nd ed. Bogotá, Colombia: Impre Andes, 1994.

Ramos, Emelda, ed. *El folklore latinoamericano y del caribe*. Santo Domingo: Editora Tiempo, 1987.

Reid, Alastair. "Reflections: Waiting for Columbus." *New Yorker*, February 24, 1992: 57–75.

Rivera, Martha. *Geometría del vértigo*. Santo Domingo: El Nuevo Diario, 1995.

———. *He olvidado tu nombre*. Santo Domingo: Taller, 1997.

———. *20th Century y otros poemas*. Santo Domingo: Ediciones Armario Urbano, 1985.

Rivera, Severo. "Milly Quezada cantante merenguera." *Listín Digital* Online, 2, no. 695, Internet, 1998.

Rizik, Marisela. *El tiempo del olvido*. Santo Domingo: Taller, 1996.

Rodríguez Demorizi, Emilio. *La imprenta y los primeros periódicos de Santo Domingo*. Ciudad Trujillo: Imprenta San Francisco, 1944. Reprint, Santo Domingo: Talleres de Impresiones, 1973.

Rosario Candelier, Bruno. *Valores de las Letras Dominicanas*. Santiago: Pontífica Universidad Católica Madre y Maestra, 1991.

Rueda, Manuel. *Imágenes del dominicano*. Santo Domingo: Banco Central de la República Dominicana, 1998.

———. *Papeles de Sara y otros relatos*. Santo Domingo: Corripio, 1985.

———. *Teatro*. Santo Domingo: Sociedad de Autores y Compositores Dramáticos de la República Dominicana, 1968.

———. *Todo Santo Domingo*. Barcelona: Palaudarias, 1980.

———. *La Trinitaria Blanca: (comedia dramática en tres actos)*. Ciudad Trujillo: Librería Dominicana, 1957.

Sáez S. J., José Luis. "Cinco siglos de historia dominicana (1492–1992)." *Estudios sociales: República Dominicana 500 años depúes*. 25, no. 89/90 (1992): 15–22.

———. "Gobierno de la iglesia dominicana (1511–1992)." *Estudios sociales: República Dominicana 500 años depúes* 25, no. 89/90 (1992): 23–34.

Safa, Helen I. "Where the Big Fish Eat the Little Fish: Women's Work in the Free-Trade Zones." *NACLA* 30, no. 5 (1997): 31–36.

Santos, Danilo de los. *La pintura en la sociedad dominicana*. Santiago: Universidad Católica Madre y Maestra, 1977.

Sención, Nicole. "La X 102 tiene veinte años a la vanguardia musical." *Listín Digital* Online, 2, no. 713, Internet, 1999.

Sommer, Doris. *One Master for Another: Populism as Patriarchal Rhetoric in Dominican Novels.* Lanham, MD: University Press of America, 1983.

Stratton, Suzanne, ed. *Modern and Contemporary Art of the Dominican Republic.* New York: Americas Society, 1996.

Tejeda, Alfonso. "El crecimiento desbordante de la ciudad." *Rumbo,* October 7, 1996: 51–54.

Tejeda, Darío. *La historia escondida de Juan Luis Guerra.* (An unauthorized biography.) Santo Domingo: Amigos del Hogar, 1993.

Tejada Ortiz, Dagoberto, Fernando Sánchez Martínez, and César Mella Mejías. *Religiosidad popular dominicana y psiquiatría.* 2nd ed. Santo Domingo: Corripio, 1995.

Tolentino, Mariannede. *Veinte años de pintura: Twenty years of painting.* Santo Domingo: La Galería, 1986.

Torres-Saillant, Silvio, and Ramona Hernández. *The Dominican Americans.* Westport, CT: Greenwood Press, 1998.

Ureña, Salomé. *Poesías completas.* 1950. 5th ed. Santo Domingo: Taller, 1975.

Vega, Bernardo. "La herencia indígena en la cultura dominicana de hoy." In Bernardo Vega et al., eds. *Ensayos sobre cultura dominicana.* 5th ed. Santo Domingo: Amigo del Hogar, 1997.

———. *Trujillo y Haití.* Vol. 1 (1930–1937). Santo Domingo: Fundación Cultural Dominicana, 1988.

Veloz Maggiolo, Marcio. *Los ángeles de hueso.* 2nd ed. Santo Domingo: Taller, 1985.

———. *Barril sin fondo: Antropología para curiosos.* Santo Domingo: de Colores, 1996.

———. *La biografía difusa de Sombra Castañeda.* 2nd ed. Santo Domingo: Taller, 1984.

———. *Cuentos, recuentos y casi cuentos.* Santo Domingo: Taller, 1986.

———. *Cultura, teatro y relatos en Santo Domingo.* Santiago: Universidad Católica Madre y Maestra, 1972.

———. *De abril en adelante.* Santo Domingo: Taller, 1984.

———. *De donde vino la gente: Novela para niños.* 1978. Santo Domingo: Taller, 1986.

———. *La fértil agonía del amor.* Santo Domingo: Taller, 1982.

———. *Florbella (Arqueonovela).* Santo Domingo: Taller, 1986.

———. *Materia prima (Protonovela)* Santo Domingo: Taller, 1988.

———. *Retorno a la palabra.* Santo Domingo: Taller, 1986.

———. *Ritos de cabaret.* Santo Domingo: Taller, 1991.

———. *Sobre cultura dominicana y otras culturas (Ensayos).* Santo Domingo: Alfa y Omega, 1977.

Vergés, Pedro. *Sólo cenizas hallarás (bolero).* Barcelona: Prometo, 1980.

Vicioso, Abelardo. *Santo Domingo en las letras coloniales: 1492–1800.* Santo Domingo: UASD, 1979.

Vicioso, Sherezada (Chiqui). *Algo que decir: Ensayos sobre literatura femenina (1981–1991)*. Santo Domingo: Editora Búho, 1991.

———. *Internamiento*. Santo Domingo: Mediabyte, 1992.

———. *Salomé Ureña de Henríquez (1850–1897): A cien años de un magisterio*. Santo Domingo: Editora de Colres, 1997.

———. *Un extraño ulular traía el viento*. Santo Domingo: Alfa y Omega, 1985.

———. *Viaje desde el agua*. Santo Domingo: Visuarte, 1981.

Ward, Philip, ed. *The Oxford Companion to Spanish Literature*. Oxford: Clarendon Press, 1978.

Welles, Sumner. *Naboth's Vineyard: The Dominican Republic*. 2 vols. New York: Apple, 1966.

Wiarda, Howard J. *Dictatorship and Development: The Methods of Control in Trujillo's Dominican Republic*. Gainesville: University of Florida Press, 1968.

———. *The Dominican Republic: Nation in Transition*. New York: Praeger, 1969.

Zaglul, Jesús M. "Para seguir releyendo, haciendo y recontando la identidad cultural y nacional dominicana: Pistas interrogantes." *Estudios sociales* 25, no. 89/90 (1992): 133–156.

Index

About the Author

ISABEL ZAKRZEWSKI BROWN is Associate Professor in the Department of Foreign Languages and Literatures at the University of South Alabama, Mobile. She teaches Spanish, Latin American civilization, and Latin American literature.

Made in the USA
Lexington, KY
02 February 2010